Praise

Misadvent

Middle

D0330419

"A once-in-a-lifetime journey, full of youthful ebullience and idealism, but self-aware too, and brave."
Colin Thubron, author of *Behind the Wall* **and**
The Lost Heart of Asia

"The brilliantly-written account of a daring journey, by turns hilarious and poignant, and a timely antidote to current misconceptions about the Middle East. Essential reading."
Jason Elliot, author of *Mirrors of the Unseen* **and**
An Unexpected Light

"A fantastic journey, full of surprising incidents and exciting encounters, in which you never know where the travellers will end up next. High-spirited and often amusing, Hemming's book also grapples with some of the big issues in the Middle East today."
Nicholas Jubber, author of *The Prester Quest* **and**
winner of the Dolman Best First Travel Book Award

"*Misadventure in the Middle East* is more than a gripping story of a dangerous expedition. It is a journey of self-discovery and an exploration of what it is to be an artist in a fractured world."
John Mole, author of *It's All Greek To Me!* **and**
Mind Your Manners

For Dad and Tom Fenwick, who in different ways made me want to do this

Misadventure
in the
Middle East

Travels as Tramp, Artist and Spy

Henry Hemming

NICHOLAS BREALEY
PUBLISHING

LONDON · BOSTON

First published by
Nicholas Brealey Publishing in 2007

3–5 Spafield Street
Clerkenwell, London
EC1R 4QB, UK
Tel: +44 (0)20 7239 0360
Fax: +44 (0)20 7239 0370
www.nicholasbrealey.com
www.henryhemming.com

20 Park Plaza
Boston
MA 02116, USA
Tel: (888) BREALEY
Fax: (617) 523 3708

ISBN-13: 978-1-85788-395-4
ISBN-10: 1-85788-395-0

British Library Cataloguing in Publication Data
A catalogue record for this book is available from the
British Library.

Library of Congress Cataloging-in-Publication Data

Hemming, Henry, 1979-
    Misadventure in the Middle East : travels as tramp, artist and spy /
Henry Hemming.
        p. cm.
        1. Hemming, Henry, 1979–Travel–Middle East. 2. Artists–England–
Biography. 3. Middle East–Description and travel. I. Title.
N6797.H3855A2 2007
915.604'54–dc22

                                                                2006024120

Printed in the UK by Clays Ltd, St Ives plc.

Contents

PART ONE: GO EAST
From the Czech–Slovak border through Turkey to Iran
1

PART TWO: DANCING AT DEATH
From Iran into Kurdish Iraq and back into Iran, illegally
119

PART THREE: BEAT OF THE DRUM
From Oman to Jordan, via Saudi Arabia,
as the second Gulf War gets underway
141

PART FOUR: ARABIAN SUMMER
From Amman via Damascus and Aleppo to Beirut,
where Yasmine is almost killed
195

PART FIVE: BAGHDAD AND BEYOND
From Amman to Baghdad, Jerusalem and home
231

"Anyone who wants to know the human psyche [...] would be better advised to abandon exact science, put away his scholar's gown, bid farewell to his study, and wander with human heart through the world. There in the horrors of prisons, lunatic asylums and hospitals, in drab suburban pubs, in brothels and gambling-hells, in the salons of the elegant, the Stock Exchanges, socialist meetings, churches, revivalist gatherings and ecstatic sects, through love and hate, through the experience of passion in every form in his own body, he would reap richer stores of knowledge than text-books a foot thick could give him."

Carl Jung (1875–1961)

Part One
Go East

From the Czech–Slovak border through Turkey to Iran

Go Home English Bastards

THE GUARDS ON THE SLOVAK SIDE OF THE CROSSING HAD had their heads shaved earlier that week. The first one to see us said "Problem" and radioed through to his superiors before ushering Yasmine out of the flow of traffic into a no-man's land bordered by thick yellow lines. He spoke some more into his radio, his voice hushed and a little tense. He sounded like a racing commentator. With the border crossing so small he didn't really need to talk into a radio, he could have just turned around and shouted at the other guards in the guardhouse, but, as he knew, talking into the radio looked good. It reminded the watching world that he was in charge. He slotted the radio back into its holster and with a series of nods and sudden hand gestures motioned us out of Yasmine, the second-hand Toyota pick-up truck I had bought with Al a few months ago.

Al was also clambering out of Yasmine at that moment, the person with whom I had left London nine days before; the other part of what had just begun.

Two more Slovak officials came over to have a look at us, hands on chins, foreheads crumpled. The shortest one stepped forward. He had a snub nose and wore a hat one size too big.

"Passport."

I handed my passport over and stepped back, trying to look apologetic and unthreatening, but at the same time not entirely sure why we had been pulled out of the flow of Trabants and Ladas heading into Slovakia. The three guards looked me up and down, clumsily, none of them seeming to like what they saw, before turning to Al. He didn't mind being looked up and down so much and their eyes remained on him as he pottered back and forth within our miniature no-man's land, whistling to himself, kicking at small stones and hopping to the tune in his head.

The guard going through my passport found a page that he liked the look of. The other two crowded round.

"Problem," he said once more, looking up at me and then back at the passport, shaking his head slowly, making sure to give each shake an exaggerated, pantomime follow-through.

The guard held up my passport and pointed at the Iranian visa stamp I had obtained two weeks ago, just before leaving London. He shook his head once more to really ram the point home, before marching back to the guardhouse. There was an ominous spring to his step: it was as if he had just found an important clue, or proof of something. The other two guards told us to get back into Yasmine and directed us to another no-man's land. Although more spacious than the last – you could really stretch your legs in this one – our new holding area was farther away from the flow of traffic entering and exiting Slovakia, and farther away from Slovakia itself, the country we hoped to cross in order to get to Istanbul, our first stop.

AL AND I WERE NINE DAYS INTO WHAT WE HAD SPENT THE last few months telling anyone who had asked or anyone who would listen was going to be a year-long journey into the Middle East. We were painters; or you could say we were artists, but there's something about the word "artist" that feels a bit exclusive, or makes you think of people with a language all of their own – one that non-artists wouldn't get – and besides, most of the time we made paintings. So we were painters.

Between us we knew very little about the Middle East. Or the "heart of the Islamic world", as we had begun to call it because we thought this might make it easier to raise money for our journey. "Heart of the Islamic world" sounded more epic than "Middle East", and less like something you'd hear about on the nightly news. So why go to the Middle East? We would be asked this almost everywhere we went, the questioner smiling as if whatever followed was going to be a little perverse.

Our journey began, like a lot of journeys, with a conversation. One afternoon, three years before we arrived at the Czech–Slovak border and several weeks before starting our different degrees at different universities, Al and I agreed that once we had finished university we would spend a year painting together. At the time it didn't matter where. We had gone painting together before but on a much smaller scale, usually for a few weeks or at most a month, and it had worked: we got on with each other, we became prolific around each other, we didn't argue too much, and best of all we could criticise each other's work and it did not hurt. With anyone else it did. Two years later and only a few weeks before the terrorist attacks on the World Trade Center and the Pentagon, we decided that for our year of making art somewhere, anywhere, we would go to the Middle East. Neither of us knew much about the area. Both wanted to know more, and at the time that seemed enough of a reason to go.

In the wake of the 11 September attacks, while the Taliban regime in Afghanistan was threatened, bombed and eventually ousted from Kabul, we were busy making homemade A4-sized proposals with grainy, internet-quality images and gutters that would always end up half a centimetre off centre, explaining what we were going to do in the Middle East. The more of these proposals we made the more culturally righteous our journey began to sound, until it was no longer the "journey", nor the "adventure". It became the "Project" or the "Expedition". Our pamphlets declared in the cold Arial font that the two young men pictured were not just going off painting in the Middle East – no, they were embarking on an artistic expedition to the heart of the Islamic world in order to alter Western stereotypes about the region. They planned to get under the skin of this area, to find the parts that didn't appear in the news. They would try to plug the gap that existed between the two visual caricatures of the region: on one hand the hotbed of modern-day suicidal terror, and on the other a more Orientalist, antique and sexually louche land of Ali Baba flying-carpet fantasy.

We sent almost a hundred of these lovingly handstapled pamphlets to companies or charities or trusts who we thought might like this kind of thing, in the hope that they'd send us money. None of them did. Most of them were worried, I think understandably, that a project involving the word "Islam" and two scruffy young artists would end up either politicised or controversial or both. Most, that is, apart from Ken Bromley of Ken Bromley Art Supplies just outside Bolton, Lancashire. He took pity on us after we sent him one of our pamphlets and agreed to give us a fifteen per cent discount on the crate of paint we ordered from him.

That meant we would have to raise most of our money during the journey. Somehow. Otherwise, according to our budget, we would run out of money just over halfway through the trip in the middle of the Saudi Arabian desert. But how could we make money while we were on the road? As two people with no experience of anything other than sitting in libraries and writing essays, making money while *not* on the road was hard enough. We would have to come up with a plan.

Lee, one of the partners at a second-hand Toyota dealership near Stroud, Gloucestershire, though both impressed and worried about what we were planning to do, did not feel that the cultural relevance of our expedition justified a discount on the pick-up truck we had our eye on.

"We can't do it without her," Al and I told each other repeatedly and a little breathlessly, the words coming out as a mantra, before both parting with our life savings and signing two of the largest cheques either of us had ever written; apart from the one for a million pounds that you write when you get your first chequebook, before tearing the cheque into tiny pieces (and putting the pieces in different bins).

WITH A BEEP AND A BURST OF STATIC THE BORDER GUARD'S radio came to life. He nodded fast at the instructions he was given, like a nodding dog in a car being driven over a cattle grid, before unwrapping a pair of latex gloves and pulling them on slowly and without menace. The only latex gloves I had ever seen being pulled on were in American teen gross-out movies. This was different, in every way. The guard moved round to the back of Yasmine and directed me to unbolt her. He began to remove objects one by one, holding each as if it was diseased before placing it on the tarmac beside him, something he did with the precision of a miniaturist.

One of the poles from my camp bed made him frown. He swiped the air with it like a man hailing a taxi in a black-and-white film, and it made a whistling sound.

Once he was done with the back of Yasmine he moved into her cab, which had filled fast since we left London and was now a kaleidoscopic mess. The first thing you saw in the jungle of tacky colour was a green, fluffy ball with a moustache and a Mexican hat sewn on it that hung from the windscreen mirror. Wedged into the handles above each door were several Disney bodyguards that Al had collected from McDonald's Happy Meals. The steering wheel cover was furry with piebald black and white splodges, another Al contribution, while all over the dash and floor were copies of *The Sun*, maps of Amsterdam and Prague, *The Aleph* by Jorge Luis Borges, Jack Kerouac's *On the Road*, the Penguin translation of the Qur'an, pint glasses, mugs, clothes, tapes, tubes of paint, paintbrushes and a leaflet entitled "What is Islam?" that had been given to us the day before by the man who ran the Czech Republic's first official mosque. In fact there were so many odd-looking things that the border guard didn't know where to start. So he didn't. Instead, he turned to Al and pointed at his trousers, tutting. They were ugly, calf-length combat trousers made from "rip-stop" material, so that if you ripped them the rip would stop, something Al had demonstrated a few times (so his trousers were covered in tiny rips, which had stopped).

Visibly upset by the state of Al's trousers, the guard had another chat with his radio before heading back to the guardhouse.

An hour later, two more senior-looking officials stepped out of the guardhouse holding what looked like our passports. We got back into Yasmine as they sauntered towards us.

"So," Al sighed as he slammed his door. "Remind me what there is to do in Bratislava?"

"Not sure."

"Actually we've got a book on it somewhere. Where did I put it?" As he rummaged around by his feet, one of the border guards tapped on my window. I wound it down.

"No," he said as he handed me my passport open at a page with a Slovakian stamp and a cross drawn through it. "Slovakia no. Go home England."

"What? What do you mean? What have we done?"

"Slovakia no. Go home England," he repeated. The other guard handed Al his passport, which bore an

7

identical stamp with a cross through it, and the two of them ambled back to the guardhouse.

Al stayed with Yasmine while I followed the two guards, waving one of our pamphlets at them.

"I don't understand. You must have got us muddled up with someone else." They looked blank. "You see, we're part of a UK cross-cultural expedition designed to..."

I was removed from the office by the two guards nearest the door. As I tried to get back in, the door was slammed in my face. Not in the figure-of-speech sense of having a door slammed in your face, that would have been fine – this door landed on my face and hit my nose. It hurt like when you hit your funny bone and you laugh and howl at the same time and for a moment can't work out whether you're feeling morphine-like happiness or acute pain.

I tried again.

"Slovakia no. Go home England," said someone inside. Again the door was shut with me on the wrong side of it, this time with my nose out of the way.

I couldn't think what to do. Then I remembered that as I was being ejected from the office, in the semi-commotion I had managed to drop one of our pamphlets onto the senior official's desk. Maybe he was reading it now. He'd let us in after that, surely.

A few minutes later I opened the door. Again it was slammed shut with me on the wrong side of it. This sequence played itself out twice more, the slam of the door getting louder and louder, until I decided to pull my one and only trump card. I went to find a payphone.

An anti-climactic amount of time passed as I changed money, bought a phonecard and went back to the payphone. Then I was ready. It was time to call the British Embassy.

Because it was a Saturday, the line went straight through to the duty officer's mobile phone. He had a honeyed,

BBC news-reading voice and was midway through a picnic somewhere in Bratislava, Slovakia's capital. I could hear birds tweeting in the background. He would be happy to help, he said, but first he had to find out exactly what the border guards' report said. Half an hour later he rang back, the birds still hard at it in the background sounding more and more like foley on a wildlife documentary.

"Look, I'm sorry to say this," he said, his voice condoling. "But it appears they think you two are, well, that you're Islamic activists of some sort."

"We're what?"

"'Islamic extremists' are the words they use. Obviously I'm not there so I have no idea why they think this, but this is what the report says. It also says you've come armed with various weapons, including a baseball bat."

"But... But we don't have a baseball bat."

"I'm afraid that's what the report says."

Silence.

"I think I know what it is."

"The baseball bat?"

"It must be my camp-bed pole. They must have thought my camp-bed pole was a baseball bat."

"Right." He didn't sound convinced.

"And we're not Islamic activists. Or extremists. I mean, we're not even Muslim..."

"The leaflets promoting Islam?"

"Oh, we were given them by a guy in Brno. Just yesterday. An imam. Well, he wasn't actually an imam, that was his friend in Cairo."

"Either way. They seem to think you two were heading to Bratislava to start a riot. Or a protest," the duty officer said slowly, still reading the report. "They also make special mention of your dress and demeanour. Apparently both

9

were unsatisfactory. Look, I'm terribly sorry, but they've done a paragraph six."

"What's that?"

"A paragraph six. It's quite serious. It means there's nothing we, as your representative embassy, can do to help. I'm afraid you'll have to turn back. If I were you I'd try to get round through Austria. Assuming they don't see the P.6 in your passport at the Austrian border. But you can't cross this border."

This was more or less the exact opposite of what I had shouted at the Slovak commander before tramping off to find the payphone. I couldn't believe it. We were being turned away from Slovakia because we looked like Islamic extremists. My brain couldn't quite process what had happened. Although I had just about worked out how to change one of Yasmine's tyres and had bought a first aid kit in case Al hurt himself, at no point before setting out had I worked out what to do if we were accused of being Islamic extremists, barred from a European country and branded with a "P.6".

I opened my passport and looked again at the miserable cross the guards had put through the Slovak stamp. A big, Basquiatesque cross there so that other border guards would see it, read the P.6 beneath it and know that we were trouble. Tearing out the page was no good, because for any border guard not new to the job the passport would feel wrong as he or she flicked through it; equally, the pages were numbered so whoever was inspecting the passport could tell if a page was missing.

As the man from the embassy told me about places we should try to see in Iran, if we got to Iran, a team of overgrown and less-uniformed Slovak border guards advanced. One of them positioned himself a foot away from me, his shoulders ox-like and his eyeballs vast and in danger of popping out. I said goodbye to the embassy duty officer and returned the phone to its rest. My hand fell away from the receiver, an umbilical cord broken, the man's mellifluous voice still ringing in my ears; the guard with the large eyeballs took me by the arm. He began to march me towards Yasmine. Another guard did the same to Al.

Feeling a wave of boyish indignation, I shook off the guard's grip. The moment I did this I knew I shouldn't have. He turned to me, his eyeballs larger than before and for a moment disbelieving, in a lovely, childlike way – it was as if he had just been shown how a toy he'd been struggling with all morning really worked – before he pushed me up against the wall and held me there by the throat. His face was five or maybe six inches from mine. His palm pressed into my windpipe, turning my voice into a helium whine. He began to chant his own version of the Slovak border guard motto.

"Slovakia no. Go home England. Bastards."

His breath smelt of crisps.

"We're going, don't worry," said Al.

I squeaked agreement.

"Bastards," the guard said again.

Cheese and onion.

"No, no," said Al. "You've got it wrong, honestly, we're not terrorists or anything. We're here to learn about your country. We're students. Really."

"Students," I squeaked.

"Students," said Al.

"Bastards," said one guard.

"Bastards," chimed the others, nodding and getting into the routine.

The man holding me against the wall let me go and we walked back to Yasmine.

"Go home England. Bastards," they shouted in what sounded like rehearsed unison.

"Go home Slovakia. Bastards," we yelled back, a bit stupidly as, technically, they were already in Slovakia.

They shouted at us some more and I felt like the dog listening to his owner in a Gary Larson cartoon as I picked out the words "bastards", "go home", "England" and the occasional "fuck off" from the clutter of Slovak.

I drove back into the Czech Republic with a sickly kind of anxiety. It was like the pause at the end of your first driving test when the instructor tells you to pull over and park the car so that you can be told your fate, only this nauseous, guilty feeling would not go away, and continued until it was less of a feeling than a state of mind.

C

Biscuits

THE DAY BEFORE - 11 SEPTEMBER 2002, THE FIRST anniversary of the suicide terrorists' attacks on the World Trade Center in New York - Al and I had sat in a mosque in Brno, in the southeast of the Czech Republic, and spoken to Czech Muslims about how their lives had changed since "9/11". One of them had called it "11/9". The mosque had smelt of polished pine. In turn, they had described how hard each of them found it to relax on a plane or in an airport departure lounge, so flying had become a last resort. As long as each man's face or clothing signified "Muslim" they would feel eyes on them throughout the journey - accusing eyes, watchful eyes, wary eyes - and enough of these would make them feel guilty. And nauseous.

I had no idea as I sat with these men in the carpeted warmth of Brno's only mosque that the following day I too would signify both "Muslim" and "Muslim extremist". Or had the two merged in the minds of the Slovak guards?

It was our first taste of the new, post-9/11 world that was forming around us: an unfamiliar world, even to itself. Although we had read about its embryonic parameters of suspicion and morality, heard stories about Sikhs being attacked because they looked Muslim or Asian-looking men being held without charge in countries where such a thing was illegal, and had tried to imagine what it felt like to be a part of the new "them", only now could we fully understand it because only now had we tasted it for ourselves.

I followed signs for the Austrian border. With seven kilometres to go I pulled into a lay-by and we both changed into suits. Each of us had packed one suit for the journey ahead: for the exhibition we had lined up tentatively in Tehran, and for the nights in palaces with princes and princesses we did not yet have lined up but liked to dream about. Because I was fairly sure that the Middle East would be hot, I had packed a beige-coloured linen suit. It was a hand-me-down with sleeves that were too long. Three kilometres before the border a Billie Holiday tape replaced Rod Stewart. One kilometre away and we pulled into a service station to fill Yasmine with diesel and buy some biscuits. She was half full anyway, but a full tank made me feel like a more pious driver.

"And we can eat the biscuits while we cross the border," said Al as we pulled up to the first checkpoint. "It'll make us look calm."

"Right."

"I mean, who eats a biscuit when they're nervous?"

"Exactly," I said. "And you should be reading something."

Al reached for the first book he could find. The Qur'an. With Yasmine rolling to a standstill and several Austrian border guards walking towards us, he shoved it into the glovebox and pulled out a European guidebook.

"Don't forget the biscuits," he hissed as I wound down the window.

Both border guards liked their biscuit and there was no "problem". In fact, all the Austrian officials we spoke to seemed genuinely pleased to welcome into their country two bookish, well-dressed, biscuit-eating Billie Holiday fans. We were waved through in the time it took to swipe our passports through a machine. I sprayed biscuity thanks at the guards and drove towards Vienna feeling the thrill of petty guilt. It was as if we had tricked them somehow, stolen a penny sweet, pinched their parking space, tied their shoelaces together. If only they knew! Then I remembered that we hadn't done anything wrong.

For a moment, it felt like we were back on track.

☾

Clothes

TWO DAYS LATER, IN BUDAPEST, YASMINE WAS BROKEN INTO in broad daylight while parked on a busy street. The bags we had left on her back seat were stolen. We spent that afternoon in Pest police station dictating reports, trying to remember exactly what was in the different bags, working out how much it was all worth, adding a bit on for the insurance and waiting several hours while our statements were translated into Hungarian. After that we were driven around Budapest in police cars.

With the Slovak border crossing still heavy on my mind, like the memory of a dream where you kill someone, being in a police car made me feel guilty and on edge. Every time one of the police officers asked me a question I felt as if they knew what we had done. Although we hadn't done anything wrong; I had forgotten that again.

Al was pissed off about losing his bag. Although he hadn't lost anything expensive, what had been stolen meant a lot to him, hard-to-replace things like his tobacco or his pipe-cleaning kit; luckily he always kept his pipes on his person. As with anyone leading a faintly nomadic existence, Al's few possessions had become his home and losing so many of them now we were on the road hurt. What he missed more than anything else were the clothes that had gone.

Although he rarely admitted it, Al's clothes were important to him and in many ways they defined him, or at least they said a lot about him. Like Al himself, Al's clothes were an unusual mixture of ordinary things. For him there was nothing showy or strange about wearing a luminous yellow FUBU basketball top beneath an ageing leather jacket, or shell-suit Adidas trousers topped by a tweed jacket. Each was a fantastic bit of clothing, he would say, so why not wear them together? If he were a chef he'd put caviar on ice-cream. He didn't do this to be sensational, or to get a reaction, he did it because it made Cartesian, rock-solid sense to him.

I had known Al for eight years and the longer I knew him the harder he was to describe. I could see that to look at he had a flattish, angular face with arctic blue eyes that people remembered and hair that was beginning to thin, while to talk to he might come across as wildly confident

or at other times shy, and if shy he might appear arrogant in that he was comfortable being silent. But that was all surface. I knew Al best when he was making art. That was when he came alive. The energy and calm certainty that flowed through him when he was creating a picture or building a sculpture were mesmerising. Any and all inhibitions disappeared so there would be nothing unusual about finding him, say, in a busy Damascene street seven months later surrounded by a crowd of fifty men as he positioned a toy tiger on the shoulder of a bemused *hajji*, as part of an installation, before dancing round with his camera, dropping to the floor, jumping up again, blinded by the need to get the best shot; nor anything odd about discovering him on the roof of a hotel in the middle of a bitterly cold Iranian night, earphones in, eyes shut, making a painting with his hands. Why? Because it expressed his subconscious feeling, he would explain, as if giving you directions to the nearest bus stop.

The Hungarian police eventually found Al's bag in the bathroom of a cheap hotel. Most of its contents had gone. The police apologised for the theft, saying it was unusual for Budapest, before dropping us back at Yasmine and wishing us a pleasant stay in Hungary.

Night was coming up fast.

"Not really how I imagined it," said Al as he started to tape up Yasmine's window, echoing my thoughts, the black plastic flapping in the breeze like a pennant.

"What do you mean?"

"This, where we are now, how far we've got. Or I suppose how far we haven't got."

"Yep."

"What?"

"Nothing."

Silence.

"How did you imagine it to be?" I asked, amazed that I hadn't asked this before.

"Well." He stopped what he was doing. "I suppose I'd pictured the pair of us more or less gliding through the Middle East, in a secure truck, making pictures about whatever we saw. Recording it all like a fly on the wall. Well, two flies on the wall. But I guess that's not going to happen. Our demeanour is... what is it?" He looked over. "Unsatisfactory. Yup. Yasmine is a target. We look like Islamic militants. Can you believe that? There are borders we can't cross because of what we look like."

"Or what we represent."

"And that changes everything. I mean, I never thought we would look like anything other than two guys in a red pick-up truck who make pictures. Harmless people. Not-a-threat people. But now we look like, I don't know, we're two Qur'an-carrying young men of aggressive demeanour and no fixed abode. And uncertain destination. One of whom has a beard," he said, glancing at me.

Even more worrying – although I didn't bring it up just then because I thought we had enough to mull over – was the idea that had been snowballing in my mind since we left London: could it be that neither of us actually knew how to make our portrait of the heart of the Islamic world? It had sounded so simple when we put it in our pamphlet that we hadn't really addressed this. Now that we were on the road, fleshing out the fiction we had spent the last year creating, defining, refining and preparing, our mission statement and everything our pamphlet embodied began to look and feel like artifice. Beyond our carefully worded sound bites about cross-cultural artistic dialogue, what should we be painting, day to day? Or *should* we be painting? Did the Czech Muslims we had spent time with in Prague and Brno constitute an atom of the Islamic world, and if so how should we be making art about them? Or perhaps it didn't matter how we made the art. Perhaps our art was no more than a device, or a way into the people and places we encountered.

We were less than two weeks into the journey and what had happened to us over the last three days had neatly blown apart my understanding of what we were doing. All of a sudden we found ourselves in an unfamiliar world where we no longer knew where we could go, what we signified or what we were doing. It was not a good feeling.

"We've got to change the way she looks," said Al as he finished taping up Yasmine's window. "Make her less inviting, so she doesn't get broken into again."

"Right."

"She looks too new. Too proud. We've got to scuff her up somehow. Make her look like a heap of junk," he said, cocking his head as he sized her up.

"And we've got to change the way *we* look."

"Yasmine first." He squinted at her. "I want her to look like a rattlebag old jalopy. A proper tank you wouldn't store anything more valuable than a spare tyre in."

"Flat spare tyre."

"And that yellow has to go. Honestly."

Not long before leaving London, in a particularly bright mood, I had painted the hood that covered the pick-up part of Yasmine a bawdy, look-at-me yellow, which, next to the cheap-red-wine maroon of her body made her stand out like a streaker on a busy street. Though the way she turned heads was not just because of her colouring. It had a lot to do with her shape.

Before setting eyes on Yasmine I had never really got off on the shape of any car; I had never bought a car magazine, never oohed and aahed as an armada of classic vehicles drove past on a Sunday afternoon, and never, ever dreamt of one day owning a Ferrari or a Porsche and feeling slick or in some way fulfilled by doing so. Cars were someone else's obsession. None of my dreams had cars in them. Until Yasmine. Looking at her made me happy in a way I did not think a metallic means of getting from A to B possibly could. It also made a lot of other people happy. Everywhere we had been with Yasmine she drew admiring smiles or gestures. Conversations began because of her, and there was something about her shape, her proportions, the curve of her bonnet when you caught her profile (or was it just her redness? – her body was very red) that made most people fall for her.

The next day in Budapest we got Yasmine's broken window and its undamaged counterpart replaced with sheets of aluminium. "Very strong," said Mikael the welder, thumping each one to prove it. Already she was starting to look like a dreadnought. From the garage we drove to an art shop where we bought several cans of spray paint and for the rest of the day, as if doing the pilot for some twisted makeover show – *Wreck My Ride* – we set about ageing Yasmine. We added rusted bruises with jagged edges that I drew shadows on with a paint pen. We covered her glossy maroon paint with a matt red that softened with time into a weather-beaten pink. Her hood turned from gaudy yellow to peat brown. We worked sandpaper over her body and added wedges of paint or invented collisions and scrapes, the paintwork of Yasmine's phantom victims still visible around each dent, and just below the driver's window we thought about drawing a line of icons depicting cars and several small animals, each one with a cross drawn through it, although we decided against that. Finally we scratched nails along the length of her body until Yasmine looked five, maybe ten years older, scarred and stolen.

Both of us felt awful doing this, Al especially so. All afternoon his face was an apologetic grimace. It was like cutting off all of your daughter's beautiful waist-long hair, badly, and yet, as we kept on telling each other, it was for Yasmine's own good. One day she'd thank us.

Only two hours after we had finished a man walked past Yasmine, pulled out his phone and when he thought he was out of earshot, made a call during which I heard him read out her number plate. He must have been calling the police, to report a stolen vehicle. I told Al. It was the best thing that had happened to us since, well, since leaving London.

The trickster spirit in both of us had come alive. Perhaps we really could change the way Yasmine looked. And if we could do that, perhaps we could change the way we looked. We got drunk to celebrate.

The next morning we left Budapest and followed the signs to Istanbul.

☾

Something It Is Not

JAMES WILDE CREAKED BACK AND FORTH IN HIS ROCKING chair, the sun catching his nest of white hair every time it bobbed into the light. Behind him the rooftops of Taksim simmered beneath a late afternoon sky that framed the sun as it lowered itself gently onto the Golden Horn.

For most of his life James had been a staff writer at *Time* magazine. He looked like a mad professor and had the wry delivery of an ageing, dried-up rockstar who had seen more than anyone else in the room. He now lived in Istanbul. On the wall behind him was a collection of black Jesuses in different states of crucifixion, each body writhing in its silent and polished agony.

"If I had to follow a religion, I think I'd be a black Catholic," he said, following my gaze, his skin looking just as pallid and pink as it had when I first met him. He spoke with a warm, North American lilt and his words, although staccato, had a kind of rhythm that made you want to listen forever. He'd been talking for some time now.

"Y'know the most peaceful people I ever met?"

Al and I were part of a seven-strong audience. None of us knew.

"Pygmies!" he whispered. "In the Congo. For two and a half months I was trying to find them. Everyone thought I was mad. *I* thought I was mad. They said I was a diseased, white gorilla who'd got lost. Ha!" He launched into a raucous, snorting laugh that came to a sudden stop as he hacked something up. "Then I found them," he went on, reaching for a tissue. "Incredible people." Again silence, everyone certain there was more to come. "Lots of bees there too. Been covered in bees. Complete blanket. Other white guys did it but they hated it." His voice was a whisper again. "You see I loved it. The more they stung, the better it got. And when you took a shit, they'd sting your arse. So I'd be standing there, bent over with my men plucking the stings out of my skinny white arse. Ha!"

"Remind me, James, why you chose to live in Istanbul," asked the serious woman two to my left.

"Best city I know. Thought about living in Vietnam but I couldn't." Another pause. "That was a bad war." He shook his head. "A bad, bad war. Those troops were gone. I was covering it for *Time* and I swear to you now, there's nothing in this world like being on a hill in Vietnam with the wind swaying the bamboo around you, the whole thing lit by the moon, some first-class opium, and you doing watch for a bunch of soldiers so smashed they've passed out. That, my friends, is something else." Another pause. "Good drug, opium. Lot of it in Iran. Better for you than the worst."

"The worst?"

"Alcohol." He looked irritated by the question. "No doubt about that. Evil drug. Nearly killed me. Killed a lot of my friends. Qur'an got that right." He paused before leaning towards me, his chair no longer rocking. "Now tell me something," he said, his pupils widening behind ever-so-slightly tinted glasses. "You're British, right? This ecstasy drug I've heard about. They say it's big in Britain." He paused again. "Tell me, is it all that?"

Talk of trance-like highs and dancing triggered something else in James's mind. He announced that we would soon be joined by Abdullah, a former alcoholic who had found salvation at the *tekke* (a building for Sufi gatherings) in Fatih, a district of Istanbul. It had changed his life. At the *tekke* Sufi Muslims danced themselves into a drug-free state of euphoria. They were what visitors to the city might call whirling dervishes, but this *tekke* was different, James explained.

"Nothing like what you see in the ceremonies they do for tourists."

An hour later Abdullah arrived wearing a black leather jacket that looked like something out of a student production of *Grease*. He nodded when I asked if he was going to the *tekke* later that night. He also confirmed that Sufism had saved him, or rather the leader of his particular Sufi *tekke* had saved him. He was a born-again Sufi. I asked if Al and I could come along. Abdullah made a call to find out.

"Yes," he said. "You can. But no photographs."

"Sure. And you're coming too, right?" I turned to James.

"Oh no. No, I don't like to any more."

"Why not?" I asked.

"I get scared by that thing."

"What do you mean?"

"You'll see when you get there. It's dangerous."

"Why?"

"You'll see."

"No really, why?"

"Because," he said, looking away as if it had hurt him long ago, and making sure Abdullah was out of earshot, "it lets you think it's something it is not."

His words played over and over in my mind as the *taksi* sped me, Al and Abdullah across Istanbul to Fatih.

WE ENTERED THE *TEKKE* SHOELESS THROUGH AN UNMARKED door. Abdullah led us down several low corridors and through a series of anterooms as he continued the lecture he had started half an hour earlier.

"In 1925 Ataturk banned Sufi dervish orders all over Turkey," he explained as we advanced deeper into the building, his voice a half whisper. "But he cannot kill them. Instead we go underground. Now, in the last years, there is a new growth. There are more Sufis now than ever before in Istanbul."

In a low-lit room with framed inscriptions jammed onto the walls with the cluttered aesthetic of a Victorian drawing room, we sat down towards the back of a sea of cross-legged men, each one wearing a white cylindrical cap. As each sat down he leant over to hug and kiss the men on either side of him on both cheeks. Everywhere I looked men smiled at each other in well-to-do anticipation.

Some prayers were said and at the front of the room one man began to tap at a drum while another plucked at a *saz*, a kind of lute. Two men started to sing, one high, one low, the microphones crackling as they pulled themselves closer. The men around us wiggled to get comfortable. The singers grew bolder and soon the two voices were weaving into and out of each other, not yet like two strands of DNA, but with a certainty that suggested they had sung together before. There were more prayers, the old men rising more slowly from their prostrations than the young, and one of the singers began to read, sing or chant – I was not sure which – passages of the Qur'an. As he did so, men in the congregation began to whisper "hai-hai" to themselves, over and over in rhythmic succession. At the same time the white-capped heads around us started to sway, looking like gulls bobbing on the ocean.

Hu means Him, or God – God your lover – Abdullah had explained, although it sounded like "hai" that night.

The singing and whispering went on for more than an hour.

"Man, I'm exhausted," Al whispered. "Think I'm going to head back."

"I'll stay," I said, sleepily.

Soon after, with Al gone, I fell asleep.

I woke to the booming thud of a bass drum. The entire congregation had moved next door where they had formed six or seven concentric circles, each with his arms over the shoulders of the men on either side of him. They looked like footballers in a series of overgrown pre-match huddles.

Coming to fast I hurried next door, got out some paper and started to draw. I was the only person sitting down. There was no audience. The men were chanting "hai-hai" in unison now and it was louder than before. Something had begun. In a gallery above, screened by wooden lattice *meshrabiyehs*, women I had not noticed as I walked in sat cross-legged watching the men. Some of them began to rock back and forth.

More drums started up and a different man began to sing, his voice thin and feverish, nothing like the soporific drone from before. Still the men chanted, "Hai-hai. Hai-hai."

The singer's voice grew, becoming louder and more shrill, until it was piercing and made my ears ring on certain notes. On a signal I did not see the circles began to sway as one, each man shifting his weight from left foot to right foot, left foot to right foot.

Then the circles began to turn slowly in a clockwise direction. "Hai-hai. Hai-hai."

Near the centre of the circles the leader of the ceremony was ducking in and out of the lines of men as they moved past, chanting at worshippers from point-blank like a sergeant major as he exhorted each man to greater heights. His eyes looked enormous behind the bulletproof bulk of his glasses. I was drawing as much of this as I could, taking in the shapes, the movement, the noise, and wanting to paint but not having my paints with me.

As the drumming and chanting grew louder, the circles accelerated. The men on the outside circle began to look out of breath. Still they went faster, the chanting becoming more frenzied.

"Hai-hai," gasp, "hai-hai," gasp, "hai-hai" pounded through it all, over and over, as a man appeared in the middle of the rotating circles wearing a black cloak and a conical camel-hair hat. I hadn't seen him make his way there. He stood very still before shedding the black cloak to reveal a white skirt and a white shirt with a black sash round his waist. The circles widened to make space for him. This forced the men on the outside circle into a canter.

"It is when he drops his cloak that he leaves the mortal world," Abdullah had explained earlier, grinning at the thought. I could see Abdullah now in one of the outer circles, his face blank and his eyes shut as the circles hurried him on. "The white is the white of death. Only in white can he throw himself at Allah, like a butterfly at the light."

The black sash round the man's waist was the conscious, nagging reminder of his setting, of his ego and of his mortality. In slow motion he crossed his arms over his chest as if about to go down a steep slide and he began to spin. His arms opened out above him like those on a corkscrew as it grinds into the wooden flesh below.

"Hai-hai," gasp, "hai-hai."

The eyes of the spinning man were empty. Open but empty. His head hung to one side as he spun faster and faster in the opposite direction to the mass of men around him.

"Hai-hai," gasp, "hai-hai."

The men shooting past allowed me split-second stills of the centre man's face. It was like watching an old-fashioned mechanised animation. Above, women rocked with more intensity and some began to moan. The room now smelt of sweat and deodorant.

"Hai-hai," gasp, "hai-hai."

It sounded like someone trying to hyperventilate.

"Hai-hai," gasp, "hai-hai."

One by one, men began to lose themselves.

"Hai-hai," gasp, "hai-hai."

Their faces went limp and their smiles hung loose as if they were drunk. Their heads lolled like flowers too heavy for their stalks. Their feet mimicked movement, the momentum and shoulders of those around them hurrying them on. Head after head bowed in submission.

"Hai-hai," gasp, "hai-hai."

A whisker of saliva formed in the mouth of one man and I watched it grow and grow, its angle jaunty as the man hurried on, his face blank, until the spit caught on the shirt of the man next to him. He too had been consumed.

"Hai-hai," gasp, "hai-hai."

On and on they went, head after head bowed in trance-like ecstasy.

"Hai-hai," gasp, "hai-hai."

The room smelt even more of deodorant.

"Hai-hai."

I felt like the one sober person at a drunken party.

Gasp.

A voyeur.

"Hai-hai."

On and on the spinning went, as the drumming built to a crescendo. The leader joined one of the circles and was consumed immediately. His head rolled about like the men on either side and the circles around him began to tighten, moving faster and faster, closer and closer, rudderless, until the singing reached one final crescendo and the circles all collided, bodies piled up in one great heap of flesh.

"Hai-hai." Gasp.

Heads and shoulders and arms were as one, and for a moment it looked like the remains of some awful massacre.

Silence.

Deodorant and sweat.

It was over. The circles retreated a little and the dervish who had been whirling in the centre began to look for his black cloak. One by one the men removed themselves from the mêlée and sat cross-legged on the carpeted floor. Each man looked exhausted. Another prayer was said and the ceremony closed. The hall emptied slowly, with devotees offering hushed and almost embarrassed pleasantries to one another, and for some time the room remained thick with the intensity of what had just happened; in the film of sweat on my forehead I could feel it still.

☾

Sensible Men

THIS SEEMED TO BE EXACTLY THE KIND OF THING WE SHOULD be making pictures about. The Sufi ceremony Abdullah had taken me and Al to ticked all of our boxes: it was the modern-day Islamic world, it was something you wouldn't read about in a newspaper or see on the news, it had nothing to do with terrorism, there were no flying carpets, no odalisques, no camels. It felt truly Islamic.

"But we shouldn't be focusing on that kind of thing," said Al, firmly, as I described what he had missed.

"What should we be focusing on?"

"Don't know. But I don't think we should be trying to make a religious portrait of the Middle East. And... Yes. I just don't think that's what we should be focusing on."

"What were you going to say?"

"I was going to say think about Munneb, in Brno. Remember? The guy who ran the mosque."

"Sure."

"And the way he answered your question about Sufism?"

Not long before we left Brno, I had asked a man called Munneb what Sufism was. His face had fallen.

"The Sufi, he is not the proper Muslim," he had replied, his words clipped. The young Saudi with shaky hands who had been listening in on our conversation had rebuked him in Arabic and Munneb had reneged.

"OK. Sufism is a mystical tradition within Sunni Islam," he had said, chided. "And no," he had continued, "there are no Sufis for you to meet in Brno."

I'd felt like a cliché – a gauche cliché, if that's possible – in expressing even a mild interest in Sufism to a traditional Sunni Muslim. It was like asking a plain girl about her famously pretty younger sister, the one you'd never met but heard amazing things about. In its mysticism, apparent lack of rules and trance-like dancing, Sufism was obviously appealing to an archetypal Western liberal mentality open to spirituality yet terrified of religion.

Perhaps because of this, but also because I wanted to know more about the ceremony I had seen, I spent the next few days grilling Abdullah in his carpet shop about Sufism and reading up as much as possible in a nearby bookshop.

Sufism was certainly closer than any other stream of Islam to the diluted and unthreatening "Eastern" religions that might find their way, in name alone, into Western interior design, chill-out albums or light exercise classes. At the same time, in its partially coded language, poetry and strange-looking rituals, Sufism had all the intrigue of a secret society. In its asceticism and brotherhood there was the purity of monasticism. But as Abdullah pointed out Sufism has no monasteries, nor does any Muslim subset, and annoyingly there were no secret handshakes.

"The Sufi tries only to take his spirit as close to God as possible," Abdullah told me the following day. "And when the Sufi is filled with this... um, how can I say, this love of Him, this incredible love. This is *ahwal*. And there are no words to describe *ahwal*. If you put together all the words in the dictionary you are still very far away."

Music and dance, although proscribed by the Qur'an, can be used to help achieve *ahwal* or spiritual states of mind, according to Rumi, also known as the Mevlana, the original whirling dervish who lived in the thirteenth century and preached through his poetry and his example a cosmopolitan kind of mysticism. He was light years ahead of his contemporaries in the way he championed monogamy, religious tolerance and an end to slavery, among other things. The poet Ted Hughes once described Sufis as "the biggest society of sensible men there has ever been on earth".

Sufism minus the music and dance first formed in the centuries after the death of the Prophet Muhammad, in some ways as a reaction to the dogmatic approach to Islam taking root throughout the Arabian peninsula, especially within the court of the Damascene Caliphate. The first Sufis felt that too many Muslims no longer strived to surrender themselves emotionally to God. Instead they focused on physical submission – Islam means, literally, surrender or submission – so to try to restore this spiritual dimension they looked beyond the Qur'an to the time of the Prophet and the ideas that surrounded him. Like modern-day historical enthusiasts re-enacting mediæval battles, they even dressed as they imagined the Prophet to have done; hence their name, Sufi, *tasawwuf* in Arabic, which is conventionally said to derive from *suf* meaning wool, referring to the coarse woollen cloak worn by early adherents. Until the eleventh century and the work of al-Ghazzali and Ibn Arabi, Sufism and its search for a God of love relatively unconcerned with dogmatic ritual were seen by most Islamic religious orthodoxy as heretical.

"But we do not just dance," Abdullah told me, folding his arms in front of him. "This is not some mystical disco." You could tell he had used this line before. "We are true Muslims," he went on. "We pray, we fast, we go on *hajj*, we give *zakat*, we do all these things."

This was confusing. I didn't know enough to distinguish between what Abdullah was saying, with his talk of pilgrimage and alms, and James Wilde suggesting the Sufi *tekke* "let's you think it's something it is not". Or indeed the scorn in Munneb's voice as he told me that Sufis were not true Muslims.

Al was right, this was not where our focus should lie. We were neither theologians nor historians. Although there is something undeniably reassuring about imposing order on your understanding of a foreign place by linking each modern-day fragment you find to its historical antecedent, that was too easy. It was what a Robert Byron or a William Dalrymple might do. Engaging with a place or a people through a historical lens like this makes the individuals you meet appear to be no more than an incarnation of some hidden archetype, while every place you visit ends up looking like a ghastly aberration from its former glory, which turns your journey into an elegy.

We were not in Istanbul to make those kinds of connections, tempting as that might have been. To engage with our surroundings only through their history and to make art that reflected this would be to blinker ourselves to what was going on around us, in real time, and it seemed that something had begun, something was in motion – and I didn't want to turn my back to it.

ℭ

Renaissance

EVERY SIX, SEVEN SECONDS A DROP OF RAIN FELL THROUGH A hole the size of a fist in the skylight forty feet above, before landing with a "quack" on the chipped stone floor beside me. A puddle was starting to form. The space smelt at different times of damp, dust and coffee, depending on whether anyone had recently ordered coffee. On one of the other tables in the café two boys and two girls in school uniform were hunched together in urgent discussion.

I was on the ground floor of an elegant and stately townhouse on the European side of Istanbul that had been turned into a café. It had been ten days since the Sufi *tekke* and my mind was staggering under the weight of the conversations and sights and experiences I had been a part of since that ceremony. I was in the café to write them all down.

Sometimes together and sometimes apart, Al and I had been sent hurtling through Istanbul making art and meeting a cavalcade of people, most of whom wanted us to meet other people who in turn would have parties to take us to, places to show us, and yet more people to meet. Everyone had something to say. Usually it felt important. We both seemed to have "sponge" written in cicatrices across our foreheads.

There was the Anglican priest bemoaning the new religious make-up of Istanbul, who had also just found out about a communist group that wanted to assassinate him; there were sleek clubs where we couldn't afford any drinks but could wear our suits and pretend we were something we were not; there were the transsexuals, the arabesk music, the acisiz arabesk music (literally, "arabesk without pain"); svelte Istanbullu boys and girls setting up artistic projects that fused fashion, music, design and art; music video directors, jazz festivals, art openings, a Turkish Oktoberfest, outdoor art installations; a kindergarten teacher who had studied Islamic art at Oxford; drunk fishermen; McDonald's workers who gave us milkshakes because they liked our paintings; *taksi* drivers who gave us melon, tea, bread, *borek*, whisky and *baklava* because they liked our paintings; a Pakistani sailor who was in love and wanted to become a Buddhist; the country's leading calligrapher; a phalanx of freelance journalists; the bitter English poet who told me I had no right to write about the Middle East until I had studied the region for at least ten years, preferably twenty – this was after I had told him I was keeping a diary – all fleshed out with talk of Ataturk, a Muslim revival, migration from the Turkish East, Kurds, the Turkish army, the looming general election, Istanbul not being where East meets West but where Turkey meets Turkey, as well as the possibility of war in Iraq. But sadly, like balls rumbling around in a tombola, these snapshots did not, when put together, reveal very much.

Apart from one conversation. It wasn't that this conversation gave away some eye-opening truth about Istanbul, or Turkey – in fact it took me far away from both – but from the moment I heard it I could think of little else. It made everything in Istanbul look like the shadow of a parallel existence, a more subdued reality.

In a bar on a street running off Istiklal Caddesi, Istanbul's elegant shopping avenue, I was introduced to a young Turkish journalist who, when he heard what I was up to, asked if I knew about the artistic renaissance in Baghdad.

"No, I don't. Which century was that in?"

"What?" he replied, eyes agog. "It's now! It's happening right now. As we speak. Really. Maybe this is the kind of thing you should see, you know, you were saying you are travelling artist."

"But what is it? What kind of renaissance?"

"A friend of mine told me about it. He said that since 1995, since this oil-for-food programme that they have in Iraq, the art scene in Baghdad has gone crazy. It has exploded. Everyone is making art. Really! Listen, in 1990 there was one commercial gallery in Baghdad. OK? Now there are fifteen."

"How come?" I asked, excited.

"I think because of the sanctions, that the rich people in Iraq, they don't want to spend their money on swimming pools, on fast cars. It looks bad for them. So now they want to buy art instead. It's the economics, stupid!" I remembered that he had gone to university in America. "And apparently in Baghdad, there is this one area, I don't know the name, but there is this one area that my friend is saying is like Paris in the 1900s. What is this famous district in Paris?"

"Um..."

"Where the artists are. You know. Like Picasso. Like..."

"Montmartre?"

"Yes. This part of Baghdad is like that. Studios everywhere." His right arm swept before him as if he was receiving an ovation. "Galleries. The best painting in the Middle East."

"What, better than here?"

He burst out laughing.

"What?"

"That is funny!"

"Yeah." I started to laugh along with him. "Why?"

"What?"

"Why is it so funny?"

"This is not the Middle East!" he said, choking, perhaps for effect. "No, come on. We are not Arabs. I mean it's the best painting in the Middle East. The Arab world. The Arab world is the Middle East. Turkey is Europe. These Iraqis have a really strong tradition in painting. But nobody knows about this renaissance. It is like a secret. I think you must find it. It is important."

"Where can I read about it?"

He reclined in his chair. We were in the garden section of the bar. Above him the Istanbullu sky glowed a stale lemony colour, much like a London sky on an overcast night.

"I don't know. It's hard. The foreign journalists that get to Iraq are too busy trying to find Saddam's secret nuclear bomb or whatever it is. Don't forget, this is the Axis of Evil. People want to hear stories about Saddam the tyrant. They want suffering. They don't want an artistic... I don't know, an artistic renaissance."

"Can't I read about it on an Iraqi website? Or an Iraqi newspaper?"

"There's very little internet in Iraq. And almost no satellite television. The newspapers are state run. So no. But imagine. Really. Imagine it now in Baghdad with all these artists, these galleries. Maybe there's an opening right now! While we have been talking." He clapped his hands together. "Boom! Maybe a picture has just been sold."

Ten minutes later the journalist made his excuses and left. He had a party to get to.

"It does sound amazing," I said dreamily to November, the young curator who had introduced us.

"So why don't you try to get there?" she said.

"What? To Baghdad? No. We can't. No way. You know how difficult it is to get into Iraq? It's almost impossible. No, Iraq's the one place we can't get to on this trip. Anyway, it'll be a war zone pretty soon, won't it?"

"I hope not."

"But no, we'd be mad to try and go."

That had been two days ago.

I was trying to get as much of this down as I could when one of the schoolgirls from the table opposite came over to my table. With a hint of ceremony, she placed a photo album in front of me.

"For you," she said, grinning, before returning to her seat. Her friend was hunched over in nervous giggles. The two boys turned round and smiled sheepishly. I opened the album. The photos, all taken inside different homes, were of her and her friends in bedrooms or living rooms posing, dressing up, pouting, dancing, laughing and sometimes looking startled. All were lit by an unforgiving, surgical flash that gave each image the feel of a Richard Billingham photograph. In each picture the group huddled in an imaginary rectangle in the centre of the image and from time to time you'd see a headscarved mother on the edge of the picture trying to get out of the way. Often she'd be cut in two by the border.

I heard the group practising their next line for some time. They changed the sound and weight of each word, rearranged the order and added new words only to discard them, before one of the boys pulled out his chair with a screech and came over to my table.

"Er. My friend. She want marry you. She say she love you." He smiled a satisfied, job-done smile and marched back to his friends. The girl looked over.

I looked again at the pictures, and in what I thought was the spirit of the moment I nodded at their table. "Why not?" I said. "Let's get married!"

My bride-to-be looked put off by this. Very put off. The mood changed. She no longer smiled. Perhaps I was meant to play hard to get. After more hushed consultation, the girl who had given me the album came over and took it back. The group got up to leave, making me feel like I'd punctured something.

Having got to the door my ex-bride-to-be stopped, turned and strode back to my table. Her poise was composed. Her walk was a coquettish strut. She drew in her cheeks ever so slightly as she arrived at my table and took my wrists, her grip firm and matronly, before dabbing cheap perfume onto the part of my wrist I'd cut if I wanted to hurt myself. Gripping the bottle of perfume like it was a weapon she smiled, looked me in the eye, dropped my hands and set off for the door. I couldn't think what to say. As she walked out into the rain, the sight perfumed by the chemicals now streaming off my wrists, she did not turn around.

This exchange, in its ambiguity, its reflection on Istanbul's westward gaze, truancy or time off, silent longing ruined by words, language, scent, ownership, marriage and the idea of Images of the girl and her home, the pyjamaed female interior, as an overture that cut through language, a calling card, her self distilled into a series of pictures – in all these things this exchange seemed to embody something that we should be making art about. It connected with a part of me that the Sufi ceremony did not. I was not sure why. Nor could I understand why the girl and the smell of her perfume made me think immediately of the artistic renaissance in Baghdad, like some distant Pavlovian association.

I went to find Al and Yasmine, and that afternoon we drove east out of Istanbul into the Turkish countryside.

☾

She Will Love Me So Much

THE GROAN AND GRUNT OF A VAN ACCELERATING FASTER
than usual made me stop what I was doing. For a moment
it sounded like Yasmine. I thought about getting up to
have a look, but stayed put. The sharp, autumnal sun was
beginning to warm me and it felt good: for the last five days
in eastern Turkey I had forgotten what it was to be warm.

Through a gap in the muddy, one-storey houses to the
right of Nazim's house, I saw a van with JANDARMA sten-
cilled on its side. The word was familiar and official, but I
could not, at that moment, remember what it meant. The
Turkish I had picked up since leaving Istanbul was more
preoccupied with getting fed or explaining that Al and I
were painters. Eh? Artists. Music artist, singer? No, picture
artist. Oh.

The van parked somewhere out of sight. There were several shouts followed by a thud-thud-thud of running boots
that sounded like they were running away from where I
was. I wondered who they were after, which villager had
misbehaved.

A minute later two soldiers came jogging round the corner towards me, their guns knocking against their sides. I
turned round. There was no one behind me. They were
running for *me*. I froze. Before my eyes was a scene I had
only ever seen in a computer game or in a film. A group of
soldiers was actually running at me. It wasn't even in slow
motion. Clunk-clunk-clunk. More shouting. Louder. They
grabbed me by the arms, pulled me to my feet and marched
me to the van. I had no idea what was going on. I tried to
get my things, but they wouldn't let me. I tried the Turkish
for "stop", "enough", "no", but they weren't interested.

They bundled me into the back of the van. Al was already there.

"Small world," he said, as the soldiers dumped me in the seat opposite.

"Right."

"And I really, really don't know what they want," he said, annoyed. "They're... I don't know. They're proper idiots," he said, making "idiot" sound like "idjut". "And they went mad just now when they picked me up. I was sitting there, painting, going nowhere, doing nothing, and they came running up at me, yelling, putting their guns in my face. Morons. Fucking morons. I kept on telling them to calm down but they were just like, 'No, no, no.'"

One of the conscripts turned round at Al's "No, no, no" and gave him a lingering look, though Al had his back turned and the look was lost on him.

"But you should have seen the guys from the village when they saw this lot coming," Al gestured at the gaggle of soldiers on either side of us. "I've never seen anyone run so fast."

The four conscripts in the back of the van reeked of nerves and you could tell they were desperate not to screw up. The hands of the soldier next to me were clammy on the barrel of his metal-butted gun and none of them would hold eye contact for more than a few seconds, their eighteen- or nineteen-year-old eyes darting around the van as if lost or looking for something.

We arrived at the barracks and got out of the van. Everything you could see in the barracks said conscripts with too much time on their hands. The lawn looked as if it had been trimmed with nail scissors. Hand-painted rocks marked out a wasteland of empty parking bays in the front. The entire compound was spotless. On a nearby hill the slogan "Country First" had been written in twenty-foot-high characters, again made out of hundreds of hand-painted stones.

We were led to the camp's commanding officers. They reclined in plastic garden furniture in the middle of the lawn, with the remains of a large and late breakfast strewn over the table looking like fallout from a food fight. Conscripts with their backs now bent in servility showed us to two plastic chairs and we sat down as directed.

"So," said the Turkish army commander, who had film-star good looks, swept-back hair and a lot of disdain. "Who," he asked, "are you?"

I looked at Al.

He looked blank.

"Um. Painters," I said. "Artists."

Al nodded.

"We're here to make a picture of the Muslim world," I went on.

Al nodded some more.

The commander leant forward and picked at a piece of meat. "If you are artist, why you are write in book?"

Artists don't write. "It's my diary," I said.

"Show me."

I handed the Turkish Harry Potter notebook to one of the conscripts, who ferried it round to the commander. He winced as he tried to read my handwriting. "You say you are artist." He looked up. "But the artist, he goes to Istanbul, or Ankara, maybe Bodrum." His voice was incredulous, hammed up for the performance. "Not here. No artist here, ever. No foreigner here, ever. These people in the village have no seen foreigner, ever. They are simple people." He shook his head. "But we army. We know foreigner!"

Everyone round the table laughed.

"If you are artist," the commander said, watching me, "then you can relax. Please. Imagine you are guest." One of his colleagues smirked, not sure whether this was a joke as well.

"Your friend does not say anything," said the commander, nodding at Al. "I think he is worried. Relax! Pretend you are at home."

"Well," I said brightly, reclining in my chair so much I almost slid off, and feeling the need to be twice as voluble with Al mute for some reason. "It's a wonderful barracks you have here."

"Yes."

The commander looked at me as if I'd asked him to do a logarithm. I couldn't think what else to say and, feeling flustered, tried to conjure up the small talk I might make with someone I had just met. Inane, harmless, conversation-starting banter that might put the person at ease, get them talking about themselves or, better still, their job. Everyone likes talking about their job.

"So," I said, sensing something was wrong but carrying on all the same, "it's a nice barracks you have here. How many soldiers do you have?"

"What?" asked the captain, no longer reclining, his colleagues sitting up as well. "What do you say?"

"Nothing."

"What do you say?" he asked again.

"I was trying to relax, like you said."

"You ask how many soldiers in barracks."

He said it loudly, shaking his head and seeming to chew over each word, not liking them. The other officers shook their heads.

"You come here," the commander started again, louder this time, "at time with every soldier in Turkish army the most high alert, all because of... of you, you and your leader. Who is this man? British leader?"

"Blair," I said quietly.

41

"Yes, Blair. The troubles in Iraq because Britain is weak with America. Like its dog! We know this. The whole world know this. The whole world laugh at you." His second-in-command demonstrated. "The Turkey army is the most high alert because there is war about to start in Iraq, when two British arrive where no foreigner go. They say they are artist, they cover their number plate with mud, they dress like poor men, they write in books, they ask how many soldier we have. It is suspicious, yes?"

He had a point.

"We're artists," I said. "Really."

He thought for a bit.

"If you are artists, you make picture, yes?"

"We love making pictures," I said, nodding. "We make pictures every day."

"OK. If you are artists, you can make picture of our girlfriends."

"Excellent. Where are they?"

"In Istanbul," he glowered.

"Right."

"But we have photos." He pulled out a passport photo from his wallet. His number two did the same. "You will make pictures of these girls. Nice pictures, OK?" They handed the two photos to a conscript, who jogged round to our side of the table. "We will pay you ten million each."

Although it was bliss to hear anyone say these words, with sincerity, when talking about how much they were going to pay us for paintings we were about to make, ten million Turkish lira got you no more than half a drink in one of the more glamorous Istanbul clubs, or three-and-a-bit McDonald's Happy Meals. I did not, however, feel we were in a position to haggle.

"And we keep your passports," added the commander.

"Right," I said. "We'll make the pictures."

"For tomorrow," he said.

"No problem. Any particular style you'd like? We can do expressionist, cubist..."

"What?"

"Shut. Up," whispered Al out of the side of his mouth. "Nothing."

Back in the village, I made a portrait of Nazim as a dress rehearsal for my portrait of the commander's girlfriend, while Al went to play football in a field with cows in it. Nazim was the elderly man who had taken us in the day before in Yeniyol, the hamlet hidden in a valley that we had driven up to late at night two days earlier and asked the first person we met if we could stay to make pictures. It had been a while since I had made a portrait that was anything more than a sketch and it was good, finally, to be able to luxuriate in every crevice, indentation and crooked line of a face. There were fewer lines on Nazim's face than I had imagined.

He had recently had a tracheotomy and I felt squeamish painting the metal hole in his neck; it was like jabbing at an open wound. It looked like the buckle of a Texan string tie. His eyes aimed in fractionally different directions and his seared hide of skin was so coarse I wanted to touch it. He wore a clean white shirt with an over-sized, pointed collar beneath a leather waistcoat.

Because of his tracheotomy Nazim could not speak properly and instead communicated in clicks and almost inaudible whispers. All the same, it was strangely easy to understand what he was saying. Towards the end of the painting he asked if I ever got bored when I made a portrait. Only afterwards, I said.

Once Al got back from playing football he began to shiver and sweat uncontrollably. The number of clothes he wore or the strength of the fire in the stove made no difference. Nazim looked worried. Al's internal thermometer was in freefall and as I began to wonder what he might have, I felt a paralysing pain in my stomach. It was as if someone was tying nautical knots with my intestine. By the time the sun had set neither Al nor I was able to think about painting, let alone lift a brush. All we could do was sit or lie very still and wait for the pain to subside.

Half an hour after sunset the power in the village went off. "Paint in that!" I could imagine the army commander chuckling to himself next to some secret power switch in the nearby barracks.

For the rest of the night Al and I lay comatose in a silvery, moonlit gloom, our thoughts anæsthetised by pain and our words reduced to an inchoate mumble. The room smelt of woodsmoke and heavy, worsted blankets that had not been washed for some time. Around us were the men we had met the night before, as well as their wives who had come to see if we were alright. It was hard to feel anything but complete safety in this blanket of watchful and mothering eyes and around me the mélange of bodies became one slowly undulating object. Wood continued to be fed into the stove and the patter of someone playing the drum Al had brought in from Yasmine melted into the hushed and chattering voices around us.

It was as close to the middle of nowhere as I could remember being, and yet I could not think of the last time I had felt this safe. Every few minutes a hand would make sure my forehead was not too hot, the touch assured. Unable to sleep and unable to think clearly, I focused my thoughts on the ebb and flow of the words and sounds in the room, their meaning hidden and their rhythm everything. Sometimes the conversation moved in time to the drum, and sometimes a female voice sang in a whispered arabesk alto, everyone going quiet as she did and starting to drift away.

THE NEXT MORNING THE ROOM WAS EMPTY AND I FELT A little better, so I began to paint the commander's girl-friend. Al continued to sleep.

The photo I had was from her graduation and she had turned her head at a perky angle and put her shoulders three-quarters to the camera, like they tell you to do in passport photo booths. It made her much easier to draw. She was pretty and looked deliriously happy that day, and even though I was still feeling ill I found it impossible not to feel by contagion some of her wipe-clean happiness as I painted the teeth and gums of her grin. Before long I was grinning along with her.

Two hours later I finished, feeling close to this girl. She was my imaginary friend or my new lover, even if we had never met and I did not know her name. What made this feeling strange was the idea that this was the same girl the commander, our temporary nemesis, the arch-baddie of the last two days, had gazed at lovingly and lustfully so many times, the same face he had stroked or kissed ten-derly. Dreamt of. Fought for, perhaps.

As I finished, a ruckus started outside. I went to see what it was. An electioneering battle bus had just rolled down a muddy track into the centre of the village, scatter-ing the resident chickens and goats.

The Turkish general election was in less than two weeks' time and the party ahead in the polls, led by a man previously jailed for Islamist sedition, Tayyip Erdogan, described itself as a moderate Islamic party. For a party that openly associated itself with the word "Islam" to be front-runner in the election was unheard of in Ataturk's Turkey. It was anathema to the nation Ataturk had moulded in his image: a jingoistic polity designed to exalt the army officer and not the imam.

The man in the passenger seat growled into a

loudspeaker, raising his voice at the end of each political point and handing out stickers to the children by his window.

A different van advertising a different political party with both a man on a loudspeaker and music came by half an hour later and a larger crowd swarmed around it. Fights broke out among the children over who had collected the most stickers.

Half an hour later again, an army van drove into the village and everyone disappeared. A different gang of soldiers tumbled out and took me and Al back to the barracks. There was no manhandling this time.

At the barracks Al explained to the commander that he had not been well and had not finished his picture. "But I'll post it next week. From Trabzon."

As the commander pondered this, I handed him an ugly, soulless painting that did, for all its failings, resemble the photo he had given me.

"Ahhhh," he said, smiling and holding the portrait at arm's length. "She will like this. Yes. It is good. She will love me so much!" The officers laughed heartily, as officers should. "OK. Here is fifteen million," he said, handing me a clump of lira as well as our passports. "It is important that you send this picture next week. We trust you with this, OK. But now, come eat with us to celebrate picture," he said, looking and sounding like a changed man.

We were led to a table in the middle of the lawn where succulent kebabs had been laid out. The sun was shining. A weight had been lifted.

Al was still feeling ill and did not want to eat; instead he sat apart from the table looking miserable beneath the seven layers of clothing and two woolly hats that he had not taken off since last night. His internal thermometer was still on strike.

The officers began to talk about Ramadan, which started in a few weeks.

"Most of us will follow it," said the commander, turning to me. I felt guilty when he looked at me. It was as if something had gone on between me and his girlfriend, the one I'd been leering at all morning. What if he found out?

"But if there is a war Turkish army will fight. Ramadan does not stop us."

I thought about saying I would pass this on to my superiors in London. Because he thought before we were spies. Sort of. It would have been a joke.

Mercifully, I kept the thought to myself.

"We do not have to do the Ramadan," he carried on. "And it is not the law to follow this. Turkey is not like Iran. We are not the fanatic!" Everyone laughed on cue. "But many, many people in Turkey do Ramadan this year. More than before," he said, his tone serious. "Everyone now is becoming more close to Islam. I think you will see this everywhere in Turkey. But it is important the people in Turkey don't forget the army."

We nodded soberly.

One of the conscripts who had been waiting on us brought over a plastic bag that had been left at the gates by a man from the village. Inside were two boxes of honey-soaked *baklava*. The officers ogled them as if they were female, cor-ing and phwoar-ing while plates were fetched.

"Beautiful," the commander sighed a little later, sucking the honey from his fingers before falling back into his chair with a post-coital, dreamy smile on his face. "We get presents like this from the village every day. They are such simple people. They give you trouble, yes?"

"No, none at all."

"Really?"

"Not a thing."

"Well, be careful."

"Why?"

"Er, the women there are very simple." The second offi-cer nodded. "They don't educate anything, they only make food, make children, make sex." All the soldiers roared with laughter. "And maybe they try make something with you. They are crazy. So are their men. Maybe they try some-thing with you!" More laughter, and some thumping of the table this time. "These men, they don't let their women sit with them in the house. Really."

I thought back to last night.

"But the problem in the villages," said the commander, "the big problem, is imam. Imam has too much power. Turkey is not Muslim country. It is lay country. You know this word, lay?"

I nodded. There was a lull in the conversation and a junior officer pulled a *saz* out of its case. Everyone watched and smiled as he began to pluck a dreamy sound that floated up into the afternoon sky, the Anatolian hills behind him looking tea-stained and autumnal.

"*Hamdulillah*," the officer next to me sighed.

"What does that mean?" I asked, leaning over.

"Praise be to God," he whispered, making sure none of his colleagues heard.

☾

VIP

"Mashallah," said the Iranian border guard as he glanced at Yasmine, smiling. With his avuncular manner-isms and checked shirt tucked into sensible pleated trousers, it was hard to imagine a less threatening or more welcoming border guard.

"What does *Mashallah* mean?"

"It is Arabic, but we use it here as well. It means, hmmm... it means God has willed it. You will see it on the buses everywhere in Iran."

"And are we, er, are we free to enter Iran?" I asked.

"Yes. Yes please, you are most welcome in Iran. Please." He pointed to the exit.

At first I thought there must be some kind of catch. Another line of checkpoints. But no, we were in. During the previous week in Turkey since leaving Nazim in Yeniyol, we had been told to expect a forensic examination of Yasmine on arrival in the Islamic Republic of Iran.

"In Iran," they would say, "every man is crazy religious man. The man is allowed no picture of girl, even if she is your mother, unless she wear headscarf. You will be locked up for many years. No cards, no chess. No games. All games illegal in Iran. No Coca-Cola, nothing American, and *no talk to girl!* Or prison."

But after twenty minutes of firm, welcoming handshakes and dutiful passport stamping, we had crossed the Iranian border.

I was about to drive off when an Iranian girl in a black headscarf and jeans with fabric drawn round her waist like a miniskirt came up to Al's window. He was fiddling with the stereo and did not see her. She knocked on the window. He stared in disbelief.

"Where are you from?" she asked through the glass in Hollywood-practised English.

"Er... Inglestan," said Al, loudly, slowly, too shocked to wind down his window.

"England! Wow. Good for you, good for you. That's a long way," she said. "Welcome!"

Al was still in shock and his window remained up. The girl shrugged, smiled and walked off.

Already Turkey felt distant.

The feeling as we drove away from the border was hard to contain: a messy and cathartic eruption of fast driving and singing and talking and music turned up loud. We had a full tank of petrol, a hundred yards of blank canvas, we could go anywhere we liked, and for the first time we felt genuinely welcome in a country while all around us was a new world unlike anything we had seen before. The Persian script looked outlandish and exotic. There was a new landscape, an Iranian landscape, different-looking faces, different clothes, different shops, different food and a different kind of Islam. Even the trees looked different as we raced deeper into the night and further into Iran. Oh, and there were now three of us in Yasmine. Stephen was perched in the middle of the backseat.

I had met Stephen for the first time nine months earlier at a travel fair in Earl's Court. A mutual friend had said "You two must meet" because, like me and Al, Stephen made his art outside and abroad. After running the idea past Al a few times, I had asked Stephen to join us for the Iranian leg of our journey. He had agreed straightaway.

Stephen was four years older than Al and me – twenty-six to our twenty-two – and had recently finished a six-year stint at Brighton Art College. He had a mane of reddish hair that, as he liked to point out, was testament to his Nordic roots. Stephen was half Norwegian. He liked telling us about his Viking forebears and the scandal of how English history teachers had turned them into barbarous rapists. He was on a one-man crusade to revise this. He had small eyes and pink skin and spent a lot of time making fun of himself in a brilliant and effortless way. Stephen was instantly likeable. If he wasn't putting himself down he was telling you breathless stories about his idols – Johnny Cash, Peter Beard, Dan Eldon – or making sure you knew how much he disliked Damien Hirst and Tracey Emin, or any other successful Saatchi-sponsored British artist. He talked about them in a familiar late-1990s British art college way, the colour draining from his face as he became a conduit for the failed artists who had lectured him at art college.

As arranged, we had met up with Stephen the day before in Doğubayazit, in Turkey, a few miles from the Iranian border. After only one night and one border crossing it felt as though he had been with us for several weeks. In a good way.

The ten-hour drive from Trabzon, near the Turkish border, to Tehran was dotted with roadblocks, each one a whirr of grinning handshakes and warm greetings of *salaam aleikom* (may peace be upon you) from Iranian army conscripts the same age as us wearing olive-green combat trousers and balaclavas drawn up double over their ears. Few seemed to be at all interested in checking our passports. Most were too busy saying "Hello" or "Welcome" and laughing at Yasmine's steering wheel being on the wrong side of the car. Had we not realised? We should take it back to the man who sold it to us! The more they pointed it out, the funnier it was. They also liked Yasmine's raised suspension. The standard Iranian police trucks were the same make and model as Yasmine, and they too had raised suspensions. It was a good thing to have, said one burly sergeant.

"For VIP person only!" he said, roaring with laughter and giving me another meaty handshake.

As well as roadblocks there were tollbooths where wide-eyed Iranian *petits fonctionnaires* would wave Yasmine through free of charge, the novelty of a car with its steering wheel on the wrong side proving too much. At one petrol station we were let off all of the 43p it cost to fill Yasmine with 37 litres of diesel because, as the man said, our beautiful car was most welcome in Iran. The government subsidised fuel in Iran, as I found out that day.

In between the roadblocks and tollbooths lay a coarse landscape leading to immense horizons. Everything had a rugged finish. Looking at it for too long would make your mouth go dry. It was what I imagined the plain of Mordor to look like. Running alongside the road were pylons not yet connected by cables and in their rusted branches birds of prey had built their nests.

Something about this bleak landscape reminded me of the no-man's land we had driven through just before arriving at the Iranian border, a sight that was hard to forget.

Readiness

ON EITHER SIDE OF THE ROAD THAT RUNS BETWEEN Doğubayazit and the Turkish–Iranian border there is a wasteland. To the left as you drive towards Iran lies Mount Ararat, where Noah's Ark is said to have come aground as the flood subsided.

It was late afternoon when we drove down this road. The midriff of Mount Ararat was coloured pink while its peak was blotted by cloud, as it had been for several days now. To the right had been a more startling sight: a mass of Turkish armoured personnel carriers, tanks, jeeps and several thousand soldiers either tending to their vehicles, pitching tents or jogging back and forth in units of twenty or thirty with their legs moving as one, so that from a distance each unit looked like an overgrown millipede.

It felt like something was about to happen.

It was late October 2002 and men and women in the news were talking with growing conviction about an Anglo-American and possibly UN-backed invasion of Iraq that was either "likely" or "inevitable". It might also involve a northern front launched from Turkey, they would add. The real question, to paraphrase the CNN or BBC discussions we had glimpsed, was not "if" this invasion took place but "when".

The more composed talking heads, not the military experts but the ageing hacks who knew the American political landscape and had been reporting on it for several decades, assured whoever was watching that this was not about Saddam Hussein's purported link to 9/11 so much as George Bush Junior wanting to finish off what his dad had started eleven years earlier. To do that, Junior had to do more than just invade Iraq, he had to get to Baghdad.

It was all about getting to Baghdad, they would say, nodding seriously and glancing at the camera.

☾

Gallery Seyhoun

WITH HIS FRESHLY IRONED WHITE SHIRT OPEN A BUTTON lower than anyone else would dare at that time of year, Nader Seyhoun had the air of a Mediterranean yacht-owning playboy. His hair smelt of someone who had just got out of the shower, possibly after an hour in the gym, and Gallery Seyhoun lit up as he walked in. One hand flicked through a string of prayer beads, keeping time as he

fired questions at the woman who had looked after us while we waited. That morning she wore cowgirl boots and a delicate, black muslin headscarf that alluded, and no more, to the whispers of grey hair beneath.

Under the watchful eye of his mother, who was not there that morning, Nader Seyhoun ran Tehran's leading commercial contemporary art gallery, Gallery Seyhoun. I had started emailing him just under a year ago when I first knew we'd be in Tehran, and after five months of e-nagging he had agreed to let us have a show in his gallery. This felt like a coup, considering that Al and I had only a handful of very small shows to our names, most of which had taken place in cafés or restaurants.

Our show in Gallery Seyhoun, which had once been graced by Andy Warhol in the days of the Shah, opened in five weeks' time and we needed to make work that Nader's clientele not only liked but liked enough to buy; we needed the money. Although we were spending a lot less now that we had left Istanbul, to live off the money we had for the rest of the year would mean Al and I had three pounds per day, each, and we were not sure how far this would get us. Perhaps farther than the Saudi desert, perhaps not. A tank of petrol in Turkey had cost us thirty-five pounds. Cheap hotel rooms in Iran cost three or four pounds. A repair to Yasmine could set us back several hundred pounds.

Like being told to be funny, now, we had to make good art, very soon.

Nader greeted the three of us like brothers, while Al and I got out the work we had made in Turkey.

"And you will exhibit these?" he asked, sifting through the loose canvases and bits of card.

"Maybe," said Al.

"Right," Nader nodded as we pulled out more work. "I think only works from Iran."

"OK."

We had not yet made anything in Iran.

"And your invitations, you must get them printed. I will give you number of the framing man. He does not speak English so I think you should go there. Draw for him how you want the frames. You must explain to him slowly, yes? I will draw you a map and soon we must get you press. We will have everyone in Tehran talking about this show! You have spoken to the British Council?"

"About to," I said, meaning I had forgotten.

"You have a lot to do," he said, looking at each of us in turn, his features wan beneath one of the gallery spots.

"So how many pictures do you think we need?" asked Al.

"Thirty. Maybe forty?"

Thirty-seven days until our show opened.

"So how's this show going?" asked Stephen, looking at the large-format photos of dreamy, cloud-clotted skies that had been hung in front of sheets of cotton.

"Oh, very nice," said Nader, his face lighting up. "I like these so much. They are beautiful, no? But they are coming down today."

"I mean are they selling well?"

"People are not buying art so much now in Tehran, I think."

"And how many have you sold?" asked Stephen. He too was relying on our show to fund his time in Iran.

"None. Yet." Nader turned away. "But there is the rest of the morning. Maybe we sell some then."

WE SPENT THE NEXT FEW DAYS IN A FLAT HIGH ABOVE Tehran surrounded by exquisite paintings, large books that you open slowly and gawp at reverentially, and furniture you didn't want to put a glass on in case it left a ring. The owner of the flat was a friend of Nader's who was away for a few days. As well as letting us stay, she lent us a mobile phone. Having a phone changed everything. It gave us a sense of purpose. We were in Iran on business with a phone.

For several days we visited galleries, spoke to framing people, met with the British Council who kindly agreed to pay for our invitations and our framing, and went to a graphic design studio to get our invitations made. The pony-tailed men there laughed because we had the word "Islam" in the title of our show. We had decided to call our first exhibition "Visions of Islam".

"There is no Islam here!" they had said.

"Right," we had replied in unison, laughing nervously. None of us had a clue what they meant. Iran was, after all, the world's only "Islamic Republic".

Back at the flat we began to look harder at books on Iranian contemporary art and watched a marathon of Iranian films. In between we went to see the girls and boys in internet cafés or fast-food joints on Valiasr Street as they preened, made eyes at each other, huddled in groups and ate without meaning it. The girls wore their headscarves right back over their heads so you could see a clump of hair at the front. Often the clump was dyed blonde, and sometimes the headscarf would fall off, the girl making a show of putting it back on like someone in a Carry On film having their bra pop open.

Slowly, we became less daunted by what we had to do, even if none of us yet knew what kind of art we should really be making.

Thirty-five days to go. One picture made.

☾

Bath Time

On our last night in Tehran Al went to have a bath in the deluxe black-tiled bathroom in Nader's friend's apartment. After half an hour he jogged out of the bathroom, a towel slowing his legs.

"Nobody take the bath, I'm still in it," he shouted, rummaging in his bag next door before scampering back into the bathroom with a canvas, a Walkman and some paint. The door slammed shut. An hour later he reappeared, grinning.

"I've got it."

"What?" asked Stephen.

"I've worked out how I'm going to paint. Forever."

"How?" asked Stephen. Al continued to hop about the room a bit.

"It's about. Hmm. Where to start, it's about a system. A system that expresses what I feel. Not what I see." He hopped some more. "You see, I've got to go somewhere photography can't. There's no point in going to a place and painting what I see. That's what the Orientalists did. They'd go to a place in the Orient..."

"Eh? Why do you say the Orient?" asked Stephen, putting down his pencil.

"The Orient," said Al.

"We're in Iran."

"Yes. The Orient."

"No. The Orient is the Far East," said Stephen, slowly. "You get Oriental cuisine in China, not Iran."

Al screwed up his face.

"Stephen, we're in the Orient. Honestly."

"We're not."

"That's not the point. The point is Orientalists, and that is what they're called, Orientalists would come here and paint what they saw. I, on the other hand, am going to paint what I *feel*. No figuration." He was still looking like he'd won something.

"What's your system then?" asked Stephen.

"Well, it's all about having the same limitations on every picture I make. Each one is on the same size canvas and I can only use the three primaries. And black and white," he said, remembering. "I use the same brush, or maybe my hand. Yes, I think my hand. Otherwise I'd have to make a decision about the size of brush. You see, it's about removing decision making. About creating limitations, like with ancient rock art. With that you have people working on a fixed medium, rock, with a fixed tool, a sharper bit of rock, and when you have that kind of limitation you get a more pure expression. You have to, really. There's more of you and less of what you're using." He paused.

"Let's see it then," said Stephen.

Al held the canvas in front of him, muttering under his breath "Can you see what it is yet?" in the mildest of mild Australian accents.

Stephen and I took in a mess of thick and expressive paint. As Al had promised there was no figuration, just joyful paint, empty canvas, marks. The more I looked at it the better it was; it was unlike anything he had done before.

"That's being in the bath, just now, listening to Cheb Khaled," said Al. "The first ever paint-feeling."

"Paint-feeling?" asked Stephen.

"Sure. They're called paint-feelings."

"Since when?"

"Since just now. That's what I call them."

"Great. Well, don't mind me," said Stephen, starting to laugh. "I've just got to get on with another of my... my pencil-arts."

"You like it really, don't you Stephen?" asked Al, still holding his painting.

"Nope."

"You do."

"Promise you I don't."

"What don't you like about it?"

"Well, there's the name, the..."

"No, no, you haven't let yourself see the joy of them. Each one, I mean I've only done one but there will be thousands, seriously, each one is this incredible account of a feeling. Like a page from a diary. I mean, how many Orientalists went to the Orient and made pictures of what they felt when they were in a bath?"

"I wonder why."

"No, really," said Al, nodding, smiling, willing him to like the idea.

"Really, it's fine. The idea's fine," said Stephen, looking at the picture again and cocking his head. "I've just never really liked abstract expressionism."

"But this isn't abstract expressionism."

"Course it is."

"Really?"

"Sure."

"I thought they always did theirs in a studio," said Al.

"Al, it doesn't matter where you do it, or how you do it. You're creating the same image. You can go and make it with your eyes shut in exactly seven seconds as, I don't

know, as you jump off a cliff, you know, 'to have a system'.
It's just," he grimaced, "it's just it's been done before. It's
like all these people I was at college with, who when they
talked about whatever they were making it would sound
amazing. And then you'd see what they'd actually made
and it wouldn't move you. Maybe if you can be there to
explain the concept to everyone who sees one of your Al-
feelings..."

"Paint-feelings."

"Paint-feelings, whatever, then you'll be alright."

Al did not seem to hear Stephen. His expression was
that of the Tehrani men and women who would cross the
road just in front of Yasmine without looking at the
oncoming traffic, as if transfixed by the other side where
they had seen something wonderful.

☾

Orientalist

ON THE DAY WE ARRIVED IN ESFAHAN, FOUR HOURS SOUTH
of Tehran, I found by chance the Esfahan Art University.
It was just behind one of the arcades running down the
length of Meydan Emam Khomeini, the square at the centre of the city. Not long after wandering into the university
I met the director, a gaunt and handsome woman who was
interested in what we were doing and suggested we come
back the following week and give a presentation. We fixed
a date.

Just as Al, Stephen and I walked into the university's
central courtyard on the appointed day, the rain stopped.
The director summoned the student body. They oozed
cool like no other group of students. Most of the boys had
long hair, carefully trimmed facial topiary and a purpose-

ful swagger. The girls preferred to slouch or pout. They wore maroon, violet, pink or go-faster-red lipstick and tracksuit hoodies or woolly hats to cover their hair. We had seen some of this *hijab*-wearing punkishness in Tehran, but nothing like it in Esfahan up to then. As the director introduced us I heard the words "Islam" and "Gallery Seyhoun" again and again in her melodious stream of Persian.

"Every student dreams of exhibiting in Gallery Seyhoun," she had told me.

At this point we had enough pictures to fill one of its four walls. It was 10 November. The show opened on 7 December.

While the three of us took it in turns to address the assembled students the director went through our work, holding up each piece in front of her like a porter at an auction. The eighty or ninety students gasped, laughed, murmured or said nothing as they took in the different pictures. Saying nothing was the worst.

After going through the paintings and collages she went through Stephen's sketchbook, holding up double-paged collages of posters, labels, tickets, photos of himself and tight, architectural drawings. Everyone laughed at the double page of a sticker of a girl with a semi-opaque veil drawn over her lips who gazed out at the classroom, longingly. The director asked polite questions about the artistic point Stephen was trying to make. Stephen became fidgety, as if asked to explain something he had said in his sleep. She moved on to another page.

"Shit," he hissed to me. "I know what's coming next." He turned to the director. "Er, excuse me. I think everyone's seen enough. Really."

"No, no, it is good," she said. "The students must see all of this, it is interesting for them." There was a hum of agreement in front of us.

"They really don't, you know."

She held up the next double-page spread without looking at it. More murmuring than usual. I craned my neck to see which page it was.

They were looking at Stephen's rendition of our border crossing between Turkey and Iran. On one side was a girl in a *chador*: a stereotyped, journalistic-photo kind of girl-in-*chador* where you don't see the face, and next to her was a line of tanks.

"You must change this," said a boy with a shaved head, glasses and a sheepskin-lined waistcoat, as he stepped forward. "You cannot say this." If he was sitting at a table he would have thumped it. "It is make everyone think we are war people. You don't understand this about Iran."

More murmurs.

"I was just putting down what I saw, you know, at the border."

"No! This is wrong. Why you like *chador* and guns? In Iran we hate the war! It makes us angry. So angry. Million die in this war with Saddam. This picture not Iran, not Islam. Is only your... your head, your mind, yes? Like Orientalist."

I winced. Enough people in Tehran had asked politely whether we were "Orientalist artists" for us to be touchy about it. As we had recently found out, there were still middle-aged European or American artists happy to work under this soubriquet: men and sometimes women who would go to the Middle East and paint stylised pictures reminiscent of what their European predecessors might have made in the eighteenth or nineteenth century. "Orientalist" in the context of painting was a byword for saccharine, idealised visions of an exotic Alice-in-Wonderland East, a place that didn't really exist where European imaginations were allowed to run riot. For many of the original European Orientalists, visiting the Orient was a big letdown. During his first visit in 1843 French poet Gérard de Nerval wrote mournfully, "soon I will know of no place in which I can find a refuge for my dreams". Everything he had seen was a watered-down version of his fantasy.

This was exactly the kind of art we didn't want to be associated with, yet at the same time I knew that if we reacted too strongly against it we would become a precise inversion of what we were trying to avoid: like three mascara-wearing teenage goths living in a straitlaced suburbia, we would end up as an extension of what we were trying to break away from, rather than something discrete. None of us was yet sure whether we could sever the link to our predecessors, or whether our respective nationalities would mean that we were forever Orientalists, technically speaking.

"But this picture has nothing to do with what I think now," said Stephen, shaken.

"And this next to it?"

"Nothing. No, not important at all," said Stephen as the boy bent down to read it. "Definitely time to move on." He tried to turn the page.

"Aha," said the boy in the sheepskin waistcoat, stepping back. "About the man being hanged in Tehran. The execution, no?"

"Look. Like I said, it's about first impressions."

"OK, so Iran is the *chador*, the war, and the execution. Bravo."

The discussion splintered and different students took first Al and then me aside. One girl did not like the way I used the posters I had torn down from walls in Qom and Esfahan.

"You cannot use the Persian word like this," she said. "You cannot use it without knowing meaning. And you don't know meaning, do you?"

"Not really," I said, becoming fidgety like Stephen a moment ago.

"But you must know the meaning," she said, her voice and face pleading. "Otherwise this art is lazy. So lazy."

For a while I tried to tell her my ignorance was interesting or that my work was faithful to the experience of being an outsider, but soon enough this no longer made sense. The girl spoke in a lovely, imploring voice and before long I agreed, completely, with what she was saying. What I had done was lazy. I couldn't defend it. I had to find out the meaning of these posters before using them.

This first day in the Esfahan Art University became a turning point in the art Stephen and I were making. Al's art was different, in that nobody accused it of being ignorant or Orientalist in a pejorative sense. This turning point for me and Stephen might have been about to happen anyway, yet that day opened our eyes to the possibility of making work that was specific to Iran and acknowledged our outsider status while avoiding the clichés of Orientalism.

This was the first time anyone in any of the places we had been working had both engaged with our work and torn it apart. It was exactly what we needed.

☾

To Die for Love

I SPENT THE REST OF THE AFTERNOON IN THE UNIVERSITY, chatting and painting with Esfahani art students. Almost every boy or girl I spoke to asked what I thought of their government, the Iranian government, the face of the Islamic Republic of Iran; and before I could answer they would tell me they hated it. Especially the way it forced you to do national service. Without going through these two years of drills, border patrols, traffic policing and possibly fighting, none of them could get a passport, and getting a passport was all that mattered because a passport gave them the chance to make art abroad; this was the escape so many of them dreamt of.

After the backwardness of the government and a future impaired by it, most conversations moved on to things that they the art students controlled. Things like what music they listened to, who they were going out with, their clothes, the art they were making or their favourite drink, all of which was trivial and throwaway, looking back on it, compared to what happened the following day.

THAT NIGHT, THE NIGHT BEFORE IT BEGAN, AN ART STUDENT called Moonlight was nervous. He could not eat. He paced his flat. The men around him, in their silence, were beginning to piss him off. They too were down to their boxer shorts and T-shirts and none of them could sleep.

"We're going to get expelled," said Arush.

"I know," said Moonlight.

"We're going to get expelled," said someone else.

"I know," said Moonlight, looking at Arush.

On the front of Arush's T-shirt was a fake Nike tick and on the back the words MANCHESTER: JUST DO IT.

THE NEXT DAY IN THE UNIVERSITY'S MAIN COURTYARD, A crowd gathered round a metal structure that looked like a pared-down stand for a tennis umpire. In the studio where I had been working the day before, Arush was busy painting Moonlight's face red. Arush's face had already been painted white. He wore white trousers and a long-sleeved white T-shirt to complete the look. They did this without speaking as the students taking part in the protest had taken a vow of silence for the day.

The seed of their discontent had been sown in the summer. Twelve of Esfahan Art University's finest students,
including Arush and Moonlight, had gone on a sponsored
university outing to Kish Island in the Persian Gulf. They
had had a great time. They had made plenty of work and
planned lots more, including pieces that involved installations or performance, and when they returned to Esfahan
the director of their university told them there would be a
competition to see who had made the best work on Kish
Island. The twelve artists refused. They were artists, they
said. There was no way they would compete against each
other. The director said they would have to get over this
and set a date for the competition, adding that it would
take the form of an exhibition. The twelve artists, led by
Arush and Moonlight, repeated that they would not compete against each other and after the director refused to
compromise, they decided to stage a protest.

As Moonlight described their not-so-tragic plight, I
realised that with no exhibition to fight he and his friends
would have staged a protest about a blocked drainpipe. As
a group, they were desperate to express some of their
chronic frustration with both their setting and the authority that appeared to castrate their dreams.

The Kish Island competition had by now become a
microcosm of everything the art students hated about the
Iranian government. They were being dictated to. In the
eyes of Moonlight and Arush, the university director had
become the government while they, the middle-class art
students, were now the downtrodden masses.

The director seemed happy to go along with this, and in
the spirit of her new role mimicking the Iranian government
she barred "the British artists" from the university on the
day of the protest. She let it be known that it was the three
of us who had organised the protest that was about to start.

Accordingly, when Al and Stephen arrived at the main gate to the university on the morning of the protest, they were told they could not enter. By chance I had taken the back entrance and got in fine. The man at the main gate explained to Al and Stephen that he had been told not to let in the British artists responsible for inciting the protest, but without any teachers to enforce the ban – all of them had taken the day off when they heard what was afoot – Al and Stephen were able to talk their way in.

Every time there is a major protest in Tehran it is linked by the Iranian government to "foreign scheming", be it the CIA, "Zionist plotters" or "British spies". It was not hard to see which of these categories we had been corralled into. For once, it would have been nice to be mistaken for Islamic extremists.

Getting ready with Moonlight and Arush in the studio were ten other artists who wore blue, yellow or green with their faces painted the requisite colour. There was one girl in the group, though I wasn't sure if she was part of the protest or was just wearing too much make-up. With the protesting artists keeping their vow of silence it was hard to find out.

I wished Moonlight luck. He was far away beneath his mask of paint and at first did not hear.

"Good luck," I said, louder this time. He looked up and nodded, his face sombre, before scribbling on a piece of paper.

PRAY FOR ME.

Outside several hundred art students sat and stood in a circle as they waited for the show to start. Pieces of paper were sellotaped to the ground. Objects picked up on Kish Island demarcated a temporary and circular stage. A tinny stereo started to play a Pink Floyd track, its sound mangled and light, and after a few chords Moonlight leapt out of the studio and began to sprint barefoot round the court-yard. His eyes were painted hollow, making him look like a ballerina on speed as he danced through flowerbeds, round trees, past people on the edge of the crowd, before hurling water balloons at the audience. No one seemed to mind. The others danced out after him, the colours of their clothes and faces startling next to the black or navy blue of the spectators and the pale, dust-coloured bricks of the university.

Roger Waters continued to croon. Workmen perched on some scaffolding nearby stopped what they were doing. Each protesting artist dragged behind him a length of coloured rope, and together they began to act out a com-plicated and silent sequence, each player representing a dif-ferent Iranian character. There was the Iranian who is always happy, the Iranian who is always sad, the dreamer, the simpleton, the comedian, the artist, the depressive, the lovers not allowed to love, the Basij or paramilitary, the devotee and the government supporter. Together they buzzed around the metal stand as if it was a hive under construction, weaving ropes into and out of it until fifteen minutes later the central figure – the depressed one, Arush, in white – was bound by the different-coloured ropes and deserted on top of the metal structure. It was as though he was about to be hung. The figures below acted out either approval or apathy before traipsing off. The per-formance finished with Arush forgotten on top of the stand. There was rapturous applause and Arush walked back to the studio.

Just as a single colour inspires different reactions in dif-ferent people – something Al had been reminded of six days earlier in Sepahan's football stadium in Esfahan when he made a paint-feeling using a lot of red paint and was attacked by a section of the crowd who bombarded him with pistachio shells and bits of wood, because red was the colour of Sepahan's arch-rival, Persepolis, something Al did not know – what we took from Moonlight and Arush's performance was unlikely to be what anyone around us took from it. With no words the performance was passive. That was its beauty. None of the protesters could be accused of serious sedition because of the wordlessness of their protest.

All the same, Moonlight was suspended from the university several weeks later. Had there been words I imagine he would have been expelled.

The *ta'ziyeh* – a traditional passion play that is part of the solemn Ashura festival and a ritual increasingly frowned on by the Iranian clergy – is acted out annually during the month of Muharram, the first in the Islamic calendar, in most Iranian villages or neighbourhoods. It is the only drama indigenous to Islam and tells the story of the events leading up to the martyrdom of Imam Husayn, grandson of the Prophet Muhammad. Men and women weep as they watch it, not because of the quality of the performance but because the *ta'ziyeh* rubs up against the most sensitive part of the Shia psyche, as much as it is possible to talk about a Shia psyche as something unchanging or concrete. The story embodies everything it is to be a Shia Muslim. To see it being acted out is like watching a televised reconstruction of the murder of your father. You cannot help but cry or be deeply moved.

In the traditional *ta'ziyeh* ordinary people dress up as the historical characters – perhaps the local butcher as Imam Husayn, all in green, the bank clerk as the wicked Caliph Yazid, all in red – while the audience sits or stands in a circle as the drama unfolds, just as the art students had formed a circle while their classmates danced in the midday sun.

The *ta'ziyeh*'s basic themes of repression, injustice, hope and tragic martyrdom were also played out during the months leading up to the Iranian Revolution in late 1978 and early 1979, as the Shah's regime fell apart.

It was only when I learnt more about this ritual that I understood quite how powerful Moonlight and Arush's performance was. I was in awe of it; all three of us were. None of us had ever made something so courageous. Not only was their performance visually stunning, artistically tight and brave, but by drawing on traditional Shia motifs it also had a semi-religious and political appeal that gave it authenticity and added bite in that setting.

The three of us made to leave the university. Unlike the day before, we now got suspicious looks from the students we passed in the arcades running round the different courtyards. We were now the "foreign schemers" or "the British spies-sorry-I-mean-artists"; the ones who had purportedly organised the protest they had just witnessed. With this encounter both silent and dictated by what we looked like and what they, the viewer, had been told about us, we were helpless. And not for the first time.

One boy stopped me. Al and Stephen kept on walking.

"Are you coming back?" he asked.

"Er, no, we can't. We're not allowed back in. We're banned."

"OK. Then it is good to meet you." He shook my hand.

"So when do you graduate?" I asked.

"This is my final year. Then I am soldier." He laughed. "Look at me." His frame was hopelessly thin. "For you I am look like soldier?"

"You'll make a great soldier." I made to leave and said goodbye. "*Khoda hafez.*" This was the same conversation I had had at least ten times yesterday. As I turned to go the boy stopped me, the back of his hand firm on the inside of my elbow.

"We are the same, you and me."

"What?"

"We are the same. When you are home, when you are in England, remember this. We are the same, you and me. That's all."

He smiled sweetly and left.

I drifted out of the university. Already I missed it. Around me the streets of Esfahan looked staid and windswept.

Opposite the main entrance to the university, like a flower grown from a seed that had blown from the walled garden we had just left, a simple, unexplained message was scrawled in black spray paint across a long and low wall: TO DIE FOR LOVE.

I caught up with Al and Stephen. Al looked morose, like he had just heard some bad news, and Stephen didn't look too happy either. None of us had eaten or drunk or smoked since dawn and we were getting close to the most uncomfortable last three or four hours of the day, the part where one of us, if not all of us, would become irritable and fidgety. It was the month of Ramadan, or Ramazan in Persian, and for the last five days we had decided to fast, so we knew what it felt like, which meant no food, water or smoke from sunrise to sunset.

"Right. Let's get out of here." Al began to walk purposefully down the street. "Where's Yasmine?"

"Yup. Let's get out of here," Stephen sighed.

"But where to?"

"I don't know," said Stephen. "Away."

☾

Pinocchio

ALTHOUGH AT THE VERY CENTRE OF IRAN, ONLY A FEW hours' drive from Esfahan, Yazd felt forgotten. Displaced Baluchi and Afghan men would drift down its streets looking lost amid the provincial Iranian smartness. Few of Yazd's original labyrinthine alleyways were any wider than a car. In parts they might be carpeted by sand, reminding you that this was a city in the middle of a desert. But most of these streets were now hidden by the tree-lined boulevards that had been inserted by the Iranian government like fig leaves to hide the Old City's ageing nakedness.

There was something soothing if not sensual about leaving the railroad efficiency of Yazd's main streets and sinking into the warm and tanned embrace of the slightly chaotic alleyways and cul-de-sacs of the Old City. Just ten strides from the main street and it was as if you had slammed a door shut behind you. The rumble of the main road was replaced by a padded and interior set of sounds and within the custard-coloured walls on either side of you were gnarled doorways, each one turquoise or emerald or blue. The streets had risen over the centuries while the doorways had not; a lot of them looked as if they were drowning. The older ones had different knockers on either side of the door, one for men and one for women. Next to some of the doors were bells that made the sound of a bird tweeting, or metallic boxes with mouthpieces where you could, among other things, announce your gender to whoever was inside.

I walked through one set of open doors into what turned out to be Yazd's Art University. I was getting good at finding art universities by accident. There I met Ruya.

She wore paint-spattered overalls and had wonderful, dark-rimmed eyes that didn't blink much. I told her I wanted to make pictures of artists. She said I would paint a picture of her, only not in the university and not just then. She had a commanding presence. If I would wait an hour she would take me somewhere where I could paint her in private. I said I would wait.

An hour later Ruya finished the still life she was working on and summoned her friend to act as our translator. This friend worshipped Ruya. She was the dowdy and plump foil to Ruya's totem of glamour and together they formed a familiar, symbiotic female double act where each girl felt they looked better next to the other but for opposite reasons.

The three of us left the university and Ruya bought some pistachios. We were now several weeks into Ramazan and Ruya was not interested in observing *sawm*, fasting. Ruya's friend was. She tutted in a "her loss", nannyish way as Ruya picked apart her pistachios, the shells falling to the ground as if she was leaving a trail.

We carried on past restaurants where sheets of newspaper had been put up in the windows to hide whatever was happening inside. In most restaurants the newspaper did not cover the whole window and at the bottom you could see rows of socked feet swinging happily back and forth. Sometimes, if you were lucky, a bit of food would fall down from whatever veiled operation was going on behind the newspaper.

Throughout the last two weeks, mainly because it was so heavily endorsed by the government, observing Ramazan had felt like an annual steeplechase in an English boarding school with most of the people we met trying to worm their way out of it. One man in Esfahan showed me a doctor's note that excused him from fasting. It said that he had injured his toe. He could not possibly fast with an injured toe, he had said.

Ruya, her friend and I arrived at Yazd's Friday Mosque. It was the tallest building in the Old City. Ruya went to speak to the man with the key to the roof; I could hear the pleading in her voice, the sweet cadence of each sentence or phrase beguiling, and before long the man agreed to let us onto the roof. His only condition was that there was another man up there with us to make sure we did not misbehave. A bored young man was summoned.

The four of us climbed the steep stairs that led to the roof, which was enormous and empty. Beyond the precipice lay a grandstand view over all of Yazd. The city looked like an ærial photograph. Its alleyways and streets were now an elaborate circuit board, while the desert beyond seemed much closer than before.

Ruya sat herself against the dome of the mosque and announced that this was where she would be painted. She told me to hurry up. The light was about to go. I sprawled in front of her with a canvas on my lap, while Ruya's friend and our recently acquired chaperone went to a different part of the roof, as instructed by Ruya. With the sun low and the moon beginning to rise I unpacked my paint, my plate, my water and the plastic bottle of brushes – the ritual by now well worn and unthinking – and started to paint.

From that moment Ruya fixed me with the same draining gaze with which she had introduced herself. Every time I looked up she was staring hard into the very centre of one or the other of my eyes. At times it felt as if she was painting me. I worked my way round her face, marking every undulation of her creamy skin and working hard at her eyes. So she knew what it felt like. I had to capture the power of each kohl-edged almond; the full, looked-after lashes around them; the lovely nougat of their centre. They were infinitely prettier than any of the male eyes I had painted during the last month and everything that set a female face apart from a male one flooded back. The eyes were deeper set, the cheekbones higher, the jaw a different shape and the curve of the eyebrows matched the shape of the eyes more precisely, but what made this face so different to any other I had tried to paint was the allure of all that was hidden. Ruya's headscarf covered her hair – not something I had a fetishistic attachment to – but it was covered, and that was enough to turn it into something special, something magical. Whether she knew this, her hair knew this or the wind had picked up on it I don't know, but just after I started to paint, a ribbon of just-washed jet-black hair fell down from beneath her headscarf. For the rest of the sitting it hung over the right-hand side of her face, shimmering a little in the late-afternoon light as an ambassador of somewhere I was not allowed to go.

Her nose led to full, rose-coloured lips and the point on either side of her mouth was dark. If I drew a line up from each they would meet her pupils exactly, which made it a classically perfect face like I remembered being taught. Just to the side of each point were suggestions of dimples, each one no more than a delicate indentation, its depth steamrollered by make-up.

As the sun slipped behind the mountains someone pressed play inside the mosque and a pre-recorded call to prayer thundered out around us. It was deafening. Ruya's friend ran off to break her fast. Our male chaperone had left long ago. The light was fading. Other mosques pressed play on their pre-recorded calls to prayer and floodlights went on to illuminate the dome above us. We were the only people there. It felt dangerous and exciting because we were invisible. Ruya was just beneath the glare of the floodlights and it was getting hard to see her face. Squinting, I threw down a thick coat of paint as a background, dropped my brush and it was done. The light had gone.

I felt the need to run. Something about the hour-long staring match that had just ended made me want to sprint round the roof of Yazd's Friday Mosque like a coil released. The intensity of the last hour evaporated into the darkening sky. The loudspeakers continued to summon the faithful as I ran, the call to prayer soaring into the evening sky and beginning to echo back from the mountains beyond the city. It had been a while – too long – since I had felt the possessive energy of someone's eyes like that.

Ruya took the canvas to one of the floodlights to inspect it.

"My nose," she sang out over the call to prayer, sounding upset. "You are make me like... like Pinocchio!"

I was determined not to let this ruin the moment. I went over to the floodlight and promised her it wasn't that bad, and no, I wasn't going to change it.

"But the eyes," she said, still poring over the canvas. "The eyes OK. You have these good."

She put down the canvas and wrote onto the back of my left hand her name, first in English then in Persian. I

thought of the girl in Istanbul with her cheap perfume.

"So you remember," said Ruya.

Ruya means dream. Not just the dream itself, but the memory of it.

We walked back to the university and for one truly dreamlike moment we held hands. It lasted no more than five, maybe six seconds and was electric.

☾

Under the Veil

STILL CLUTCHING MY PAINTING OF RUYA – THE MEMORY OF the memory of the dream – I went to find Al and Stephen in the restaurant where we usually ate in Yazd.

As we had done every evening for the last week, each of us told the tale of where we had been that day, what had happened, whom we had met and what they had said, before wandering out into the street three hours later, full after another round of the local Arso-Cola, kebab, bread, grilled tomatoes and herbs we did not know the name of. At our favourite juice place each of us ordered the house speciality: banana milkshake with a Snickers bar chopped up into it.

It felt good to be creatures of habit, even if it was a temporary habit; the longer we were on the road the more we craved these moments of routine.

Our show in Tehran now loomed large and we had to get back to the capital to tell people about it, frame it or, in Stephen's case, make it. He had begun several pictures but had finished nothing. I had several large pictures to both start and finish, while Al was a man of leisure with more than fifty paint-feelings in the back of Yasmine, each one finished by virtue of being started.

"No, I can't work back into them," he told Stephen. "That's the whole point."

"You mean..."

"Yes, Stephen. They have a point."

"I wasn't even going to say that."

"Let's just see how everyone reacts to them in Tehran," Al said, half to himself as he scooped a nugget of Snickers from his milkshake. "Right?"

"How they react to your paint-feelings?" asked Stephen. "Yep."

"But why? You're not going to change them if people don't like them."

"I might," said Al, sounding interested by the idea.

"Of course you won't. You don't listen to a word either of us says. Why are you going to listen to anyone who comes to the show?"

"I don't know," he said, sounding nonplussed.

"You see, what I still can't understand," said Stephen, frowning, "is how you can sit here and defend all of them. I mean, do you, or do you not, after everything we've said, see that some of your paint-feelings are better than others?"

"No. Not at all. You can't judge them æsthetically, Stephen. No one paint-feeling is better than another."

"Bollocks."

"They're not," said Al, speeding up. "Really. This is not about investing my work with some universal æsthetic of what looks good or what doesn't. It's not about prettiness. It's about rejecting that! To say one is better than another is... I don't know, like looking at a wall of tiles in a mosque and saying, 'Well, some of them are amazing. But that one in the middle and to the left a bit is awful, and there's that one four along and seven down on the left...' Every one of these paint-feelings is an expression of my emotion in a place, and so they all have a certain value. They're like tiles. If you think the concept's crap, then they're all crap."

"Right," said Stephen, beginning to smile to himself.

"They're winners, Stephen," said Al, grinning back at him. "All of them. You just haven't seen it yet."

"No, I haven't. I just can't help thinking you're doing this because of your *Orientalism* book." He screwed his face up. "You want to make art that an academic in Oxford would want to have a wank over."

"You haven't even read it!"

"What, *Orientalism?*"

"Yes."

"Well, I started it. That was quite enough." Stephen did his guilty face. "That's not the point. Here you are, in Iran. And just think about some of the things that have happened to you, to all of us, over the last few weeks. Think of those poems you were given the other day about depression, about being unemployed, about not being allowed to have sex with your girlfriend. They're some of the most powerful poems I've ever read. Really. They're just... I don't know, they're incredible. And then you think of Moonlight and Arush, or any of those students. Think of what they were talking about. You've got the chance to make art about some of these incredible themes, things that actually matter! Come on. We've lived our whole lives without anything to... anything to really fight against. We haven't had a war. We haven't had... um, Communism, Vietnam, equal rights. What can you go on a march about in London? Tuition fees. Great. And here we are for the first time with people who have something huge to fight against, something to make art about. It's proper freedom-of-speech stuff. It's things you take for granted back at home. And don't forget that as a foreigner you can say things that Moonlight or Arush can't. You think of all that, and for your part of the show in Tehran you want to exhibit random, non-figurative paint because, wait for it, it expresses your subconscious feeling."

"It's not random paint."

"Come on Al, you've got a responsibility to these people. Right now there's nothing, and I mean nothing, in those paint-feelings that says Iran. You could have just sat in a studio in London for a month..."

"Stephen," said Al, pausing to think, "shut up. I am not obliged, because I'm now in 'The Orient', to make art that is political or has Oriental-looking motifs. 'Aw look. There's a mosque, everyone. We must be in the Middle East.' That's crap. Such crap. Why can't you see that? What I'm trying to do is get away from that, I want to make the kind of art I'd make in London. Otherwise I'd just end up reinforcing stereotypes or doing what everyone else does! And as for a responsibility to these people, what's that about? These people? Moonlight is a brilliant artist. He doesn't need me to speak on his behalf. I hate the idea that we can somehow speak for someone like Moonlight better than he can."

Al and Stephen carried on for a while, both of them going through the motions of the same argument they had had most evenings, with me switching sides like a turncoat.

At one point Al said something about Iranian artists being the best in the region, the most conceptually adventurous, and it made me think of the artistic renaissance in Baghdad. Did they do more conceptual work there? I didn't know. I hadn't been able to find out anything about them. All I had was the remembrance of one half-drunk conversation, but it was enough. I now had an image in my head of the Baghdadi street the young journalist had described, the one that looked like Montmartre in the 1900s. If I thought about it long enough the image would for a moment become animated and flicker like an old film.

We got back to our hostel. Our room was not much bigger than the three beds in it and was lit by a single halogen strip. Next door was an ageing Afghan with a wooden leg who had a pot of honey that he let me and Stephen dip our bread into every morning. He too had decided to give Ramazan a miss. Al was still fasting. The marathon runner in him had decided he was going to complete the course no matter what.

"Let's just concentrate on getting people into the gallery," said Al as we lay on our beds.

"Right, concentrate on getting people in," said Stephen, slowly, sleepily.

"But how?"

"Don't know."

"Nor do I."

"Great."

Silence.

I began to doze off.

"Maybe the name of the show isn't right," said Stephen. "Give people what they want," he said as if chanting a mantra.

"Yeah," said Al.

"What they'd expect us to do."

"We could call it 'Three idiots in the Middle East'."

"And make the whole show about stereotypes."

"Yes! But not everyone would get it."

"Nader would love it," said Stephen.

"He would, wouldn't he?" said Al.

"We could have Axis of Evil in the title."

"Um. 'Bicycling on the Axis of Evil'?" said Al. "Stephen, you could get on a bike."

"I'll put you on a bike."

"Or how about 'Iran, the Land of Repression'?"

"And..."

"And veils," said Al.

"'Land of Repression and Veils'," said Stephen in a deep American drawl.

"'Repression and Depression'."

"'Depression and Veils'."

"'Lifting the Veil'."

"Been done."

"'Behind the Veil'."

"Been done."

"'Under the Veil'."

"Again."

"Guns."

"*Guns.*"

"Guns."

"We need guns."

"Definitely guns."

"It's the Middle East, we can't not have guns," said Stephen.

"Although I haven't seen a gun since we got here," said Al, sounding short-changed.

"Really?"

"Yep. No guns yet."

"But guns would be good," said Stephen, wistfully. "A big rack of them."

"Guns and terrorism."

"Or puns," said Stephen. "Guns and puns. I want more puns in my titles."

They both thought for a bit.

"There's a picture I could call 'Iran and ran and ran'," said Al. "Something about running away from the religious police, maybe?"

"They've been disbanded."

"Oh." Pause. "You sure?"

"Yup."

"Oh well."

"What about... Actually no."

"Er."

"Yeah."

"Something about a queue-wait?" said Al, sounding optimistic. "You know, waiting in a really long queue."

"Eh?"

"Queue-wait. Like Kuwait."

"Great idea, Al," said Stephen, rolling over. "You know we're not actually in Kuwait?"

"It's an idea, Stephen. You know. Just putting it out there."

☾

Dog

WE ARRIVED IN TEHRAN A WEEK BEFORE OUR SHOW OPENED with no studio, nowhere to stay, nothing framed and a lot of art to make. Panic was beginning to set in. Not a pre-exam, I've-done-the-work-I'm-just-feeling-a-bit-nervous kind of panic, but proper sleep-losing, irritable, the-show-might-be-cancelled-because-we-don't-have-enough-work-and-we'll-run-clean-out-of-money panic that tastes a lot like fear.

The most important item on our to-do list was the studio. Once we had a studio we also had a place to stay, in that there was no floor we would not sleep on.

Stephen and Al went to look up people and places in the centre of Tehran who might be able to help while I went to the British Council. It rented its premises from the British Institute of Persian Studies (BIPS) and after some negotiation the people at BIPS agreed to let us stay in their

spacious and empty set of rooms above the British Council offices, as long as the British Council paid for it. They kindly agreed to do so and suddenly – a word I don't like to use but this really was sudden – we had a free apartment with three bedrooms, each one larger than anything we had shared during the last month, a studio, a kitchen, a kettle, walls dotted with British plug points and a cupboard with a pot of Marmite in it. None of us could quite believe it.

"But there are rules," said Khalman, the man who lived in the lodge to the BIPS fortress. He was disagreeable and squat. He was also our new landlord. "You are now on the property of the British Embassy and you must behave accordingly. Absolutely no women in your apartment. If you drink, you do not leave the building. Most importantly, from eleven each night until seven in the morning a dog is let out."

"That's nice. What's he called?"

"No, no. He does not answer to anybody. Except for me. And he is trained to bite. Hard."

"How hard?"

"What?"

"Well, thanks again," I said, turning to leave.

"I don't think you have done this before, have you?" he said in a different tone of voice.

"What haven't we done?"

"This. What you're doing now. Going somewhere and putting on an exhibition."

"Um," I said, taken aback, and in my hesitation answering his question.

"You didn't think of arranging a place to stay before you got here? Or having your pictures ready before the week of the exhibition?" The scorn in his voice was fantastic.

"Nope."

"And what were you going to do if this didn't work out?"

"I think," I said, searching for the right cliché, "we were going to cross that bridge when we came to it."

He raised his eyebrows and looked away.

"Let me make this quite clear now," he said, turning back. "I mean what I say about the rules. You break one and you are out."

☾

The Night Before

4 A.M. THE EXHIBITION OPENS TOMORROW. FOR THE LAST three days I have been phoning a long list of people and telling them about our show. "*Salaam aleikom. Ingliz baladi?*" At which point the person tells me they speak either English or French or both. As well as Persian, of course. If they speak both English and French, which is what usually happens, they ask which I prefer, making me feel like a linguistic half-wit as I am reminded that I am, if there is such a word, monolingual.

Ramazan ended yesterday. Al ate a lot to celebrate and is now passed out on his bed after smoking too much of his pipe. Stephen is in his room staining and touching up his pictures. He says they'll be ready by lunchtime tomorrow when we load everything into Yasmine and go to hang the show. It opens at six tomorrow evening. After our initial panic it looks like we may have enough work, just, although we could still do with another week to prepare, as well as more money.

Ten days ago Al spent the British Council framing money he had been allotted – which he said was less than his fair share because Stephen had taken more than his due, something Stephen disputes – on getting a carpenter in Esfahan to make his frames. It would be cheaper, Al had said, and the wood was good. He drew careful plans but didn't explain them properly. None of the frames the carpenter made fitted any of Al's paint-feelings. They weren't actually frames. They came out as meticulously constructed wooden platforms that you might put a figurine on, each one smaller than any of Al's paint-feelings. He couldn't use them for anything. Instead, he bought some cheap black frames from the open-air frame place near Tehran University. Stephen says they look tacky. I agree. Al says frames aren't that important. Stephen sighs.

We have also spent a large part of the week handing out flyers for the show. One of the best places to do this is in Tehran's traffic jams as we plough back and forth between the framers, the gallery, the photo lab and our studio, because the cars on either side are always tightly packed so you are usually no more than a few inches away. This makes it easy to hand flyers to people you get chatting to in the traffic. Sometimes when the traffic speeds up you can do moving flyer handovers. They're the best. Our most stuntman-like yet was at 50 kilometres an hour, which was worth the potential collision because the car we were aiming for was expensive. Right now we like people who drive expensive cars.

Earlier today the disagreeable man who guards the BIPS fortress, the man with the dog, told us we can no longer stay in the apartment because of the art journalist girl he saw leaving our apartment, our drumming earlier in the week that had woken him up and the occasion two nights ago when we missed his curfew by ten minutes, so this is our last night here. The show opens in fourteen hours. I don't know where we will sleep tomorrow but we have plans, most of which involve being waited on by flunkies in one of the expensive hotels that we will be able to afford with the vast sums of money we make from the show.

Outside I can hear the dawn call to prayer. It is three or four miles away and it is the first call to prayer I have heard since arriving in Tehran. It reminds me I need to sleep.

Allahu Akbar!
Ash-hadu alla ilaha ill-Allah...
God is most great!
I testify that there is no god but God.
I testify that Muhammad is the Prophet of God.
Come to prayer!
Come to success!
Prayer is better than sleep!
God is most great.
There is no god but God.

☾

Showtime

NADER HUNG THE WORK AND IT LOOKED GOOD, BETTER than any other show I had been a part of. In different ways, the three of us had taken on the criticism in Esfahan Art University and the pictures up in Gallery Seyhoun avoided the most obvious pitfalls of Orientalism. It was strange to feel this good about a show I was a part of. Every other time I had walked around a show just before it opened I would be overcome with a post-natal loathing of what I had made, but not this time.

In the hour before the private view began, while everyone else went home to change, I began to think about how this body of work, our first exhibition on the road, related to what we had set out to do. How did it fit into our "Portrait of the Heart of the Islamic World"?

The answer was not very well – although it wasn't the work that was at fault but the concept we had dreamt up before leaving London.

The main problem was the term "Islamic world". With some fifteen million European Muslims living north of Granada and west of Istanbul, it felt anachronistic or just wrong to talk about the Islamic world as a geographical unit. It was much better and more accurate to talk about a body of believers, the *ummah*. That way you would not imply that any Muslim living outside a predominantly Muslim country was in some way an exile or part of a diaspora community.

The other problem with the label "Islamic world" was that neither the people we were meeting nor the places we were seeing were "Islamic". "Islamic" means of Islam; that is, of the Qur'an or the hadiths, the sayings of the Prophet

Muhammad. It implies something immutable. While most of the Muslims we had met were trying to follow Islam, they were not Islam itself. As one man put it to me, "You must think of Islam itself as a beautiful bright light and we the Muslims are the moths that are all drawn to it." The faith of no two Muslims was the same. Each had his own or her own necessarily unique relationship with Islam, which might change, fractionally, over time as any believer might fall into or out of religion as a result of something that happened to them, or something that did not happen to them. But, put simply, the fact that someone described themselves as a Muslim did not imbue them with any given characteristics. This felt important. So instead of talking about the "Islamic world", were we making a "portrait of the centre of the Muslim world"? Or perhaps it was better to talk about the plain old "Middle East"? Better still, the "post-9/11 Middle East"?

Outside Gallery Seyhoun workmen dug up the street. Behind them the words BACKSTREET BOYS and DJ SCOOTER had been spray painted in joyful lettering on a pink wall.

By six o'clock people started to arrive at the gallery. We handed round orange squash and *baklava* while a BBC film crew led by Kaveh Golestan – a Pulitzer prize-winning cameraman who tragically died a few months later when he stepped on a landmine in northern Iraq – filmed some footage. Soon after a smaller film crew from the Tehran School of Journalism turned up. Al announced that he would not be giving any interviews.

"What?" asked Stephen, starting to laugh.

"My art speaks for itself," said Al.

"Right. Your paint-feelings?"

"Sure."

"Piece of piss. Anyone can understand them."

"Just because you don't," he said, grinning back. Al and Stephen could now generate laughter just by looking at each other.

Stephen and I spent the evening answering questions into dictaphones or microphones and moving about politely, talking to people, watching, tense; and deep down waiting for the onslaught of expensive-car-driving collectors.

Between seven and eight the gallery verged on being half full but nothing more. I kept watching the door, willing it to spew forth an army of rich-looking people, but they never came.

At ten thirty Nader looked at his watch and told us it was time to go. Like someone being stood up on a date, the three of us were sure that the missing hundred people would turn up any minute now.

"Five more minutes?"

"I can't," said Nader. "The gallery is meant to close half an hour ago."

We had sold nothing. Not one thing.

"It is OK, though," said Nader as he looked for his keys. "It was National Student Day today. All of Tehran was like a traffic jam because of the protests." We nodded solemnly. "And it is raining."

"Raining?" said Stephen, incredulous. "How's that going to make a difference?"

"It makes a big difference! When it rains in Tehran people stay at home. And anyway, the opening is not important, it is what happens during the week. Sometimes, you know, I sell most pictures here after the show has finished."

We all suspected Nader of white lies as we sat in a scrawny hotel with the rain pelting down outside, chewing over what had just happened. It was difficult to work out what had gone wrong, not least because the three of us believed in the show like it was a religious cult. The people we had spoken to liked the work. You could see it in their faces, feel it when they congratulated you, hugged you, winked at you or talked about how clever a certain piece was. Often they would read meaning into a piece that you had no idea about, like the man who took my picture of a Yazd doorway to be a comment on the Iranian Revolution because it had both the old and new street signs on it. "Like the old and new regimes!" he had whispered, drawing close. "Side by side, one a little higher than the other but *over the same door!*"

This suggested people wanted to engage with the work and were able to project themselves into it, and by extension into us. If they could buy into it emotionally, why not physically? Was it our pricing that had gone wrong? Nader thought the work was well priced. Our foreignness? He also said Tehranis preferred to buy art from Iranian artists, but that implied there was a steady stream of foreign artists exhibiting in Tehran. There was not. Our show was only the third exhibition by foreign artists anywhere in Iran since 1979.

Unable to work out what had gone wrong, we went to bed feeling a sense of chronic anti-climax. Although we had not touched let alone smelt alcohol for the last five weeks, the three of us woke up the next morning feeling hung over.

☾

Street Cleaner

"YOU ARE FRIEND OF THE ARTIST?" SHE ASKED.

"No, I'm one of them," I said.

She did not look convinced. She had come to the gallery to interview the three British artists.

"Really, I am."

She looked even less convinced.

"I promise you. I'll do a picture for you. I'll do a picture *of* you."

"But you are not like the artist."

"What do you mean?"

"Your hair. An artist has beautiful hair and beautiful clothes. Your things are not beautiful."

I wasn't sure what to say.

"Why is your hair like this?" she said, gesturing at my not outrageous but certainly uncombed hair.

"I don't know. Perhaps you can pretend it is smart."

"Yes, but for an artist to make beautiful things, he must have beautiful person. Otherwise he makes dirty things, bad things. These hair is like hair of someone else."

"What kind of person?"

"I don't know, person with bad job," she said, her young, prefect's demeanour beginning to wobble.

"Like what?"

She looked down at the table. "Maybe you can make clean the streets?"

She pulled out a dictaphone from her bag, smirking to herself. "Let me see. Is this working?" she said to it in an impersonation of someone talking to herself. It shrieked as she wound it back and the machine parroted her words back at her.

"Good. OK. What is... um." She looked at a long list. "What is your idea about Iran?"

I told her well-worn things about how I liked it, how everyone we had met was extremely hospitable and no, it was not how I imagined it would be. Also, that I was interested by how different the Iranian version of Islam was to what we had seen in Europe or Turkey.

"And what is the colour of Islam?"

"What?" I blinked.

"The colour of Islam?" she said more slowly.

"Blue?"

"And the colour of Zionism?"

"Zionism?" I asked. She nodded. "What's that got to do with this?"

"It is important for the readers," she replied, looking defensive and for a moment confused. "This is newspaper for Iran. Zionist state affects Iran."

"You mean what is the colour of Israel?"

"No, no, there is no Israel," she said, a furrow working up from between her eyebrows. It looked uncomfortable on her unblemished face. "It is Zionist occupied state."

"Oh."

"For me the colour of Islam is white," she said. "And Zionism it is blue. What is your favourite colour?"

"Red."

"How many colours in the world?"

"Three thousand and two?"

"How many pictures you have make?"

"Nine hundred and sixty seven." She did not trust her dictaphone so scribbled it down.

"That's a guess, by the way."

She wrote that down too.

"And how many pictures are there in the world?"

"One and a half billion."

"The colour of death?"

"No colour."

"What colour is there after black?"

"I was meant to say black for death, wasn't I?"

"What colour is there after black?"

"No colour."

"OK. Death is black," she said to the dictaphone, *sotto voce* as before.

"That's not what I said."

"What would you paint if you were a blind man?" she went on.

"I wouldn't paint."

"OK. And is painting your favourite thing?"

"Yes."

"After that what is your favourite thing in life?"

"Not sure if you can print it."

"Does not know," she whispered to the dictaphone, her ally in all of this. "Why do you make art?"

"To make something beautiful," I said. She looked up. "But I haven't got there yet," I said hurriedly.

"Maybe it is possible if you make your hair beautiful," she said, her teacher's pet air faltering once more.

"Maybe."

"OK. Now. Do you think it is possible for an artist from the West to know the..." she searched through her notes. "Wait. The metaphysic of East? The metaphysic of art in East, sorry."

"Well, I don't think there is a metaphysic of art in the East. There's no single metaphysic behind Western art, and anyway, I don't like dividing the world into the East and the West." She said nothing, so I carried on. "How do you define each one? Does Japan have the same artistic metaphysic as Syria? And is Thailand the opposite to... I don't know, to Mexico? It doesn't work. There's no nation or person or thing that is purely 'Eastern', just as there is none that is purely 'Western'."

"No," she said. "There is an Eastern, Islamic idea that the Eastern artist knows. It is there from when he is born. It is inside him. It is there when he make his art."

"But why is the art in Iran so different to, say, that of Saudi Arabia?" I asked, guessing a little because I knew nothing about Saudi Arabian art.

"Because the Arab is different. He does not like art so much."

Comparing Iran to Saudi Arabia was a direct hit. I could see it on her face. Never confuse an Iranian with an Arab, as I had been told several times now.

"But Saudis are as Islamic or Eastern as you get, surely. Or what about a place like India, that's Eastern, isn't it?"

"Yes."

"Well, Indian art is very different to Iranian art."

"The Eastern artist is different person to the Western artist," she said, starting to raise her voice. "They are from the two different worlds."

"Wouldn't it be better to talk about an Iranian artistic æsthetic instead of an Eastern one? I mean, if you have to talk about an artistic æsthetic at all."

She smiled. "I think it is difficult for you. These are things you cannot see, it is because you are the Western artist."

I physically bit my tongue and it hurt.

"OK," she went on. "Explain me this picture." She looked down at her notes some more. "*Recruitment*. What is meaning of *Recruitment*?"

Recruitment was a collage of two posters on a piece of card that I had made to look like a section of wall. One of the posters advertised a sixth-form crammer in Qom that promised to get you into university no matter how little work you had done. All you had to do was be able to foot the bill. On top of it I had stuck a poster advertising a lecture on morality by one of Qom's leading mullahs. Most of the hugs I got at the private view – each one followed by a conspiratorial "bravo" – came from people who had just seen *Recruitment*. The young journalist did not like it. She said I should not be making art that used a poster advertising a religious lecture.

"It is not for art to do this," she said matter-of-factly.

Recruitment was the best thing I had made in Iran. That didn't make it at all good, but it was certainly better than anything else I had made. The red and the green and the grey fused together in a way I had not planned, and its polarised duality of meaning was something I could only fully appreciate now that the piece was in a frame and people were reacting to it. Its meaning hinged on whether or not the viewer understood Persian. For those who did, it might be a reflection on Iran at the beginning of the twenty-first century, where university symbolised a desire to get out, to succeed, and so a crammer stood for a quick fix, the handle on the emergency exit. The religious lecture was the pious vanity designed to cover this crudity, this reality, and it was beginning to peel off. To anyone who did not read Persian it was a picturesque section of wall somewhere in the Middle East with several weathered posters attached to it. The writing was probably Arabic. Such pretty script! The text had become an exotic code.

The disapproving young journalist finished her questions and left.

As each of the major Iranian newspapers came to interview us, their reaction to *Recruitment* marked them on a political gauge. The conservative journalists would stand in front of the piece tutting, while the more liberal ones would say nothing and smile, which I took as tacit approval. One journalist asked for a picture of me standing next to *Recruitment*. I asked Nader if I should do it.

"No way," he said when I told him which paper it was.

FIVE DAYS LATER OUR EXHIBITION CAME DOWN. AL'S PAINT-feelings were its undisputed celebrities and almost all of them had sold. Everyone we spoke to singled out the wild freedom and expressiveness of Al's paint as the highlight of the show. One newspaper said, "They made you think Braithwaite was on drugs." Which he was not. An elderly collector said this kind of work was perfect for Iran. "Because in this country, we love to escape," he said, grinning as if he had let me in on a secret. "It is what we dream of at night."

Between us we sold two-thirds of the work and, although it was not the "sell-out show" that artists the world over dream of, we had made a small amount of money. Enough to go and play for a week.

$$\mathcal{C}$$

Real Iranian Handicraft

THE BLOCK OF FLATS IN A QUIET STREET IN NORTH TEHRAN did not look prepossessing from below. I could feel adrenaline flood through me as we followed Marjan, Nader's friend whose flat we were staying in, through the hallway and up the stairs.

"Marjan," said Stephen, sounding like a student asking a teacher something he had been taught long ago but had since forgotten. "What's the punishment for being caught with alcohol?"

"About, let me see, fifty lashes."

"Really?"

"Probably more for a foreigner," she said, grinning. "Hope you guys are excited. Almost there."

We continued up several more flights until we reached a door. *The* door. An unlikely looking, worn, wooden thing that opened to reveal a low-lit secret garden of sleek, black, backless dresses, light house music you might get on Fashion TV, a view sweeping over all of north Tehran, vodka, DJ decks, and a black-and-white checked floor that made me think of New York, all of it fleshed out with boys and girls of dazzling beauty. It was by far the most luxurious walled garden we had stumbled into so far.

"Welcome to the real Iran," said Marjan, triumphantly.

Two of Marjan's friends walked in after us, slamming the door and removing their headscarves with an abracadabra flourish before shaking their hair into place and tossing their coats onto an abattoir of dark, expensive-looking fur. The flat smelt of at least ten different perfumes all battling for supremacy. Most of the men we could see had shaved heads. Not because they were doing national service – their parents had got them out of that – but because it looked good, and in many ways it rubbed in the fact that they were never going to do national service. It was ironic.

Dazed, and for a moment confused, we gawped at it all. Just as we were beginning to feel we weren't glamorous enough or pretty enough, Marjan handed each of us a tumbler of iced vodka. Everything began to feel fine. The vodka tasted better than I remembered vodka ever tasting.

Everyone there was a well-off student, and a lot of the people in Tehran at that moment were students or of student age; sixty per cent of the Iranian population were then under the age of twenty-nine.

Most of the girls at the party read art and the boys read subjects like electrochemical engineering that would lead directly to a job.

Farzad, the first person I spoke to, was different in that he read English. After introducing himself he began to talk about Iranians growing out of Islam and how they wanted to innovate, not imitate. I told him about a Hugo Boss strapline. He did not laugh. I felt stupid. Instead, he moved the conversation seamlessly on to *American Beauty* and from there on to postmodernism, deconstruction, *The Waste Land*, Foucault, Derrida, Sartre, before ending up at *Eyes Wide Shut* where, with all of his urbane and Western learning, he found the idea of someone letting his wife appear in a film that involved nudity incomprehensible. He thought Tom Cruise must have been medically insane to let Nicole Kidman be seen by so many men, naked or not. The whole thing confirmed the amorality of America, he concluded. A friend of his joined us.

"So," I asked the friend, "what are you going to do when you leave university?"

"Oh, I don't know." He looked at Farzad. "Open a shop maybe."

"Great. Selling what?" I asked.

"I think condoms. There's a real gap in the market for that in Iran right now, don't you think? I could have a nice big sign. 'Hosein's Condoms'. Illegal sex is a growth industry in Iran, I've heard. How about you?" asked Hosein, looking at me. "Actually no, don't tell me." His voice became confrontational. "You've left university. So now you're here in Iran. But why would anyone come to Iran?"

"I wanted to see it," I said.

"Really?"

"Sure."

"But..."

"It's a great place," I told him.

"What?"

"Iran. It's a great place. I like it."

"How..." He paused. "How can you say that? Iran is a shithole. A total shithole. Why would anyone come here when they could go to America, or Europe? Somewhere modern. I don't understand! Oh, maybe I do. You're one of these Western guys who likes the mystery of the East. Magic carpets, yes? Ali Baba? You like being in the Third World, don't you?"

"No, I don't. I mean, I do. I mean, it's not..."

"You're going to America, aren't you?" he said, turning to the girl who had just joined us. She nodded.

"Her English isn't so good," Hosein said, putting an arm round her. "But she just won the Green Card to America."

She nodded again.

"How come?"

"Green Card lottery. The prize is a Green Card to America," he answered for her. "Seriously. It's my favourite thing about living here. We have the chance to escape. One day I'm going to win the Green Card," he said, pausing to look away. "That or I'll run away."

We all looked out of the window at the snow-covered mountains that ran east–west to the north of Tehran. Dotted over them were orange streetlights that twinkled like fairy lights.

"Man, you've got to go skiing," said Hosein, more relaxed now. "It's the only thing to do here. One of them, anyway." He squeezed the shoulder of the girl next to him. She arched her body towards him, elbowing him lightly in the ribs. "Let's go skiing. Tomorrow!" he added.

"Noooo," she whined in one long, sweet sound that slid down an arpeggio as she sang it out. "I cannot. Doctor."

"What?"

"Doctor." She looked embarrassed and eventually touched her nose.

"Oh, yeah. OK, you can come," he said, pointing at me. "Or have you had a nose job recently?"

A boy with gelled hair came up to our group. "Hello, hello, how is everything this night?" he asked me, grinning hard and ignoring Farzad, Hosein and the girl who had recently had a nose job.

"It's good, we were just talking about going..."

"OK, listen," he said, eyes fixed on me. "I want you to do something, yes? It is so funny. You must guess what country I am from!"

He looked Iranian.

"Iran?" I asked.

"No!" he said, still grinning.

"Really? OK, you are Turkish?"

"No."

"Azerbaijani?"

"No."

"Afghan?"

"No."

"Pakistani?"

"No," he said, looking offended.

"Are you an Arab?"

"No!" he said, looking seriously offended.

"I give up."

Hosein spoke to him in Persian for a bit.

"OK," he said, less upbeat. "I am Iranian. But my friends say I look American."

I looked more at his face. He still looked Iranian. After an uncomfortable silence he headed towards Stephen and Al.

"What a dick," said Hosein, tutting.

KATYA WORE A PURPLE SUIT WITH A FAT, SILK TIE THAT HUNG loose and half undone round her neck. She was the most beautiful girl in the room, knew it, and spent a lot of time walking round and dipping into conversations before pulling out fast. After a number of circuits she sat herself down next to me, making sure to glance away as she did, as if she had something important to look at over in the opposite direction, a blank stretch of wall.

"So," she said after a while, turning. "What do you do?" Her voice was a tired drawl. Eventually her gaze drifted over to my side of the sofa.

"I'm an artist," I said, immediately wishing I hadn't. It sounded awful. Pretentious. "I make pictures" was bad too. "Painter." That's what I should have said.

She continued to appear bored. From certain angles her face looked drawn, giving it a hint of heroin chic.

"What about you?" I asked.

"I am an artist," she said.

"Oh. And what kind of art do you make?"

"You cannot explain it." She looked away. "Anyway. What art do you make?"

"I paint, and..."

"Ah," she said shaking her head. "You do not understand."

"Eh?"

"You cannot see that logic is a barrier to freedom."

As I began to stammer an answer she stood up, preened a little and walked away. Ten minutes later she came back, sat down, and with clumsy hands shoved a joint in my mouth. She smiled and set off again. For the rest of the night our conversation stuttered forward as we passed each other. Katya was very good at having the last word.

"How are things?" I asked.

"Depends what you call things," she said, before walking off again. Every time she said something the intonation of it threw me, and as I tried to work out what the stress of the words might mean she would disappear.

"Why did you come to Iran?" she asked ten minutes later.

"To know what Iran is," I said, feeling for a moment good about my answer.

"Ha! You do not understand."

Because Katya had been to our show, this might have been an interesting or even serious criticism. Then again, it might have been put out merely to create the illusion of a brilliant and intellectually ravishing mind that could weave wonderful and mysterious paths far beyond the rumblings of what went on between my ears. For a few seconds it worked, giving her time to get away.

"Are you happy?" I tried half an hour later.

"Only when no one asks if I'm happy."

Walk away.

"Do you like finishing conversations?" after another half hour of preening.

"Always."

Walk away again.

It was past midnight when I found Al and Stephen in the room with the coats listening to a boy coming out. He could not bring himself to tell his mother, he told his audience. A girl standing near the door whispered to me that he'd already come out and was giving this speech just because the two foreigners were there. She was called Mehraneh. We went next door and danced. She danced brilliantly. It was strange to think she had lived all her life in a country where dancing with anyone who was not a member of your family was illegal.

The party was starting to lose momentum and the people around us no longer moved with the elegance or self-conscious stealth with which they had started the night. When nobody was looking, Mehraneh and I sank into a sofa with its back to the party. No one could see us. In front of us was the view over north Tehran. She talked about the relationship she had just come out of and described her distrust of men, especially foreign men. I fidgeted a bit. Iranian girls knew all about foreign men, she said, turning to me. They knew that foreign men always fall for Iranian girls. She had gone out with a foreign man once.

I moved the conversation away from foreign men on to simpler things, things neither of us had been thinking about that night. The conversation slowed, and our words began to feel heavy, while the gaps in the conversation grew and grew until we found ourselves floating in a shared and pristine silence. Everything around me sobered up, as if a lens had been brought into focus. I felt adrenaline kick in. Mehraneh turned towards me, the moon lighting the arc of her cheekbone and her left eye glinting in the gloom like something precious.

Less than a minute later, perhaps feeling someone watching, she pulled back and there ended the sweetest, most dreamlike cocoon. A cocoon within a cocoon. I could hardly believe what had just happened. I wanted to tell Al and Stephen. Around us the room was empty apart from the figure standing over us. Mehraneh's brother looked more tall and broad than when I had met him earlier that night. Mehraneh disentangled herself fast.

"We're going," said her brother and seconds later they were gone.

Although we spoke a few times on the phone, I never saw her again.

It was three in the morning and Al and Stephen had already returned to Marjan's. There was nowhere to sleep at the party flat, so I decided to drive back to join them. As Yasmine sailed down the orange-soaked, empty avenues, I sang along to whatever was playing on her stereo. Her suspension seemed to have grown by several feet.

THE NEXT MORNING I WOKE UP WITH NO IDEA HOW I HAD found Marjan's flat that night and cross that I'd let myself drive in that state. Even if the moment with Mehraneh had felt like a cup of coffee in the way it woke me up, my breath still stank of alcohol and if I had been stopped by the police I would have been in trouble.

Once Al and Stephen were up we piled into Yasmine and drove north. Before long Yasmine was in four-wheel drive for the first time since leaving London. Four-wheel drive would be important in the Middle East, Lee the Toyota salesman had assured us, what with all the tough driving out there and the desert. I think he imagined the region to be one big sandpit.

It made no difference how-many-wheel drive we had that morning, as there was no way we were getting to Dizin, the more capacious of the three ski slopes above Tehran. The snow ahead of us was eight feet deep. It had started to snow in Tehran as well.

We turned back to the Shemshak resort and parked Yasmine between green Nissan Patrols with ski racks on their roofs. House music thudded out of their stereos as yet more rich, good-looking young Iranians got into ski boots, tightened American flag bandannas over their hair or applied extra, sometimes sweat-resistant layers of make-up. Several girls walked past with their hair out. It was shocking. We stared like perverts.

At the entrance to the resort was a painting of a bearded skier in flared salopettes slaloming down the mountain next to a portrait of the grinning Supreme Leader, Ayatollah Khamenei, in his Jay Jopling black-rimmed glasses next to the caption: 'I CONSIDER SPORT AS A NECESSITY FOR THE HEALTH OF EVERY ONE'S MIND AND BODY AND I AGREE WITH IT.'

A hundred yards away was a sign exactly the same size with a shorter message: 'DIESEL: FOR SUCCESSFUL LIVING.'

"Hey man, have some of this," said the boy in front of me in the male queue for the resort's only chair lift, a diesel-powered relic from the 1970s. He offered me a worn 7-Up bottle. The male queue was eighty or ninety people long. The female one had three people in it, of whom one was wearing a beard. In his left hand I could see a few notes with Khomeini's visage gazing out beneficently that soon made their way into the pocket of the man operating the lift.

"Thanks." I took the bottle. "What is it?"

"Jack Daniels," he said, as the chilled liquid hit the back of my throat. He and his two friends were on snowboards. All three carried Walkmans: Pink Floyd, Nirvana and the ubiquitous DJ Scooter. As we queued, one of them began to build a joint. With surgical precision he held a lighter to a small block of resin, before getting out a penknife and shaving wafer-thin flakes into a fold in his jacket near his left shoulder. His body shielded the operation from the breeze. With the knife and block of resin stowed and his left arm set at an awkward angle, he emptied half a cigarette into the same fold in his jacket and mixed its contents with one hand, before piping the mixture into a waif of Rizla that fluttered like a moth held by one wing. Somehow he kept it all in.

The queue inched forward. He tore off a square of his ski pass and rolled it into a roach. Two licks, left–right, right–left, and he was done. He got out his lighter one more time and took a triumphant drag on his masterpiece, gazing up at the mountain carpeted with sun-kissed snow. After the gloom of Tehran, just looking at it was like an hour-long shower. The expression on his face needed no caption.

We were less than twenty yards from the ski-slope officials, but none of them seemed to mind.

At the end of the day, the boy who could roll a joint in
a queue with one foot on a snowboard took me and Al
back to his house for some light après-ski. Stephen had
already gone home after Al had dared him to do a jump.
He had fallen. Soon after, he had left in a sulk.

One by one we climbed in through our host's window.

"What's wrong with the door?" asked Al.

"Um. I got a little drunk some days ago. I fell down,"
the boy explained. "I know the key is down there somewhere." He nodded at the man-doing-a-star-jump-shaped
hole in the snow beneath the window. "Though I still can't
work out what I was doing in the window."

In the background was music downloaded from the
internet: mostly anonymous chill-out trance. We talked
about whether there had ever been a sequel to
Trainspotting. He promised me there had. He had a soundtrack called *Trainspotting 2* and, for him conclusively, his
pirate DVD of *Trainspotting* came on two discs, one of
which was marked "Trainspotting 2". We agreed to dis-
agree. On the wall was a hand-sewn embroidery of a luscious, tanned and naked women who looked like Sophia
Loren.

"My aunt made that for me when I was a boy," he
explained. "You see, I grew up in the 1980s, just after the
Revolution. She wanted me to know about real life," he
carried on as he hunted for mugs for the whisky. "That's a
real Iranian handicraft for you."

⌒

Agnostic Depressed Hippie

"I CAN'T REMEMBER WHO THIS GUY IS," SAID AL, PULLING ON his coat. Marjan began to hunt for her headscarf. Outside it was snowing again.

"Ali Reza? Oh, he's amazing, you'll love him. The dervish who lives outside Tehran. Remember? The place I went on Millennium Eve when the police caught us and thought we were having a political gathering. Like you would on Millennium Eve."

"Sure. And what's a dervish?" asked Al, woolly hat in place.

"I don't know," she said, looking thoughtful. "A kind of Sufi, I guess."

An hour later I was in Yasmine following Marjan in her Kia Pride as we drove east out of Tehran. In the back of Yasmine was Memat, who was gregarious and fun and who wore a pirate headscarf that made him look like Wolf out of *Gladiators*.

"Oh, my God, this smoke is BEAUT-I-FUL!" he said, choking on a joint in the back seat. "Wow. OK, listen now. I have a story for you guys. You know that everything in this world is like a body, yes?" The best thing about driving at night with stories coming from the back seat was that you didn't have to nod or say yes the whole time. It was like being tucked up in bed and it felt good. "The world is a big body and you know that every body has a heart?" Memat went on. "Yes, you know, a big heart. And when you feel sexy, your heart goes ba-boom, ba-boom, yes? Ha-ha! OK, well, the world has a centre, a heart, and this heart, it is Iran! Really. I know this, OK. It is true. Look at 1963, this cannot be coincidence."

"What happened in 1963?" asked Al.

"You don't know this? Come on. Really, you don't know this?"

"Really."

"It's the year Kennedy die and... and... the year Khomeini left Iran! The heart was feeling very sexy then, you know, it was beating like crazy. You are blind not to see this. There is proof too. Scientist proof. These events are organised by the same people. Everyone knows the world is run by these people. Only ten people. And the heart is Iran. That's why they want to fight Iraq now, because it means they are more close to Iran."

"Why don't they just invade Iran?"

"What?" he spluttered. "No, no, no. If they do this everyone will know where the heart is. They are not stupid, these people!"

Memat went on like this until we arrived at Ali Akbar's house, peddling both standard and bizarre conspiracy theories. A lot of them had become familiar over the last few months in Iran: the CIA orchestrated 9/11, the British are running Iran, the Zionists are about to take over the world, Bin Laden is in fact Bush, Bush is in fact Bin Laden, the Bilderberg Group run the world as well as the Zionists, 9/11 never happened and so on.

Ali Reza, the *soi-disant* dervish, had piercing eyes, spongy eyebrows, long hair and a beard the colour of elephant tusk. If he had trimmed the beard and put on a turban, he might have looked like Khomeini. If he had kept it long and combed, he might have looked like Gandalf or Saruman. Equally, if he had messed it up he would have looked like a tramp. He was a casting director's wet dream. He had, it turned out, been in several films before the Iranian Revolution, although everything in his life changed when Ayatollah Khomeini and his coterie took over.

The room surrounding Ali Reza had a student feel to it and smelt of cigarettes and joss sticks. There was a jumble of chairs, rugs, abstract black-and-white photos, clocks, piles of books, overflowed candles, lamps, drapes, ashtrays and music coming from a computer that at first looked out of place in this setting. On several walls were badly painted murals in garish, primary colours that had been put on too thin. Next to the basin was a bleached black-and-white photograph of a proper-looking Iranian family with the pouting head of Mick Jagger cut out of a magazine and stuck onto the face of the baby. Ali Reza chuckled when I asked him why.

"Why not?" he replied.

It was a secret garden; and again the Iran of mullahs and gender segregation and anti-Israeli rhetoric felt very distant.

Ali Reza sat in one corner, his eyes hidden in the shade of his brow, with half a dozen people by his feet. As well as being a budding actor, Marjan told us, he had been a brilliant advertising executive in Tehran before the Revolution. He confirmed this in a deep, American-sounding drawl, his words muffled by his beard.

"Then the mullahs came," he said. "So I left. I went to a village near the Caspian."

"What was it like there?" asked Stephen.

"Special place," he said. "Nothing like Bournemouth. That's near the sea as well."

"Bournemouth?"

"I used to live in Bournemouth," he said, straightening in his chair.

"Really?"

"I was a mod. I had a scooter and everything. You are from England, yes?"

"Yes," I said.

"Wow!" said Memat. "Ali Reza, you meet with Princess Diana in England?"

"What? No," he said. "No, I didn't. I doubt she'd been born when I was there."

"That is something though," Memat said turning to Al, eyes widening. He had given up on me. "You know about British government, how they kill her? Also she was Muslim woman with Muslim baby. I read she was talking to Queen of British about becoming Muslim. Maybe she had lived longer Queen of British is Muslim as well and then, who knows..."

"Man," said Ali Reza, turning to face Memat, who immediately went quiet. "You talk a lot of shit."

For several hours we talked and smoked and drank, until Ali Reza arose from his throne and began to herd everyone outside. Fifteen of us followed him like willing acolytes across the snow towards what he called his music house. We threw snowballs at each other. Ali Reza's dog, who was not allowed inside the house, raced around kicking up snow that made a hushed, crunching sound as it was sent skywards. Inside the music house were several drums, a keyboard and various metal objects that you could either bang or ding. Al and I were given a conga and a bongo, Ali Reza took an electronic keyboard, and a man with a hippyish waistcoat took a sitar-like instrument. Everyone else sat down to watch as we started to play.

Discord soon gave way to a coltish kind of harmony and after a few minutes there was rhythm. It grew as the four of us became a part of it. Whatever it was we had between us began to build and build until after only a few minutes it was out of control. I was drowning in it, drumming as hard as I could. My mind felt swamped. I could not think straight. Then it would relent and the sound quieten. Exhale. In the background there might be an occasional lonely note from Ali Reza that would remind me of the *muezzin* in Qom's most holy shrine as he began to call the faithful to prayer. I had been allowed into its innermost courtyard, a place reserved for Muslims, where I was also allowed to paint. I had no idea why. As I made my painting and was offered food and drink and greetings by passing pilgrims, the *muezzin* whispered *"Allahu Akbar"* (God is greater than everything) into the shrine's tannoy system at intervals of three minutes for half an hour. It was as if he was not so much calling the faithful to prayer but offering prayer as a suggestion, or as an aside.

The room was silent but for the patter of one finger, my finger, on a drum. Then the man with the sitar joined in. Gently. Me, him and Ali Reza would hold it and tame it, enjoying the momentary sense of control before Al came in and it would start to buckle. With no direction other than an unspoken and collective urge to get back to where we had been and the numbing intensity of that, we sped up. The bodies watching us bobbed back and forth as the sound continued to build, louder and faster – more elaborate too – until once again it was a colossal, pounding thing. Boom-dada-boom-dada-boom-dada. It filled the room and in the cold I could feel sweat form on my forehead.

Still we went faster. I looked over at Stephen in the audience. He had passed out. For a moment I fell asleep as well, waking up to find my hands still drumming, something I would never have thought possible before. I felt like the Sufis in Istanbul had looked. But it was different now because I was part of it: I was no longer a fly on the wall.

In the tenth century, Abu al-Faraj al-Isfahani wrote the *Kitab al-Aghani* (Book of Songs) in which he described *tarab* as the absolute goal of poetry and music and song. *Tarab* is the loss of inhibition brought on by art, a kind of drunkenness that might look like someone being entered by the Holy Spirit in an Evangelical church, or a Sufi reaching *ahwal*.

Early the next morning we finished. Most of the audience had fallen asleep and I had no idea how long we had been playing. The room fell silent. The four of us looked at our instruments and then at each other.

"That," said Ali Reza in the deepest drawl possible, "was some trip."

The rest of us muttered agreement and went to find places to sleep. Outside it was snowing. I fell asleep in front of the fire next door beneath a grey, worsted blanket with Ali Reza's kitten beneath my arm.

THE NEXT MORNING I TOLD ALI REZA ABOUT OUR exhibition.

"So you had interviews?" he asked.

"Sure."

"And what did they ask you?"

"Oh, lots of things. Like what I thought of Iran."

He smiled. "And what did you say? That we're a bunch of agnostic depressed hippies? Living in a system designed for children?"

"Not exactly. I told them I thought it was a friendly place."

"Hmmm. I guess it is for you. You come from the place everyone wants to escape to. You're like ambassadors from paradise. Just don't forget all the shit that goes on," he said, beginning to mumble. "Just never on the surface."

I felt guilty about how much we were enjoying Iran. It seemed to suggest that we were blind to what lay beneath the veneer of friendly slapstick with which so many Iranians greeted us. This was the day-to-day reality we experienced, yet so often it disguised a much deeper and more debilitating melancholy.

"One journalist asked me what I thought the colour of Islam was," I told him.

"Dumb question."

"I know."

"It's green," he said.

"Really? She said white."

"White? Well, whoever this girl is, she thinks only of death. In Islam, white is the colour of death. That's very Iranian of her."

"Are there other colours I should know about?"

"If you like, black is the colour of Shia rebellion. Red can be important too."

"So there is no colour of Islam?"

"No, no. Islam means different things to different people. Maybe it shouldn't, but it does."

"With the Qur'an it is difficult to make opposite arguments," said Ali Reza. "But with the Qur'an and the hadiths, then you can start. Using only the commentaries on the Qur'an I think it is easy."

"The commentaries?"

"The modern commentaries you pick up anywhere. Every mullah and ayatollah writes a commentary."

☾

Fatimah

IN JORDAN HALF A YEAR LATER, WITH THE INVASION OF IRAQ well under way, the twelve-year-old daughter of our host Daqlala asked me whether I knew that the destruction of the World Trade Center had been predicted by the Qur'an.

"Um, I didn't, no."

"It is." She looked impatient.

"Everything is in the Holy Qur'an," said one of her many brothers who was sitting nearby.

"We were taught about this passage in school," Fatimah explained. "There is a paper that was sent to all the schools in Jordan. Look. It is from Mecca, you can see on the top of it. An interpretation. A commentary."

She handed me the paper.

"Show me the passage," I said, passing her my pocket Qur'an. It had an English translation running alongside the Arabic.

"Here," she said once she had found the *ayah* or verse. "It is in the *surah* (chapter) of, how do they say this, Repent-ance, *ayah* 109." She straightened her back and changed her intonation as she declaimed the text. In translation, these *ayah* are as follows:

> *Which is better, the person who founds his building on consciousness of God and desire for His good pleasure, or the person who founds his building on the brink of a crumbling precipice that will tumble down into the Fire of Hell, taking him with it? God does not guide the evildoers: the building they have founded will always be a source of doubt within their hearts, until their hearts are cut to pieces.* (The Qur'an, 9:109–110)

The connection between this passage and what happened on 11 September 2001 was at best tenuous. If someone had suggested these *ayah* implied four planes would be hijacked by a group of suicidal extremists and flown towards three targets on the east coast of the United States at any point before the actual event they would have been dismissed as lunatic. It was a *non sequitur*. The text did not predict the event. But by linking these verses to the events of 11 September 2001 in retrospect, the attack was being made out to be divine. A victory. A visual proof.

In their Qur'anic context, these *ayah* refer to a mosque built in Yathrib (later Medina) by recent converts to Islam who had previously fought against the Prophet. Their mosque was a rival to that of the Prophet, and the Qur'an urges all believers to boycott it.

There was an *ayah* I came across several months later that I wished I could have shown Fatimah, or rather the men in Mecca who had sent the commentary to her school:

> ...*it is He who has sent this Scripture down to you (Prophet). Some of its verses are definite in meaning – these are the cornerstone of the Scripture – and others are ambiguous. The perverse at heart eagerly pursue the ambiguities in their attempt to make trouble and to pinpoint a specific meaning – only God knows the true meaning.* (The Qur'an, 3:7)

☾

Different Things

"SO TELL ME," I STARTED, WONDERING HOW BEST TO PHRASE it. "Because I've been trying to work it out. What exactly is a dervish?"

Ali Reza grinned beneath his beard. Everyone else was still asleep.

"An excuse for being mysterious," he said slowly. "A dervish is what people want him to be. Different things to different people. Some of the people here have their own ideas and they attach them to things I say, or to things I don't." There was another contemplative pause. "You see, people believe what they want to believe until there is something to show them they're wrong. Yes? It's like how Iranians talk about living in America. They call it paradise because they want to believe it is paradise, and until there is something to show them it isn't, they continue to believe it's paradise. Different things to different people. Especially when you have little to go on."

THAT AFTERNOON ON THE WAY BACK TO TEHRAN WE TALKED with growing conviction about the need to push ourselves further, and to try to find more of these secret gardens.

"The thing is," said Stephen, "we can get to a lot of these places. In the way that other people can't. I reckon the one thing we've really got on our side is the way we look."

Al started to laugh.

"No, seriously Al. Think about it. No one can ever quite work out what we are. That's got to be a good thing. You two especially," he gestured at me and Al. "You've been, what have you been, you've been Islamic extremists in Slovakia. Henry, you've been a street cleaner. Al, you've been a tramp. Quite a few times, actually. And we've all been British spies." He started nodding to himself. "Think I'd be quite good as a spy."

"You'd be useless," said Al.

"Can't imagine you making much of a spy."

"Be better than you."

"What would you do as a spy? You'd be asked for a report on Iran and you'd send them a whole load of paint-feelings." He put on his Al voice. "There we go. That's another fifty done. Should do it, eh? What do you mean, you don't understand them? They're my Al-feelings. I mean paint-feelings. They express my inner emotions, how can you..."

"And what would you do, Stephen? You'd send in a whole load of tea-stained photos of yourself."

"Be better than your paint-feelings. Anyway, stop changing the subject, Al. This is important."

"Honestly, you'd be the world's worst spy, Steve."

"Shut up, Al. Like Henry was saying, we've got to get ourselves into more of these secret gardens. And don't forget, it's Christmas soon. Also got to find somewhere good to celebrate Christmas."

Part Two
Dancing at Death

From Iran into Kurdish Iraq and back into Iran, illegally

English Man

I WENT ARMED ONLY WITH A NAME. DANA. IT OPENED THE
metal gate with a buzz and a click and I was led into a room
that smelt of furniture polish and was full of large, plastic-
coated sofas that had not been sat on much. A glass of tea
was put on the glass of the table in front of me.

But how to sit? With decorum. Presence too, but nothing that might look like arrogance, please, that might put
him off and I was certain one of the people walking past
would be him. Appearances were important. I had nothing
else.

Upright, I stared in a haze of *politesse* at a television
screen with the news being read in Kurdish. Men and
women trotted past. Polished shoes clicked on polished
floors and a man with neat hair brought me more tea.

I was shown into Dana's office. He looked bedraggled.
He wore a polo-neck. He was on the phone and waved me
to another bank of shiny sofas. As directed, I perched on
the edge of a plastic-coated throne more grand than anything in the waiting room. Behind Dana's desk was a green
flag emblazoned with a fist clutching a red rose, the logo of
the Patriotic Union of Kurdistan, the PUK, one of two
groups that ran the Kurdish, semi-autonomous, north-
eastern region of Iraq that had been independent of
Saddam Hussein's Ba'athist government since 1991. The
PUK controlled most of Kurdish Iraq as well as the border
we hoped to cross. This was its Tehran headquarters.

When we first arrived in Iran we had no intention of
going to Kurdish Iraq. We barely knew it existed. It was
only during the last few weeks in Tehran that we heard stories about British or American journalists who had managed to cross into Kurdish Iraq. It was almost impossible to

get there, everyone said, what with the war about to start. Only a handful of the best-connected, smoothest-talking foreigners were able to do it. Jim Muir, the BBC correspondent in Tehran, told me flatly that we had little or no chance of succeeding, and before long this aura of exclusivity had seduced us, totally, until getting into Kurdish Iraq was the only thing any of us could talk about. It seemed to be the ultimate secret garden, and getting there had become a test of how far we were prepared to go in our bid to create an original portrait of the Middle East.

Every time Stephen or Al mentioned Kurdish Iraq I thought of Baghdad. I had stopped telling them about my conversation with the Turkish journalist because they were bored with it. Understandably. It didn't change each time I told it, yet for me it had become something else in the last few weeks. Not in fact, but in terms of what part it might play in our journey. It was all about the scale of what we had set out to do – make a portrait of the entire Middle East – which was, now that I had had more time to get my head round it, unwieldy to the point of being unrealistic. I was beginning to see that instead of trying to create an exhaustive account of the region, we might be better off moving in the opposite direction in terms of scale; instead of trying to create a thousand-page tome, perhaps our year-long expedition could be condensed into a single *haiku*. It might be a drawing, a photograph, an action, an installation, a conversation. Or just a moment. But if it was to happen anywhere surely it would be in Baghdad, in the heart of the unreported artistic renaissance.

Baghdad was beginning, for me at least, to be the Emerald City and Mount Doom rolled into one. I was certain that if we went there, exactly how to distil the journey into one action or one moment would be obvious. All we had to do was get there.

Although Kurdish Iraq was not Baghdad it was close, and there might be a way of getting from Kurdish Iraq to Baghdad.

"So you want to cross into Kurdish Iraq?" asked Dana.

"Yes," I said, nodding.

He scanned my face, his head moving from side to side. "This is not possible," he said.

"I want to cross that border." I nodded. "So much."

He looked at me again. It was a long way from the passionate, articulate and above all winning speech I had practised earlier. His eyes roamed the room as he lit another cigarette.

"Now," he said, walking over to me. "Here is some paper. Put down your name, your detail. Maybe something happen. Or no." The biro landed on the table with a clack.

"What about my friends?" I asked. Al and Stephen were, at that moment, elsewhere in Tehran.

"What?" said Dana, spinning on the polished floor with the gait of an ice skater.

"My two friends. The ones I told you about on the phone."

He looked as if he had just received news of a death. A family death, perhaps.

"What friends?" he asked, staring a little over my head. Maybe his brother.

"The two friends I am working with."

"Two more? No, this is not possible." He took away the paper. "You say it is one person," he said, angry, pointing at me, "that you were photographer. I telephone the border. I give them dates. I say let this photographer over, please. Now there are two more? No way. This is finished." His eyes narrowed for a moment. "I cannot understand this. You come here with, I don't know, you are from no, no organisation, no TV, no newspaper." He paused. "Who are you?"

"What do you mean?"

"WHO ARE YOU?" he shouted. "You speak English?"

This was it. The moment I had to perform: a chance to redeem the mediocrity of what had gone before and I knew it then, not later on, glum, sat down with Stephen and Al and explaining to them why we would not be going to Kurdish Iraq.

The silence grew as I gawped at the enormity of what was going on. "I'm... I don't know, I'm an artist." It wasn't enough. "An English artist."

"WHAT?" His face was red. "AN ENGLISHMAN?"

"No, that's not..."

"DO NOT EVER say that. EVER! YOU COME HERE AND SAY YOU ENGLISHMAN? I cannot believe this. How dare you! I AM KURD! So what? You are not Englishman. YOU ARE PERSON!"

He turned to the two men sat on a sofa opposite and explained what had happened in Kurdish. One shook his head gravely. The other looked at me as if to say, "How could you?"

"He thinks it is like England ruled the world," said Dana, in English for my benefit.

"No, no, wait. Don't be angry," I said, standing up to be at the same level as him. A vein was bubbling on the left of his forehead. "Please. I am not here to insult you. I am not proud of being English, forgive me. I am grateful for your help. So grateful. I only want to get to Kurdistan and to record what is happening there, to show everyone what is happening for the Kurdish people. Now. At this important time for Kurdistan." I moved towards Dana. "I said Englishman as a mistake. Forgive my mistake. Please. Understand what I am saying. I talk about my friends only because I cannot leave them. That is like betraying them and I cannot betray them, you must see that. We want more than anything to go to Kurdistan, otherwise why am I here?" His shoulders relaxed a bit. "For a holiday?" His shoulders relaxed some more.

He went back to his desk and made a call. One of the mustachioed men on the sofa opposite who was listening to what was being said nodded at me.

"It is OK," he said.

Dana came over, new cigarette in hand. "Put the names and the details on this paper."

This time he placed the biro on the table and it made no sound. I wrote down three names and three passport numbers and paused at the word nationality. Dana looked over.

"Problem?"

"I have to write my nationality," I said, staring at the paper.

"And?" asked Dana.

"I am no longer an Englishman."

The room was silent for several seconds that felt like an age as Dana began an apoplectic, red-faced roar of laughter. The men opposite did likewise. The laughter grew and grew, the sound meaty and raucous. Dana thumped me on the back so hard I almost slid off the sofa.

"Ha! You are a good man! You can come to my country!"

The men opposite nodded.

"Good man," said one.

"Good man," said the other.

"You are Kurdish man now!" said Dana.

"Great," I said, nodding and patting him on the back, gently, making sure not to thump him off the sofa.

He wrote down a telephone number on a piece of paper, came close and told me to ring the number when we got to Kermanshah, a mostly Kurdish city near the

Iran-Iraq border. The man we should speak to was called Taha. He would tell us whether or not we could cross.

"Write nothing else on this paper and when you have called the number, throw away this paper, yes?"

"Sure. And then he will take us to Kurdish Iraq?"

"I cannot say."

I later found out that the room was bugged, which made this exchange a hundred times more exciting and about as close as I would ever get to living out any pre-pubescent James Bond fantasy.

At ten past nine on Christmas Day 2002, in a hostel in Kermanshah in western Iran, there was a knock on the door of our room. Al hid the bottle of Lauders whisky we had drunk the night before and opened the door. It was the hotel owner. There was a call for "Emin". Not Tracey. I ran downstairs, the blood pumping to my head like an alarm clock.

"You have permission to cross," said the voice on the other end of the line. "Come to PUK office. There is man here who will take you to border."

As instructed, we left Yasmine at the PUK office in Kermanshah and three hours later we arrived at the un-official border crossing.

The point where Iran became Iraq was marked by a flimsy gate painted in Iran's national colours: red, white and green. The two countries had fought between 1980 and 1988 in the Iran–Iraq War and although it had finished as a stalemate with no territorial gain for either side, the Iranian government claimed victory because Iran had fought in self-defence with the aim of maintaining rather than expanding its borders. But what a Pyrrhic victory. The war had cost more than a million lives, of which the major-ity were adolescent Iranian conscripts with plastic keys tied round their necks. The keys had been issued to them by the Iranian government free of charge so that when they got to heaven they would get in without any trouble.

On both sides of the border, over the pockmarked landscape, ran slug-like trails of coiled barbed wire and craters where no grass would grow. There were no trees and little vegetation. On the Iranian side of the divide, clusters of flagpoles had been planted like emaciated birches next to portraits of Khomeini and Khamenei. Hidden in this forbidding scenery were machine-gun positions with thatched roofs and large-calibre nozzles aimed at the other side of the desolate valley.

Men in black, baggy, MC Hammer trousers with cummerbund sashes round their stomachs – *peshmergha* troops, armed Kurdish fighters, whose name literally means "those who face death" – took our names on the Iraqi side of the border and soon we were in a taxi with Iraqi markings heading west. Taha, the man from the PUK who was escorting us to Sulaymaniyah, was in the back seat next to Stephen and Al. We had made it. It was Christmas Day. I had forgotten it was Christmas Day. The car bounced a lot, putting me on the edge of my seat, while outside it was starting to snow. The windscreen wipers moved with a rubbery quack and wiped only a small section of the windscreen.

The landscape in Kurdish Iraq was different to Iran – blank, green and rich – while the towns or villages we drove through were more harsh than anything we had seen in Iran. The buildings, many of them rebuilt after being destroyed by Saddam in the 1980s during his Anfal campaign against the Iraqi Kurds, were crude and angular while the roadblocks were proper roadblocks, unlike their mostly adolescent equivalent in Iran. Irregular troops not in uniform with large guns and even larger dogs would look hard at our passports before peering through the window at our faces.

At this point in the inspections a pattern emerged. After moving without comment over Al's face and Stephen's face, whoever was inspecting our car would stop when they got to my face and start to talk fast at our driver and Taha. They would argue for some time and take my passport away.

"They ask if you are from Afghanistan," Taha would say to me, grinning. "Or if you are Arab." He grinned at most things. Or, "They think you are Bin Laden!"

Which brings me on to my appearance. Not the beard, nor the clothes I had spent so long fussing over in the name of assimilation, partial assimilation at least, or just not looking English, but what was at the heart of it: the one thing I could never truly disguise.

My eyes are small, dark and a little narrow, meaning growing up in England has been dotted with people asking where I was from. England. No, but where are you really from, where are your parents from? England. Well my mum is half-Scottish. And your Dad? England as well, I mean he has a Canadian passport but he's lived all his life in England, his family are English. Usually I would ask the person where they thought I was from and they would say cold places like Russia, or Mongolia, which made more sense from the age of about nine when I found out that my mother's great-great-great-grandfather was Russian. I decided he was to blame.

I did not try to explain any of this to the men manning the roadblocks.

At most roadblocks the guards would call over their friends to come and have a look, and like doctors asking colleagues for a second opinion, they would all scratch their chins and hum as they stared.

"Bad, isn't it?"

It was like being a painting up in a gallery having abstruse or idiotic meanings read into you and not being able to do anything about it. I was mute within their labels; labels I did not yet know. We were in a new state with its own nuanced parameters of suspicion, and what had allowed me to blend in from time to time in Iran made me an object of suspicion in Kurdish Iraq. I later found out that this had a lot to do with the terrorist group Ansar al-Islam, run by the then little-known Abu Musab al-Zarqawi. At that time they were based in the north of Kurdish Iraq and were known to recruit pale-skinned foreign fighters from Chechnya or central Asian states ending in -stan; as explained by my Russian ancestor, I was able to pass for one of these men.

At each roadblock the tutting cooled only after Taha, whom they knew, insisted that I was not a threat. He provided the sobering caption to the otherwise wordless image.

SEVERAL DAYS LATER, WHILE I WAS HAVING BREAKFAST IN THE dining room of our hotel and Al and Stephen were yet to surface, two men wearing thick black jackets began to stare at me. After five minutes of this I became fidgety and went over to their table to ask if anything was the matter. Neither spoke English. The one who was doing most of the staring led me by the arm to his friend several tables away.

"Your friend is staring at me," I announced.

The chief starer gave his side of the story. His grip on my arm remained firm.

"This man says he saw you yesterday," our arbiter announced.

"And?"

"And he was not sure where you were from or what you were doing here. He thought maybe you were an Arab, yes?"

"OK. But do I look like an Arab?"

"Um."

"Do I? I don't know any more."

"No, not Arab. Maybe somewhere else. You know, not from here. It is OK, don't be angry." The man smiled.

"This hotel has other foreigners staying in it. Why doesn't he stare at them?"

"Yes, but they are different, you know, they are American or British."

"Well, so am I."

"Yes, yes. What? British, really?"

"I can show you my passport if you like," I said.

"No, please, it is OK. You say British. There is no problem." He continued to smile. "You have British passport?"

"Yes. But do you think this man will stop staring at me when I sit down?"

"Maybe. But it is his job to watch, you know? He is bodyguard to prime minister. He must watch people who are maybe suspicious." The chief starer nodded at me. I nodded back. We returned to our tables.

I'd met a man called Shirko yesterday who not only looked like a Kurd but was a Kurd. He came and sat down with me. The prime minister's bodyguards relaxed. We were soon joined by another Kurdish man whose two bodyguards sat themselves at the table next to the prime minister's bodyguards. The two sets of bodyguards nodded at each other. The new arrival was a friend of Shirko's and a *peshmergha* commander.

"Bodyguards are important now," the commander announced. Shirko explained that his friend had survived several attempts on his life.

"It is true," the commander interrupted. "Some years ago Ba'athists bribe my wife. They get her to poison me," he went on, slicing through the poached egg in front of him. "One night she put poison in my food. She has the mixture wrong. So I live." He grunted. "Always she is bad cook."

You could tell he had said this before, but it didn't make him laugh that morning. There must have been times, drunk and with his friends, when the low-lit bevy of bear-like men had been lost in red-faced laughter and thumps on backs so hard that everyone slid off their chairs, but that morning he did not smile.

"So is it easy to travel from Sulaymaniyah to Baghdad?" I asked.

The commander choked on his food. Shirko smiled and shook his head.

"Not now. No, no. This is not possible now."

"You will be killed."

Both men smiled at me.

"Right," I said, blushing, and feeling like an especially ungrizzly twenty-three-year-old artist a long way from home in a semi-war zone who was missing Christmas with his family.

"You must be careful here," the commander went on, nodding at me before getting back to his egg. "You look like you are," he lowered his voice, "like Islam fanatic. And if you stay here, as Englishman, you are target for Islam fanatic too. They try to bomb this hotel some months before. I think, yes, I think it is good you keep your head down," he said, stooping to catch some yolk. "I think you are very unfortunate!" He was starting to laugh now. "The Englishman who looks like Islam fanatic! Or maybe it is better for you to look like this. It is like a disguise... I don't know."

☾

Facing Death

HERO TALABANI – MRS TALABANI TO YOU AND ME, THE most powerful woman in Kurdish Iraq, the wife of the PUK leader Jalal Talabani who later became President of Iraq, the woman who ran KurdSat, the first and at that time only Kurdish satellite television station, which was based in Sulaymaniyah – sat facing the three of us in KurdSat's canteen. Shirko had just joined us. The light in the canteen was unforgiving and the room smelt of cigarettes. Mrs Talabani's hair was streaked silver. Her face was lean and attractive.

Her father had been a senior member of the KDP (the Kurdistan Democratic Party), the group from which the PUK splintered in 1975, and in 1977 she had gone to live with PUK *peshmerghas* in the mountains. She had lived with them as an outlaw to the Iraqi Ba'athist regime until 1991 when the PUK, led by her husband, won UN-recognised semi-autonomy from Baghdad. During the 1980s she had filmed some of the atrocities that had gone on during Saddam Hussein's brutal Anfal campaign against the Kurds.

"But nobody wanted these pictures," she said, her voice calm. "'We don't want anything against Saddam,' they told me. They were so against Iran they want to support Saddam."

"Someone showed it eventually?" I asked.

"Channel 4 in England."

"It has changed now," said a Kurdish man with a beachball of a belly who sat next to her. "They'll take anything that's anti-Saddam. Anything at all." He raised his eyebrows and smiled to himself.

Mrs Talabani proceeded to take us on a guided tour of the KurdSat headquarters, leading us through rooms stuffed with screens and machines and eager-looking boys and girls.

"None of them have the qualification," she said, pointing at a particularly eager twenty year old. "The best-qualified person here is, let me think, boy on the second floor. He did a week's work experience in Baghdad. No one else has any training in this," she said, waving at a bank of machines nervously. "They have all taught themselves. This is special thing for them. For the first time there is Kurdish TV and you can see it in Turkey, in Syria, in Iran, in Iraq. No government can stop it. They cannot destroy a million satellite dishes."

At that moment there were more than twenty-five million Kurds in the Middle East, making them the fourth largest ethnicity in the region behind Arabs, Persians and Turks. They constituted the world's largest ethnicity without a nation of its own, but Mrs Talabani did not pine after a Kurdish nation – a "Kurdistan" – as I thought she would. Instead she described herself as a Kurdish Iraqi, making sure to put the words in that order. Beyond that there were countless layers of more personal, more emotive identities, but just then, talking to three foreign artists visiting the KurdSat headquarters with a war against Ba'athist Iraq imminent, she was a Kurdish Iraqi.

Both the PUK and the Kurdish population of Iraq had suffered appallingly at the hands of Saddam Hussein, yet the polyglot history of Iraqi cities like Kirkuk or Mosul or even Baghdad makes this Kurdish acceptance of Iraqi-ness less strange. In each of these cities Sunni Arab, Shia Arab, Turkoman, Kurdish, Jewish, Assyrian, Chaldean and sometimes Roma communities had lived side by side for many centuries. They might not have lived every day of this coexistence in a halcyon coma of sharing, mutual love and pyjama parties, but they had lived side by side, and this made ethnically defined pogroms or ethnically divisive propaganda harder to sustain, even during Saddam's "Arabisation" programme that saw the eviction of Kurdish communities from cities like Kirkuk and the insertion of Shia Arabs in their place.

The last hundred years of living within different, culturally centralising nations had pulled the Kurdish people apart, but before our eyes in the KurdSat headquarters this process was being reversed. For the first time in Kurdish history – which for the twentieth century reads like Armenian, Brazilian Amerindian or Jewish history, in being a tragic catalogue of state-administered or at least state-ignored repression or genocide dovetailed by the prospect of a brighter future by the end of the century – a satellite television station was articulating and in many ways creating a modern Kurdish identity. Kurds all over the Middle East were tuning in and nobody could stop them.

As we left the KurdSat building, Mrs Talabani did two things that fundamentally changed our time in Sulaymaniyah. She generously arranged for us to stay for free in the five-star Sulaymaniyah Palace Hotel, without which we would have run out of money; and she told us to go and visit Amna Suraka, the Red House. This was the former Ba'athist barracks where Kurdish rebels – the *peshmerghas* – had been imprisoned, tortured and executed. Mrs Talabani said we should see the drawings there.

THE NEXT DAY I WENT TO FIND IT. THE RED HOUSE WAS empty but for two guards who looked after the place and a family of pigeons with feathers going right down their legs, which made them look more friendly than their London-based cousins. The two guards were sitting in the gatehouse watching a VCD of *peshmerghas* dancing in a line. I sat with them for a few minutes and watched nine Kurds in full *peshmergha* uniform, arm in arm, kicking their legs in unison as if doing a reduced cancan. In front of them was a teenage boy who led the dance and flicked a white handkerchief back and forth in front of him.

One of the men from the gatehouse took me to the main building. Its flesh-coloured, bullet-ridden exterior gave onto charred passageways that in their decay looked like a building under construction. After a succession of identical, pared-down corridors, the gatekeeper led me into rooms without windows where I saw the first of five sculptures by a young Kurdish artist. With a blindfold tied tight round his head, a sculpted figure crouched at the foot of the stairwell. The gatekeeper acted out Ba'athists kicking him as they passed, his shoe stopping just short of the plaster of Paris each time. Another sculpture was of a *peshmergha* with his hands bound behind his back, who hung by the join in his binding from a hook in the ceiling. The innate, muscular tension of his body had arched his limbs into a curved, taut shape so that he, it, commanded the space. We went next into a room divided by iron grilles. Again there was no daylight and the gatekeeper mimed in unmistakable gestures that this was where the prisoners were held before being executed.

As my eyes adjusted to the dark, I made out drawings by men about to die that had been scratched onto the wall. The walls were the colour of charcoal and each scratched line came out yellow, giving the images the look and feel of prehistoric petroglyphs.

One drawing was of a mosque with long, meandering verticals that curved as the arm behind the hand had run out of space. Every arch and indentation of the building had been included, the act of recall exaggerating each detail and making the mosque appear bloated. Elsewhere there were flowers, or women; but not splayed women with diagrams and arrows of what was about to happen to them as I had seen elsewhere, instead mother women, or sister women.

Then, in a darker corner, I saw a picture that was unlike any of the others. In it a man with a trimmed beard and a turban sat cross-legged in front of the Qur'an. Next to him was a carefully drawn candle, the lines of its light spreading far over the blackened wall. The man's expression was anxious and his eyes, though drawn with only two marks, were unbelievably tense. I traced the lines with my hand to let my arm feel what the arm of the prisoner who had made this might have done, this man whose identity I did not know beyond his status as rebel, freedom fighter, guerrilla, *peshmergha* or insurgent, depending on your perspective. As I looked harder, concentrating more on the power of this line, the tart beauty of it, the expression of the figure, the gloom of the space around me, the rotten smell of it, I could feel this man eyeing death. Staring it in the face. Eyeballing it. Taunting it. The thought grew, spiralling and rooting me to the spot. The drawing and its provenance and the space around me fed off each other like a Mexican stand-off until the tension became unbearable. My head wanted to explode. I could not think straight. Everything about this drawing shook me. It was the most powerful drawing I had ever seen. It made every drawing I had ever glimpsed in a gallery or on someone's wall seem pedestrian and I couldn't think what to do, other than to draw it for myself.

With the man from the gatehouse lighting successive matches, I copied the image into my sketchbook. Each match lasted about twenty seconds and after thirty matches I was done.

The gatekeeper led me outside. I was exhausted. The sun was shining, though little of the snow had melted. Back at the gatehouse the other guard continued to watch the VCD where nine *peshmerghas* stood, arm in arm, kicking their legs in unison as if doing a reduced cancan. Suddenly, it made me think of a conversation in Istanbul with James Wilde.

☪

Fucking Crazy

"Yeah, I remember being in Iraqi Kurdistan, back in the early 1990s. Was covering the war there." James rocked a little harder in his chair as the Istanbul skyline glittered behind him. "Bravest people I've ever known, the Kurds. Fearless. And y'know an extraordinary thing happened when I was there. I was with *peshmerghas*, somewhere south of Sulaymaniyah, and we start getting bombed. Huge explosions going off all round us." He waved his arms around a bit. "BOOM! BOOM! BOOM! Like nothing else. Presents from Saddam. So we all took cover, scared to shit. I thought I was going to die. Then after about half an hour of this, these guys I was with just run out into the open. Bombs going off all around them. And they start dancing. I've never seen anything like it. A kind of Kurdish dance. They put their arms round each other and start to dance in a line. The bombs exploding all around them and they just kept dancing. It was insane. It was as if they were staring death in the face and just laughing. Pissing themselves laughing!" He shook his head. "Never seen anything like it. Half of them died. Died dancing."

He looked up. "That's what *peshmergha* means you know, facing death. Bravest people I've ever met. Fucking crazy as well. Maybe you need a bit of that to be that brave."

☾

Illegals

A WEEK LATER, WITH MEMORIES OF THE RED HOUSE AND dancing in the face of death scarred onto each of our unconscious memories, we left Kurdish Iraq and returned to Iran.

This was not as easy as it sounds. The border crossing through which we had entered Kurdish Iraq was unofficial, which meant that in order to use it you had to have your name down on both sides of the border at least two days before you planned to cross. Taha, who was still looking after us, spent a week trying to navigate this bureaucratic assault course from a temperamental telephone in Sulaymaniyah. On our first attempt at getting into Iran we failed because Taha had not got both sides in sync. It was another four days before he managed to get our names down on both sides of the border for the same day with the required two days' warning. By then there was a new problem: both Al's and my Iranian visas had expired. Getting two new ones would mean flying back to London, something we really could not afford.

The Iranian army captain inspecting our passports had a wooden leg and what might have been a blind eye. He stared at each of our visa stamps for what seemed like an age. We held our breath. He scanned each of our faces, as if they were barcodes. We continued to hold our breath and with a grunt he waved us through.

Iran felt familiar and homely, even though we were now there as illegal immigrants. Once again we were surrounded by the friendly slapstick and welcoming arms, gestures and expressions that had been our day-to-day experience of making art in Iran. It felt instantly more safe and less tense than Sulaymaniyah. The possible invasion of Iraq seemed to be somebody else's business, a rumour, something far away; and I no longer looked like a member of Ansar al-Islam. That was particularly good. Though perhaps the best part of being back in Iran was being reunited with Yasmine; we had all missed her in our own way and she had spent Christmas and New Year's Eve on her own, something I felt strangely guilty about.

From Kermanshah we set off for Bandar-e 'Abbas on the southern coast, just under two thousand kilometres away. Our plan was to get on a boat and cross the Straits of Hormuz to Arabia. I was excited about this. So were Al and Stephen. Arabia represented a new world, in every sense, a geography articulated by a different language, a different climate and a people racially apart from the men and women we had been among for the last few months.

After at least ten roadblocks where our passports were inspected by grinning Iranian conscripts, none of whom noticed that our visas had expired, we reached Esfahan where the man running our hostel spotted the expiry date. Our passports were confiscated and the following day two secret policemen arrived to interrogate us. Al and Stephen were nowhere to be found, so I was taken alone to an empty room in the hostel and questioned, carefully and intelligently.

They asked why I had studied history at university if I was an artist. Good question. They also made it clear they were more interested in Al because he had gone to Oxford, whereas I had gone to Newcastle. People who went to Newcastle were less intelligent than those who went to Oxford, they told me; Stephen as an art school graduate was of no interest to them, they added, which was a bit unfair, I thought. Like talking about your famous friend and feeling more and more invisible the longer you do so, I answered their questions about Al's friends at Oxford, why Al had read Geography and what Al's other interests were. After several hours of delicate rhetorical probing, they concluded that we had not crossed the border with Kurdish Iraq illegally and that chief spy suspect Al was in fact not a spy. Later that day we were given special visas that allowed us two days to get out of Iran.

Just over a week later the three of us were in Muscat, the sleepy, softly spoken capital of Oman, the Arab state on the southeastern tip of the Arabian peninsula where men wore the long traditional dishdashers, souks smelt of frankincense, the light in the middle of the day was like staring at the sun through cheap sunglasses, and we were guests of an Omani Princess.

Iran and Kurdish Iraq soon felt like the blurred vestiges of a dream.

Part Three
Beat of the Drum

From Oman to Jordan, via Saudi Arabia,
as the second Gulf War gets underway

Saba Disco

"YOU DID NOT KNOW THIS? EVERYONE KNOWS THIS. OMAN is most gay country in all world." The taxi driver swivelled around in his seat. It was hard to tell whether he was proud of his assertion or making fun of it. "And you know our Sultan has no children?"

"Right."

"Yes. *He has no children.*"

"Sure."

"You understand?"

"Got it."

On our second night in Muscat we were taken to a club that we would not have been let into were it not for Princess Susan al-Said's seventeen-year-old daughter who was looking after us that night. Her mother was putting us up in a beautiful and abandoned former antiques shop in Old Muscat. It was, for all of us, a vision of what an artist's studio should be. Every detail reeked of bohemian decay: from the white walls that lumps of plaster would fall from with an urgent-sounding crash, to its rooftop view over the city, its crumbling battlements, the roomy size of it, the dank smell, the mosque next door, the fans that rumbled like old jalopies as you fell asleep; even the studded chests piled up in the corner and the doors that had been pillaged from villages in the desert added yet more mise-en-scène. Qur'anic *ayah* had been carved into some of these doors, branding each patinated and wobbling surface as if it were a slave.

We had taken a boat by night from Bandar-e 'Abbas on the Iranian coast and woken up the next day in front of the dazzling Dubai skyline. Dubai was the slick and sleek financial capital of Arabia, a city that towered over the rest of the region like an enormous raised, middle finger to every Orientalist from Chateaubriand to Bernard Lewis who had written about an "Arab mind" inherently unable to organise or sustain something this dynamic. Swapping Iran for Dubai was a shock. It was like leaving a run-down country house inhabited by an aged and aristocratic couple to go to stay with their neighbours, *arrivistes* in the refurbished lodge at the end of the elderly couple's (four-mile) drive. The geographical proximity of the two made this contrast even more extreme.

From Dubai we had driven to Oman, where we met Princess Susan on our first night. She was traffic-stoppingly beautiful, tall and slender with skin that shone. Talking to her made you feel inadequate, or short, or badly dressed, or all of the above. Twenty years ago, as a model originally from Alaska, she had fallen for and married one of the nephews of Sultan Qaboos.

Within half an hour of us meeting her Princess Susan had offered us both a place to stay and an exhibition of the work we would make in Oman.

Everyone in the club that her daughter had just got us into was either royal, rich, beautiful or, as was often the case, all three. Along with most of the grandchildren, great-nephews and great-nieces of the Sultan of Oman's closest siblings – because of the Sultan's lack of an heir, all potential successors to the Sultanate – we spent the night jumping up and down to Eminem's "Lose Yourself" or Punjabi MC's "Mundian To Bach Ke", the floor fillers of the night. Stephen was a bit nervous. Al threw himself into dancing, swiping the air with the Omani walking stick he had bought a few days ago and rapidly clearing a space around him. As usual, I was somewhere between the two.

We were outsiders here. Everyone seemed to know one another. They all had stories about each other. There were cliques. There were certain people who would not talk to each other. There were watchful eyes, and every time an Arabic song came on the young Muscati glitterati abandoned the dance floor. They would dance only to Western pop.

At the end of the night Princess Susan's daughter went home while the three of us hung around. The crowd at the club thinned and a well-dressed Omani boy in his late teens who we had got to know a little suggested we go to the Saba disco. None of us knew it.

"I've heard it's really good," he said. "Not far from here."

We got into his car; he had a driver. Twenty minutes later we walked into the Saba disco, where we were met by a sight that was as hard to describe as it was to forget. If there was an Omani circle of hell, this was it. Everything you could see as you walked into the Saba disco was low-lit, green and fleshy. It was rammed full of bodies, all of them glistening with sweat. Corpulent Omani men in white dishdashers staggered back and forth in a carnal stupor, while between them slid armies of barely clothed Chinese and Filipino girls, three or four to every man. There were no Arabic girls. It was a bizarre, low-budget vision of paradise; a brothel-cum-harem staffed entirely by Filipino or Chinese girls because, as we were later told, they offered the "best fit" for the average Omani man.

The smell was suffocating. You could taste the sweat in the air, swill it round your mouth, name the vintage. Dry ice was being pumped in from the back of the room, making the taste stale and adding to the cheap-horror-movie feel of it all. Bodies moved badly to Britney Spears songs that had been turned up loud, louder than you could talk because you didn't need to talk – words might ruin it – and everywhere we looked we could see men being petted like dogs by expressionless girls. As we gawped at this, four women emerged out of the gloom to press flat, ill-defined bodies up against us. They felt like plastic fruit: cold and lifeless yet firm. We got out fast.

The boy who had taken us there apologised, saying he had no idea it was going to be like that. None of us quite believed him. We got into his car and his driver set a course for our studio. Neon lights, KFC, McDonald's, Pizza Hut, Hardee's and Subway rolled past the window as our host described his twenty-year-old Omani friends who would sit around all day watching American or European porn before trying out what they had seen on Chinese or Filipino prostitutes. None of his friends had girlfriends. They barely got to speak to Omani girls.

Unlike in Iran, this gender segregation was not enforced by the state, nor was it obligatory to wear *hijab* in Oman; instead both were demanded by society and in vogue, and that seemed to carry more clout.

"These friends of mine, none of them have real girlfriends," our host corrected himself. "No Omani girl will touch you until you're married. And that's the problem. I mean, do you blame the society that keeps the men and the women apart, like they are two different species?" He was starting to sound like a Middle Eastern Carrie Bradshaw tapping out the title of her "Sex and the City" column. "Or do you blame the porn that, you know, makes them want to do this. It turns them into animals. I don't know. Maybe men are animals anyway."

The four of us pondered this.

"Well," said Stephen, "Oman is changing."

"Sure is," said Al.

"Yup, Oman is changing," our host nodded. "If it carries on like this, with all the foreign porn and the prostitutes, we won't be the most gay country in the world much longer."

☾

The Sky Is About to Fall on My Head

A MONTH HAS PASSED. OUR MUSCAT SHOW OPENS IN A FEW hours and above me, with a kind of pathetic fallacy so obvious it is, for want of a better word, pathetic, the sky has turned a sickly purple. Last night the wind blew over two doors in our courtyard. One of them smashed a pot. Everyone in Muscat says rain is on the way, which is unusual for this time of year, and I have an ache in the pit of my stomach that has nothing to do with the rain, the show or anything I've eaten.

Talk of an invasion of Iraq has become urgent. Even in the political island that is Oman, both expats and Muscatis are anxious about what might happen. Nobody knows the depth of xenophobia the invasion of Iraq might unleash throughout the region. Three days ago an estimated ten million people worldwide demonstrated against the proposed invasion of Iraq – apparently two million of them in London – and the three of us are now receiving a slew of emails and phone calls from people in England who say we should come home. They make it sound as though a hurricane is about to hit and that we are the only ones stupid enough to be outside, still, after all these warnings.

"From Oman, we plan to cross Saudi Arabia to Jordan, where we have our next show lined up," I have typed over and over; or, "We will react to the war in Iraq when it starts, if it starts." By which time it'll be too late, they all write back.

I got an email yesterday from Paul Bergne, Tony Blair's special envoy to Afghanistan during the recent coalition campaign against the Taliban. I had spoken to him before we set out about the places we planned to go. He thinks we should "be out of the Arab World within the next two weeks". He knows more about the region than I do, or ever will, and to act directly against this advice feels like the definition of naïveté. A great big I-told-you-so waiting to happen. People we talk to in Oman don't know what to say when we ask them what to do. None of them will tell us "You're fine, carry on as you are", and yet all we want is for someone, anyone, to say that. Just one person. Then the three of us could sleep again, we could concentrate on our art and the show that is about to open. But instead everyone says no more than "Be careful".

For now we have decided to wait until after the show to work out what to do: whether to be sensible and postpone the project until after the invasion of Iraq, or to drive into Saudi Arabia and towards the eye of the storm, as originally planned.

Yesterday Hassan, an artist we met several weeks ago, came by to see the work.

"It's a good show, guys. Really, it's strong," he said. "And some of it makes me think of the work I'm doing right now."

"What kind of work?" asked Stephen.

"About death," he said, looking at each of us accusatorially. "I can't stop thinking about death right now. I've been dreaming about it for some time. I have this sense of, how can I say, of the sky being about to fall on my head. You know this?"

"Yes!" said Al. "I've been feeling that for months now. That feeling of the sky about to fall on top of you. Like there's nothing to keep it up."

"That's it!" He nodded. "And I feel it so strong right now. Sometimes I can't sleep I think about it so much."

What Hassan and Al said triggered a passage from the film *La Haine* in my head: "Heard about the guy who fell off a skyscraper? On the way down past each floor, he kept saying to reassure himself: 'So far so good... so far so good... so far so good.' How you fall doesn't matter." The man pauses. "It's how you land!"

Although I haven't seen the film for four years, this passage and the image it conjures have come back to haunt me, pixel sharp and untouched by the vicissitudes of time, and ever since, the words "so far so good" have been in my head like a migraine.

☾

That Which Is Beautiful

THE SHOW OPENED WITH A SPEECH BY SHEIKH KHALFAN AL-Esry. He had just returned from *hajj* to Mecca and beneath his *imama* or turban his scalp was clean shaven. Standing in the courtyard of our studio that night, with five flaming torches lighting its darkened corners and a crowd of Muscati high society gathered before him, he praised with the practised calm of a professional speaker the timing of the show, and how with war looming there was a special need to try to further our understanding of foreign cultures. This was the root of all tolerance, he added.

Sheikh Khalfan paused.

In the background the Billie Holiday tape I had set up mumbled sweet nothings into the Muscat evening. A breeze was beginning to cool the courtyard. Stars above were presenting themselves one by one as if for inspection.

The Sheikh commented how the Qur'an describes the need to do that which is beautiful, for God loves those who do beautiful things. The audience went "Mmm", and the seven mosques of Old Muscat began once again their intricate a cappella for the last prayer of the day. Polite laughter rippled over the Sheikh's audience at the timing, and he excused himself to go and pray.

That night we sold enough paintings to keep us going for at least another four months – assuming we were still in the region that long.

☾

Mashallah

TWO DAYS LATER, ONCE AL AND I HAD DECIDED WE WOULD cross Saudi Arabia, I got a call from Princess Susan.

"Have you heard the news?"

"Heard what?" I asked.

"The British man," she said.

"What do you mean?"

"The British man who was shot dead at a traffic light in Saudi. Today. He was in his car and he got shot. Dead. He was at the wheel of his car. Today in Riyadh."

I relayed this to Al and Stephen.

"When do you leave for Saudi?" she asked.

"Um... today," I said.

Nothing.

"And this happened because he was British?" I asked.

"I don't know," she said, sounding exasperated. "But I mean, work it out. The war's about to start..."

"OK, OK."

"I want you to be careful, you hear?" Perhaps because I felt a chill as she said this I thought her voice trembled. "I'm worried about you guys. Really worried. You look too British. You should paint something onto that car of yours."

"Yasmine."

"OK, Yasmine," her voice warmed. "Paint something onto Yasmine so she doesn't look so British."

Although, like us, Yasmine looked reasonably British in her Omani setting (being one of only three cars in the country with their steering wheel on the right-hand side certainly helped), she would have looked lost on the M25. She did not look fully British. Nor did she look Arabic, Persian or Turkish; in fact, all four of us were now marooned in a visual no-man's land. To muddy the waters some more, I made a stencil that said *Mashallah* in Arabic and sprayed white paint through it onto both sides of Yasmine. *Mashallah* means, literally, God has willed it. We had seen it on buses in Iran. On average, fifty-three people died every day on Iranian roads.

One night in Iran, eight hours after we had left the Esfahani immigration office with special visas giving us two days to get out of the country, *we* had nearly died on an Iranian road. There had been a roadblock made up of concrete boulders that straddled the motorway in such a way that you had to slow down to get through the opening in them. The aperture was narrow. It was snowing. I braked hard – too hard – and we began to skid. I had no control over Yasmine's direction or speed as she shot through the opening in the concrete barriers. A metre to the right or to the left and she would have smashed into the barrier at a hundred kilometres an hour.

Mashallah was also something you might say to the mother of a beautiful baby, to help ward off the evil eye, and as Yasmine was our beautiful baby this seemed right.

As well as adding *Mashallah*, I sprayed a light coat of paint over Yasmine's number plates so the letters were only legible if you got close. Al's finishing touch was an Omani newspaper with a large picture of the anti-war demonstration in London that he placed on the dash, in case our disguise did not work.

"What else, what else?" Al sighed, eyeing her up.

"How about... Actually no."

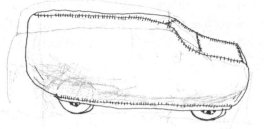

"How about," Al started, "a cover. So we can cover her up at night."

"Like a giant *abaya*?"

"Yes! One of those big covers where all you can see are her tyres poking out at the bottom."

We found a man in the outskirts of Muscat who made an *abaya* for Yasmine. It fitted perfectly. It was neither too tight, nor too baggy, the kind of thing a conservative mother would want for her daughter going unchaperoned to her first teenage party. Yasmine was now as well disguised as we could possibly make her.

We went to say goodbye to the Baluchi tailors who lived next door to our studio. Most evenings they played cricket outside their shop with a tennis ball, which sometimes they would hit onto our roof. The head tailor asked where we were going.

"Saudi."

His face fell. He started to rifle through the contents of the cupboard behind him.

"Why? Is that bad?"

"Wait," he said, still rummaging in the cupboard, before reappearing a little out of breath holding three *shalwar kamises*, shirts and wide-legged trousers: black for Stephen, peach for me, cream for Al.

"You must wear these in Saudi," he said, handing them over. "It is important." He continued to look anxious.

"And tell no one you are British. OK?"

We nodded like three children being told off and went to say goodbye to Princess Susan and thank her for everything she had done for us. Which was a lot. After that we left Muscat.

"So far so good," I mouthed to myself as Yasmine roared towards Dubai.

After one night in Dubai on the roof of the Majlis Gallery, Al and I said goodbye to Stephen. He would fly to Yemen before heading back to England several weeks later.

"Al, take care of yourself," Stephen said, giving him a hug. "Henry." He turned to hug me. "Take care of Al." And with that he was gone. Again we were two.

Night fell and Al and I crossed into Saudi Arabia. After a few kilometres I pulled off the road and we changed out of our jeans and collared shirts into the *shalwar kamises* we had been given. They felt wonderful. The crotch was down by your knee, the *kamise* was free flowing, and there was something about the feel of these clothes, in both their unfamiliar shape and their second-hand smell, that reminded you every few seconds like a gentle nudge in the ribs that you were somewhere you did not know.

I thought back to the Slovak border and began to wonder what the guards there would have thought if they could see us now. Obviously if we had turned up at the Slovak border wearing *shalwar kamises* in a truck with *Mashallah* on its side brandishing multiple translations of the Qur'an – there were now six copies of the Qur'an in Yasmine – we would have been turned away faster than a bull trying to talk its way into a china shop; and yet part of me wanted the Slovak guards to see us as we were now. I wanted them to understand how much had changed in the way we saw ourselves. Our collective ego had taken an almighty blow at that border and what had happened there had turned our world upside down. We now took in every new setting with an obsessive eye for detail and saw each border crossing as a chance to reinvent ourselves. Not just a chance but a reason. Each crossing was a point of exchange, a way in and a way out, a door that is neither open nor shut.

For several hours the road was empty. At around midnight a car with blacked-out windows accelerated past Yasmine before slowing right down, forcing me to overtake. Not long after it overtook again, hovering parallel to us for some time, its occupants invisible behind their darkened windows, before slowing down as before. It did this four times, Al and I getting more and more on edge with each successive overtaking until the car sped off towards the horizon. Again the road was empty.

We drove on in silence for a bit.

"So far so good," I said, staring ahead, my words flat.

Across the horizon the sky flashed white with lightning and not long afterwards it began to rain. We pulled off the road to camp for the night.

☾

Nemsa

THE SAUDI DESERT LOOKED DIFFERENT BY DAY. IN PLACES IT had crept onto the road and would cover a line and sometimes a lane; always it was looking to take more. Armies of orange sand kicked up by the wind would scuttle across the road, right to left, and on into the desert as if late for an appointment. The sand to the south was long and flat and its apparent infinity scared me. It made me think of a story I was told long ago with a Nordic hero who is challenged by an equally Nordic god to drink the contents of an enormous goblet. What he doesn't know is that the goblet is fed by the sea, and as hard as he drinks – and he drinks for days – the level does not shift. The story left a helpless sensation. I felt that if I walked into that desert no matter how far I went it would be impossible to reach the other side. More sand would keep on appearing the further I walked. The thought of it made the road beneath Yasmine feel precious, like a lifejacket during a storm.

As the sun reached its peak, Al made a painting. He propped the canvas against the dash and would spit on it when he needed to thin the paint. There were more cars on the road now and Yasmine got lingering looks unlike anything she would get in Turkey, Oman or Iran. For a moment I longed to be in Iran. The cars that overtook us were brand new SUVs or ageing, American-issue Chevys or Lincolns or Lexuses. Some of their older relatives lay abandoned in the desert. With their peeling, bone-white paint, they looked like skeletons. Scattered around them were tyres that the desert had not been able to destroy, while in the distance you could see herds of wild, black-haired camels. The ones with two humps when heading left looked like the Arabic for Allah, although really they needed a man walking behind to complete the look.

The road emptied once more and soon I was back in my driving head, a place that was maybe one-third sleep and two-thirds concentration. As we thundered towards Riyadh, I churned over the same set of questions and doubts that had been there since the show in Muscat. These usually began with the possible, or by now probable, invasion of Iraq, which in turn would make me think of Baghdad, which of course would make me think of the artistic renaissance going on there.

Just before leaving Oman I had found an article about it. The one I had been dreaming of. Proof.

The article had been posted on 2 January 2003 in the *San Francisco Chronicle* and was entitled "In Baghdad, Art Thrives as War Hovers". It was everything I wanted.

There was a description of a place called the Hewar Gallery that came replete with "long-haired artists with goatees and three-day stubble. Elegant women with distracted eyes and languid hauteur. Highbrow bohemians gossiping and glancing at the latest paintings and sculptures." The article even talked about the "discreet clinking of coffee cups" that went on in the gallery. But how do you clink a coffee cup discreetly? I had to find out. The article had gone on to compare the Baghdad art scene to that of Paris, or Berlin, or New York, and had described Iraqi art as the strongest in the region. Everything was as the Turkish journalist had said, and it was as much a relief to know that this Baghdadi renaissance actually existed as it was frustrating to think that we would not be able to see it for ourselves.

Every thirty or forty kilometres we would pass a run-down petrol pump manned by Indians or Pakistanis. Because of our *shalwar kamises* no one at these pumps doubted we were from "Nemsa", the country that the wife of the Austrian ambassador in Muscat had suggested we adopt as our own.

"It means Austria," she had said. "But no one knows where Austria is!" She didn't seem to mind this. "If they do know, Austria has no war with anyone, so no one has war with you." She paused. "Sometimes it is good that nobody knows who we are."

The men at the petrol pumps would ask if Nemsa was in Kazakhstan, or Uzbekistan, or Pakistan, and I would nod and sound vague, adding that I did not speak much Arabic. Which was true. Some of the truckers or petrol-pump attendants could speak a few words of Persian and, as members of a phantom central Asian state, so could we. Exchanging pleasantries was the only thing we could do in Persian; fortunately it was the only thing anyone expected us to do.

At every roadblock the Saudi policemen or Saudi soldiers we met would laugh or nod at the *Mashallah* painted on the side of Yasmine.

Because of the British man who was shot dead at the traffic lights, when we got to Riyadh I slowed Yasmine to a crawl fifty yards before each traffic light so that we were never hemmed in, nor could anybody get a good look at us.

Nothing happened in Riyadh.

"So far so good," I mouthed to myself as we accelerated out of Riyadh towards Mecca.

THE ROAD EMPTIED ONCE MORE AND AGAIN THE DESERT ON either side was bleached of life and colour. Yasmine smelt of heat. Al dozed off. His dream-filled head began a familiar cycle as it drooped slowly further and further forward before suddenly jerking back. And then started to nod forward again. Like a faulty metronome. I would measure time by it.

Once every few hours as we continued towards Mecca, sometimes more, sometimes less, I would be hit by a crushing sense of being in freefall. It had been with me intermittently since Muscat and that conversation with Hassan. Maybe once every two hours, and only for a few minutes, I would suddenly feel like the man in *La Haine*, plummeting down with my stomach left high above me. It was the same feeling I'd get if I thought about death or infinity for too long: my mind would feel on fire. Boiling with the sensation, I'd slow Yasmine right down as it felt dangerous to drive in that state, and as she rolled to a standstill the feeling would disappear, just as unexpectedly as it came.

After ten hours of driving night fell and the landscape on either side of the road became more rugged and steep. Crusts of mountain reared up and as the road began to meander Al woke up.

Just after a sign saying "Makkah 20km" the road split: non-Muslims to the right, Muslims to the left. Regardless of the fact that Christians and Jews had lived side by side with Muslims in Mecca during the lifetime of the Prophet, and that nowhere in the Qur'an or any of the hadiths does it say that the city of Mecca – as opposed to the holy shrine within it – should be off limits to non-Muslims, Mecca was for us a forbidden city.

We had crossed the girth of the Arabian peninsula in little more than a day; Bertram Thomas, St John Philby or Wilfred Thesiger would have groaned at the thought.

We turned right, away from Mecca, and after a few kilometres pulled off the road for the night. Yasmine was at last silent. It was warm and there was no sign of the rain that had pelted us the night before. Lit only by the moon, Yasmine looked too heavy for the snowy carpet of sand beneath her; instead she seemed to hover above it like an overgrown magic carpet.

In the distance we could hear dogs barking into the night, and beyond a mountainous ridge to the south the lights of Mecca turned the sky a warm mango yellow, though it was the stars above us that lit the sky that night as we fell asleep.

☾

They Ran So Fast

BOTH FAISAL AND MOHAMMED WERE IN THEIR EARLY
twenties. Although originally Indian, both had lived in
Saudi Arabia for most of their lives. Faisal had stunning
eyes. The outline of each was smudged as if in a charcoal
drawing. He was the quieter of the two. Mohammed was
loud and lecherous and had the swagger of a motorbike
courier.

Both of them worked at the *Saudi Gazette* in Jeddah and
had been dispatched to do a piece on us by Lawrence
Wright, from *The New Yorker* magazine, who was living in
Jeddah while he researched his book on Al Qaeda.

Sitting in the thick-carpeted foyer of a smart hotel Faisal
got out a yellow pad and began to take notes in a laborious
longhand, while Al and I told him about what we were
doing and where we had been. An hour later he sighed
and said we should take a break.

"So now we will show you Jeddah," Mohammed
beamed.

"Absolutely," said Faisal, pausing to look us up and
down as politely as possible. "And is there somewhere you
guys maybe want to go. Like to tidy up?" We were both still
in our *shalwar kamises*. Men in Jeddah wore either dishdashers much smarter than the second-hand clothes we
were wearing or, like Faisal and Mohammed, they went in
for fake Hilfiger tops, baggy jeans, bright white trainers
and denim jackets cribbed off MTV.

"Can't we go like this?" asked Al.

They looked at each other.

"I suppose," Mohammed trailed off. "It's just..."

"No, fine. If you want to go like that, do," said Faisal.

"OK."

"But you look like, I don't know... you look like two Pakistanis."

Mohammed smirked.

"It's true. Two tramps!"

In a show of solidarity with Jeddah's expat Pakistani community, our *shalwars* remained on as we cruised round the city with our hosts talking over each other in their rush to explain how clean and modern the city was. We drove past the most shiny or most new shops – Guess Jeans, Armani, Marks & Spencer, Benetton and Next all in a regimented line – as well as the most Western streets and the city's tallest fountain. It was very tall. Our innate and possibly Western fascination with decay and ruin was put on hold.

With Faisal and Mohammed in the cab I forgot all about our Saudi traffic light routine, and at one point towards the end of the afternoon we pulled up at a red light. Rather than stopping fifty yards before it I drove into the traffic, as any other car would. Soon we were hemmed in by other cars and like a recovering claustrophobic I became jittery as I realised what had happened. I couldn't concentrate on what Faisal was saying. It was a slow light. The slowest light in Saudi Arabia.

To the left I noticed a man with a trimmed beard and a clean dishdasher. He looked over at us and began to walk in our direction. He avoided every other car and continued straight at us. Why us? Why, oh why was he heading for us? And why hadn't the light changed? Al saw him as well and we both became very still.

Faisal, who was in the passenger seat, continued to chat about the trainers he had recently bought and the girl who had just dumped him. I think the trainers were to help him get over the girl. He had also written some rhymes and was about to start "flowing" when the man got to the

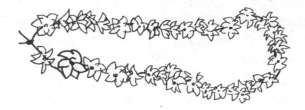

passenger side of the car. He knocked on the window. Faisal wound it down. The man shoved his hand into the cab, towards me on the driver's side. Hanging off his index finger were two garlands of jasmine flowers. They smelt fantastic: a taste of somewhere else.

I bought the garlands for a dollar and Faisal hung them from the windscreen mirror. They bobbed merrily from side to side as we drove away, filling the cab with their haute couture decadence: I found out later that Chanel No. 5 is no more than the juice of thousands of pressed jasmine blossoms. Faisal explained that Yasmine and jasmine were the same thing, and the same word, and that just as Issa and Jesus should sound much more similar than they do (Issa is the Muslim name for Jesus), Yasmine and jasmine should sound identical. It was our fault he said, nodding at me and Al. Something to do with the way we wrote our ys.

With Yasmine smelling of jasmine, we drove to Al-Baik Chicken.

"Like KFC but with better chicken, and they give you unlimited bun refills," said Mohammed as we walked into its air-conditioned splendour.

Mohammed and Faisal talked about the family section of the restaurant, just behind us, where you could take a girl on a date.

"But the family section in McDonald's, man, that's the best," said Mohammed.

"Yeah," sighed Faisal, his eyes glazing over. "It's special. They have the curtains there. You just pull them across your booth and yeah." He clapped his hands together. "No one can see what you are doing."

"Do anything you like, man," said Mohammed, eyes widening.

As we later found out, this wasn't as risqué as it sounded. In Saudi Arabia, doing anything you like meant something a little more tame than it might elsewhere. A nineteen-year-old Saudi boy Stephen met when he got to Saudi Arabia a few weeks later, who was known among his friends as a rebel and a rule breaker, solemnly told Stephen "I've done it all," adding *sotto voce*, "except for the big three: drugs, alcohol and intercourse. But yeah, everything else, I've done it."

Next stop on our tour was Jeddah's brightest and best mall. It looked like any other mall I could think of and the four of us stood in the middle of it, listless, with Al and I wondering out loud what you were meant to do in a Saudi mall. Groups of women walked past cloaked completely in *abaya*. You could see no eyes and no skin; it was the first time we had seen so many women covered like this.

As each woman strolled by, Mohammed gave us a running commentary on whether or not she "wanted it".

Two shapes draped in black passed us.

"Wow! Did you see that?" asked Mohammed, wide-eyed.

"No, what?"

"Those two girls, man. Oh my God! The one on the left, the way she pulled in her *abaya* as she walked past! Wow, wow, wow! A girl only does that if she really likes you and did you check out her arse? It was popping out! *Wallah!* You know if she really, really likes you, she'll walk past again and pull it tight over her front, you'll see her tits just hanging out, I promise."

She didn't walk past again.

"So have you guys lived here all your lives?" asked Al as we walked on.

"Most of them, yeah," said Faisal.

"I was studying in Australia for a year," said Mohammed. "In Melbourne. Then 9/11 happened. Had to go home after that," he said.

"Right," said Al. "Because of the reaction?"

"Yeah, sort of."

I nodded gravely.

"That's awful."

"I know."

"Really bad."

"I mean, I don't blame them," Mohammed went on. "I'd probably do the same, but yeah. They would just run."

"What?"

"The girls, man. The girls. Really. Think about it. I'd be in a club in Melbourne, and they'd be like, 'So. What's your name cutie?'" he said in his one-size-fits-all girl voice. "'Er, Mohammed.' 'And where are you from, Mohammed?' 'Saudi Arabia.' 'Right. And what are you doing in Melbourne, Mohammed-from-Saudi-Arabia?' 'You don't want to know.' 'No, really, tell me.' 'I'm learning... actually no, let's talk about you.' 'No, come on, tell me what you do.' 'Please can we talk about you?' 'No.' 'OK, I'm training to be a pilot.' And they would just run. So fast. I'm telling you, man, world records were broken out there." He put on an announcer's voice, "'And now, for the fifteen-metre Run Away from a Muslim.' So yeah, after 9/11 I pretty much had to come back. Wasn't getting laid any more."

That night Faisal and Mohammed took us to a secret beach outside Jeddah. Faisal promised me it was haunted. He said there was an old man who lived in a boarded-up house nearby and that one of their friends had spoken to him once and he had said his heart had stopped two years ago. He wasn't there that night. Faisal also warned me not to take a piss in a particular part of the beach because there was an angry *djinn* who lived there. Apparently the spirit had punched one of his friends last time they were there.

Along with four of their friends we chatted and danced to a drum until the sun rose. The next day we drove north to Jordan.

☾

Orfali

THE ORFALI GALLERY, WHERE WE HAD ARRANGED VIA EMAIL to have an exhibition in Amman, was run by Rana. Our show was to open on 28 March. Twenty-six days' time. Nobody knew whether the proposed Anglo-American invasion of Iraq would be underway by then, although some of the people we spoke to thought it might yet be averted. Even I bought into this. Al did not.

As ever, we had a month before our exhibition opened and no work to exhibit.

Like Nader in Tehran, Rana ran her space with her mother in the background. Rana's mother spent most of her time in a black office chair that had an adjustable back and well-oiled wheels. She would roll back and forth over the gallery's expansive parquet floor between the office and the television, where she flicked between Al Jazeera, Al Arabiya and sometimes, to see if they were getting it right, CNN. On days when Rana's mother was not in the gallery Rana would smoke inside. If she was in the gallery Rana would smoke outside.

"But I am worried about your show," said Rana, eyebrows furrowed. "If the war starts no one will come. Really, you guys." She called us "you guys" a lot. "Not to a show by British artists."

"But," Al started, "I've heard about shows that were going on during the last Gulf War that did alright. Everyone was so bored of sitting inside watching television. They wanted something to go and see."

"Yes, but this is different. Really. First, everyone knew that Saddam had done something wrong in 1990. This time, he has done nothing wrong. Second, we watch it this time on Al Jazeera, Al Arabiya, you know, we have it in Arabic. Not just CNN. And everyone has a satellite dish. Not before. Also *intifada* was not happening during this other war against Saddam. It is different now. The situation in Jordan now, it is very tense."

Rana told us we should carry on making art as if the exhibition was going ahead. We had to be optimistic, she said. She would get the invitations printed with the evening of 28 March as the night of the private view. If the war started before then, the show was off.

She asked what we had planned for the rest of the day. I told her who we were having dinner with.

"Oh, you are lucky," she said, taken aback. "He is," she paused, not sure how to put it, "He is the most loved in Jordan. He is one of the best men. Really. Everything he says is, *yani*, he is the best speaker," she said, using the Arabic equivalent of the Western teenager's "like" or "that is to say". "And he is very, how is this…" she was struggling for the right word, "warm." She shook her head. "But we don't see him any more."

C

Noble Art

MY FATHER USED TO BE AN EXPLORER; ALTHOUGH CALLING him "my father" sounds a bit formal, a bit Victorian, the kind of father you address as "sir" in an American film. Then again, saying "my dad" doesn't quite work here. Either way, the person partly responsible for bringing me into the world ran the Royal Geographical Society for twenty-one years which, among other things, meant he was involved in a number of different scientific projects around the world.

One of these was the Badia Programme on sustainable development, based in Jordan's eastern desert. This was partly the brainchild of HRH Prince Hassan bin Talal, the younger brother of the late King Hussein, who had been heir to the Jordanian throne for thirty-four years until the succession was changed in the weeks before his brother died.

In 1992 King Hussein of Jordan was diagnosed with cancer and began to receive treatment. In 1998 he spent six months in America with his American wife, Queen Noor, as he underwent his final and most severe course of chemotherapy. By the winter of that year the surgeons said there was nothing more they could do. The King would die. He flew back to Jordan in January 1999, where his last significant act before he died several weeks later was to change the line of his succession from his younger brother, Prince Hassan, to one of his sons, Prince Abdullah.

To explain his decision King Hussein wrote an open letter to Prince Hassan, laden with accusation and oblique allusion, which was broadcast on Jordanian television. Rana described the nation's shock. Everyone had assumed

Prince Hassan would succeed his brother and in their minds had begun to make the transition. His replacement, Prince Abdullah, King Hussein's half-English son, was little known in Jordan and could hardly speak Arabic. He was, however, a military man and had married a Palestinian, the beautiful Princess Rania. Before King Hussein's letter could be fully explained its author died and Prince Abdullah became King Abdullah II of Jordan.

Just as we arrived from Saudi Arabia, my father had flown into Jordan to attend the annual meeting of the Badia Programme. That night Al and I went to the hotel where he was staying and the three of us were driven to the palace complex for dinner with Prince Hassan. Our driver wore military uniform and said little. Once we entered the royal complex we were driven over bumps, past sentry boxes, down long, empty roads lined by palm trees and banks of snow, through gate after slowly opened gate, past more soldiers in red berets, until finally we pulled up at Prince Hassan's house.

The contrast to the Saudi desert and the threadbare Ammani hotel that had been our visual vernacular for the last ten days was acute. Everything around us – the log fire, the trickling water in the courtyard, the strength and hue of light, the perfumed cleanliness of it all – was for us an extravagant treat.

Prince Hassan, as Rana had suggested, was a staggering mixture of urbanity, learning and wit. He had written seven books, received twelve honorary doctorates and had one of the warmest laughs I have ever heard, a lovely roar of laughter that made everyone who heard it inflate a little.

The conversation that night was both agile and erudite and while it was hard for either me or Al to bluff any kind of intellectual parity, at no point did it feel like a lecture.

There were a lot of things for Prince Hassan, indeed any Jordanian, to be gloomy about at that moment, but he did not wallow in them that night.

The war in Iraq was about to start, as it had been for several months now. The country's economy was in a rut. The second Palestinian *intifada* was in full flow, and there was talk of an exodus of refugees from both Palestine and Iraq into Jordan. Some people we spoke to thought that a Palestinian exodus might trigger another Palestinian uprising in Jordan. More than half the Jordanian population was Palestinian. Then there were the concerns about the country's oil supply, as well as its dwindling water reserves.

Meanwhile on a personal level, although he did not mention it, Prince Hassan continued to be silenced by the Jordanian media, or rather by whoever controlled the Jordanian media. Although he gave half-hour interviews to the BBC's *HARDtalk* and had regular slots on Radio 4's *Today* programme, Prince Hassan of Jordan could not get his name so much as mentioned on Jordanian national radio. We had a twenty-minute slot lined up. Something was amiss.

Several times that evening Prince Hassan returned to his favourite theme, the *leitmotif* of the night: the idea that there existed in the Middle East at that moment a calculus between fear and hope. The continued prevalence of fear throughout the region – be it in the Israeli elections earlier that year that saw the right-wing Likud party come to the fore; or in a series of villages in southwest Saudi Arabia not long before September 2001 where nineteen willing martyrs were recruited; or indeed in any of the regimes in the Middle East whose head of state was afraid of freedom of speech and what it might bring – this prevalence of fear was one of the root causes of extremism. It was compounded by a blinkered nationalism that stopped most Middle Eastern leaders from discussing and so realising a shared, regional interest. With the intonation that suggested it was one of his favourite slogans, Prince Hassan told us: "I am, you see, a great believer in the noble art of conversation."

Towards the end of the evening Princess Sarvath, Prince Hassan's wife, told us about the planes with American markings that bellyached over the capital every day, each of them destined for secret bases in the Jordanian desert. Recently they had been re-routed over the palace complex instead of the nearby Palestinian refugee camps.

"Why's that?" I asked.

"Well," she said, echoing Rana's words exactly, "the situation now in Jordan is very tense."

C

Georgie

HER FLIGHT ARRIVED AT DAWN ON 14 MARCH. EIGHT passengers got off the plane and the airport was deserted as Georgie strode through the Arrivals hall. She was tall, with a mane of orange hair unlike anything we had seen since leaving London, and had once been a model. She was now a filmmaker-composer-photographer halfway through her Master's degree at Goldsmiths College London, who oozed energy and said "yeah" a lot in a breathless kind of way.

I knew Georgie from university and she had agreed to join us long before anyone knew Iraq was going to be invaded. During the last few weeks in London she had been surrounded by people who did not want her to go to Jordan with the war in Iraq about to start. Jordan was in the Middle East and for many people "war in Iraq" sounded a lot like "war in the Middle East". Indeed, for subeditors the world over, there was nothing that remarkable about interchanging the terms "Iraq" and "Middle East" for added impact, or replacing "Israel–Palestine" with "Middle East". Which was strange. If there was a strike in Caracas you would not read about it the following day beneath the headline "Strike in South America". Nor would unrest in Kashmir imply "Unrest in Asia". But for the people who wrote these headlines as well as those who read them, the Middle East was different. It appeared to have its own set of rules and to exist outside the realm of orthodox Western analysis. This particularism was at the very heart of almost every Western misconception about the region. It also meant that it had taken a lot of determination on Georgie's part to get on the flight to Amman, much more than it had required for me and Al to remain where we were.

After being put up for several days at the generous expense of Prince Hassan in a deluxe and deserted hotel in Aqaba, Jordan's seaside resort, the three of us drove north towards a village perched high above Petra. We had the name of someone there who might have a place for us to stay.

The night before we left Aqaba, President George Bush of America gave President Saddam Hussein of Iraq forty-eight hours to leave his country (leave Iraq, not America). We were seventeen hours into this ultimatum when Yasmine broke down. Her clutch had gone. She limped along on the hard shoulder to a nearby garage somewhere between Aqaba and Petra and was soon up on bricks.

The garage floor was a quicksand of thick, gloopy oil that had claimed screws, fanbelts and oil drums over the years; where there was neither oil nor grease there was dust. Above the desk was a picture of Mecca next to a picture of the Dome of the Rock and a hadith that warned you about the unclean spirits lurking in the loo.

The puckish mechanic who set about fixing Yasmine spoke good English. He was garage jester, garage leader and garage spokesman, and everyone there deferred to him.

An hour into Yasmine's repair an Iraqi truck driver came to have his clutch fixed. Without saying a word the mechanic led me and the Iraqi by the forearm into a wide open space. I had told the mechanic we were British, not something I had shared with many other people over the last few weeks. He handed us each an empty bottle.

"Now. Break bottle and fight! Britain against Iraq! Ha-ha-ha!"

I laughed awkwardly at the Iraqi truck driver and then at the ground. The burning, pot-holed ground. It was mid-day and this wasteland of tarmac and rubble was bright. You had to scowl to focus on it.

The Iraqi truck driver grinned and said he would cook the three British soldiers some lunch. I went with him to his truck. From the row of compartments that ran along the hem of his vehicle he produced an epicurean array of pots, pans, eggs, garlic, lemons, tomatoes, beans, olives, cheese and courgettes, before cooking us all an enormous omelette.

That afternoon Georgie took a series of photos of men hanging around the garage. She climbed into the cabs of Egyptian, Iraqi, Syrian or Jordanian trucks, smiling at all the truckers, until she had a gaggle of wide-eyed followers. Soon everybody wanted to teach Georgie Arabic, or take her for a ride in their truck, or be photographed by her. Once the sun had dipped beneath the horizon she began to take photos with a torch, getting her subject to sit very still, opening the shutter on a ninety-second exposure and shining a torch over her sitter's face so that only the parts lit up appeared in the image.

That evening the mechanic finished repairing Yasmine's clutch and told me to come with him while he took her for a test drive. As we sped away from the garage he became angry.

"You must look after her."

"What do you mean, who?"

"The girl!"

"She's fine, isn't she?"

"No, she is not," he accelerated, the rev count up beyond number four. "You cannot say this. These men she is with." His voice was pleading now. "They are bad men. All day they drive and think bad things about women. That is all. Never they have girl in their truck. Never. They think of this girl Georgie like something they see on the internet. You know, the girl like... without the cloth. You don't understand this! And this boy she is with now, al-Qaeda, he is bad." This was the latest of Georgie's sitters. Everyone called him "al-Qaeda" because he claimed to have been linked to the recent militancy in nearby Ma'an, which was rumoured to have been stirred up by trans-national *jihadis* on their way to Iraq.

"These men who drive truck, they are like the bee," he went on. "The bee with beautiful flower. They want the, what is this thing..."

"Pollen?"

"Yes, pollen," he said, memorising it.

We got back to the garage, where I found Georgie sitting on the stairs. Nearby, Al was asleep in the mechanic's bed. He was ill that day. Two steps down from Georgie was "al-Qaeda" in his camouflage jacket and white *imama*, looking just like bin Laden in his videos only without the beard. The boy was about nineteen. His friend sat next to him.

171

I squeezed in between Georgie and "al-Qaeda" boy and tried to remember what it was to feel paternal and protective over someone because of their gender. It felt ridiculous, perhaps because Georgie was taller than me and may well have had broader shoulders, although we never measured them. Also because she had an aura of fearlessness – not in a tough and bristling way, but in the sense that she was not fazed by "al-Qaeda" boy and his possible intentions.

As I sat there wondering how to be protective in a male kind of way, the boy leant over my legs and handed Georgie a keyring. He said that his friend had made it in prison.

"Present for Georgie," he added, smiling.

"Wow. Thank you," she said, inspecting it. "That's sweet of you."

The stitching said *Allahu Akbar*, Allah is the greatest.

"And why is your friend in prison?" I asked.

The boy smiled at me. "He kill man."

He got out his knife to show me how his friend had done it, stabbing the air and twisting the blade as it drove into an imaginary body. The metal flashed in the dull, halogen light. Outside, I could hear the mechanic fire Yasmine's engine. Almost there. The boy pushed the blunt side of the blade onto my leg to snap it shut and looked up at me with a lingering grin as if to say he knew something I did not. He knew plenty of things I did not, I wanted to tell him, thousands of things, but this look suggested this particular thing was something I really ought to know about. We stared at each other. I tried my best to look menacing.

Georgie woke Al and the three of us went downstairs to see Yasmine. Her clutch was fixed. As we made to leave, "al-Qaeda" boy became frantic and started asking Georgie to come and stay with him in Ma'an. She said no. If she wouldn't stay with him in Ma'an, then could she at least get him a visa for Australia? Georgie had decided to elaborate our Austrian alibi, although Australia's contribution to the imminent invasion of Iraq was fairly well documented in the Arabic media, making it a not very good alibi.

With "al-Qaeda" boy looking heartbroken we pulled out of the garage and drove towards the village high above Petra. Yasmine's new clutch worked perfectly, however in his final adjustments the mechanic had messed up her wiring so that every gauge on her dash and both her indicators were dead. It didn't matter. We were moving, the engine worked, the headlights worked and the three of us were in one place. As Yasmine rumbled into fifth gear Georgie looked at her watch.

"Twenty-two hours to go," she said.

"Till what?" moaned Al from the back seat.

"End of the ultimatum."

"Christ. I'd forgotten," he said, sliding back into the voluptuous immobility of his dreams.

☾

Beginning

IT WAS OVERCAST IN AMMAN ON THE FIRST DAY OF THE WAR. The night before, bombs had fallen on Baghdad while Georgie and I were staying with a friend in Amman; Al had spent the night in the village high above Petra.

From the moment we woke up it was on the radio and in the newspapers, there was no escaping it, the Second Gulf War had begun. I felt empty and a little winded. Up until that morning I had held a stubborn and perfectly unfounded conviction that something would happen to stall what to everyone else was inevitable, and now that was gone all I could do was wait for the war to finish and create a new, perhaps equally blind faith that the invasion would be quick and painless.

Georgie and I went outside to Yasmine. Just before we got in, Georgie's phone rang. We hovered in the street while whoever was on the other end asked if she had heard the news. Yes, she had. And why wasn't she on the next flight out of Jordan?

Opposite was a café full of students watching the latest from Iraq. One of them spotted us. I saw him lean towards his two friends and point at us. All three looked over. Soon the whole café was looking at us. Lips were mumbling, jaws jutting, eyes steeling over, and soon the male students were drifting out into the street in twos and threes. There were about fifteen of them standing ten yards away. They conferred among themselves for a few minutes, then one by one they began to shout at us.

"Fuck you!"

More muttering.

"Sonofabitch!"

"*Allahu Akbar!*"

More muttering.

"*Jihad!*"

It was neither hysterical nor chanted. It was actually a bit tame: it was as if none of them had ever shouted "*jihad*" at a foreigner before. They were all a bit too middle class for that. Not proper *shebab*, not real players. But the longer it went on, like an orchestra warming up, the more confident they became. Still none of them would advance from their position on the other side of the narrow street, as if held back by an engrained notion of hospitality. It would have been much easier had we been on a television screen, then they could have really yelled.

Just as the volume was picking up, Georgie finished her call and we got into Yasmine and drove to the gallery.

Rana had been up all night watching Al Arabiya's live feed to Baghdad. Beneath her eyes were great, purplish bags bordered by lines that looked like scars.

"The show is off," she said as we walked in. "And you must fill Yasmine with petrol," she added, remembering. "Go right away. Everyone is buying petrol like crazy. There are these queues and..."

The nineteen-year-old Palestinian boy who worked part-time at the gallery came with me.

"Did you watch it last night?" I asked as we pulled away from the gallery.

"For some time, yes."

He continued to stare ahead. Around us Amman looked miserable in the spitting rain.

"What do your friends think about it?"

"They are angry," he said, with feeling, "but, I don't know, what can they do? We can watch it on the television. But so what? Al Jazeera. Al Arabiya. Abu Dhabi. These all bring sadness. Nothing more. One of my friends, he says he will not go to McDonald's now. As protest."

"Right," I said, nodding, and for some reason thinking of Stephen who I thought would have been proud.

"I stopped going to McDonald's some months ago. As protest," he said. I nodded some more. "I am in protest against their fries. I go Burger King instead."

I was on edge and it took a while for this to sink in.

He turned to me, "I think maybe it is better you speak to my Jordan friends. They are more angry about this war in Iraq. I am from Palestine. We have like this in our country for fifty years. The Iraqis, they have it for one day now. The Jordanians, they have it never. I think maybe they are jealous."

That afternoon Georgie and I drove to Umm Seyhoun, the village perched high above Petra where we had left Al the day before. Umm Seyhoun had been built by the Jordanian government in the 1980s and the Bdul, the Bedouin tribe that lived in the ruins of the Nabatean city of Petra, Jordan's chief tourist attraction, were both forced and lured out of their caves into the new village.

That evening a wedding got underway and because Umm Seyhoun was small everyone was invited, including us. A stocky Swiss girl called Anne-Marie was getting married to one of the men from the village. He smiled a lot. She looked jittery. They met when she first visited Petra and he had been her tour guide.

There had been talk of the wedding being postponed because of the outbreak of war in Iraq. Some villagers thought it was insensitive to celebrate with Baghdad being bombed, but enough people thought it was more important not to be cowed by Bush–Blair aggression, so the wedding party was not only going ahead, but everyone there was determined to have a good time.

The three of us arrived at the long goat-hair tent that had been set up in the centre of the village. It was about ten o'clock. Georgie was taken off to the female side of the party in a nearby house where the bride was having henna painted onto her hands and feet, while Al and I were led into the cavernous male tent and shown to a space deep within a long line of men facing the open side of the tent. Fires kept us warm as tray after tray of tea shuttled past. The air was thick with the smell of fire and whisky. In front of us a mob of men danced maniacally, all of them spurred on by a singer, a drummer and several fridge-sized loudspeakers that the youngest boys would hug, giddy on the adrenaline of it all, each of them going wild as the bassline shook their bodies.

To my left a man played a flute, while to my right a youngish, well-built man more drunk than anyone else in the tent toppled towards me. His head landed on his hands. He looked surprised and took a while to focus on me. Job done, he began a monologue. It started with an account of his time in jail: he had been let out after convincing the guards he was mad. Not, for him, a catch-22. He rolled onto his side to show me the tattoo he had done on himself while in jail. It was the worst-drawn tattoo I had ever seen. He must have been pie-eyed when he did it.

"It is for my first wife. She is Americi. She is here as tourist and then we are married."

After being married for two years and living together in America, they had called it off. He did not say why. He was still in love with her though.

"And I tell this to my new wife. OK. The mother of my children and... she... she knows this. Yes? You know she know..."

"Sure. And where's your second wife from?"

"Ah?"

"Is your second wife Jordanian?"

"Jordanian? Ha-ha-ha! Yes. Yes, she Jordanian. Jordan First! She is from this village. This is... I do not love her. I have never love her. I love another woman and she is my girlfriend now. Sometime, my wife ask me about my girlfriend. She know, yes. And when she ask me, I..."

"What?"

"I..." He swiped the air. "Yes. Like this to her." He stared at the ground next to me as if it was a *djinn*. I had never before heard someone describe to me how they beat their wife. I had only ever read about it or seen it in films and I couldn't work out how to respond. "And if I do like this to her," he carried on, "she does not ask about girlfriend."

He grinned, pulled out a miniature of whisky and sucked it dry. It was plastic and it hollowed as he aimed it at the sky, willing some drop of sweet lukewarm nectar to come and caress the back of his throat. He dropped it to the ground.

"But the war, the war, it is... bad thing. So bad. You are here, yes, and you are from?"

"Nemsa," I said.

"Yes, yes."

"Well, half-Austrian, half-British."

"British, yes. OK, that is OK because you are here, you are my friend. You are guest of Umm Seyhoun. Everyone here now is look after you. Even when we have no tent, no goat, we are still Bdul! We still have this, this hospitality, yes? But I, ah. Really. Um. I want only one thing."

"What's that?"

"To kill British."

"OK."

"Or American. It is important to kill this man."

"You think?"

"Yes. I think this is the best thing. The people in Iraq, they are like my brothers. They are like this." He thumped his heart with his hand so hard that he fell backwards.

Another tray of tea came by. One of the drunk man's friends squatted down next to us, grinning. His English wasn't so good.

"But why?" the drunk went on, having propped himself on his elbow again. "Why the American soldier does not fight Iraqi soldier? Only he fights civilian. Why this? I have seen it on Al Jazeera. There is proof. If there are Iraqi soldier, Americi do not kill them, they want only to kill the women, the children. Always the children."

"Maybe they..."

"No. It is true. They try to kill only the women and the children."

"It may be that..."

"Why? Who does this? They are not human." His face was knotted into a question mark. "But it is OK. There is bin Laden. Sheikh bin Laden good man. Very good man. And strong!" He seemed less drunk for a moment. "Three hundred eighteen members al-Qaeda, and the American he has killed two! Just two. There are maybe a million American soldiers and they kill two al-Qaeda! Ha-ha-ha. *Wallah.* Now there are three hundred sixteen al-Qaeda. So what? Tomorrow there are thousand. Every day they are in Iraq they make a thousand more like this. America cannot win this. Bin Laden is too strong. Oh my God, he is the best man. Really. Really, I do not know how to say this. He is Khalifah over all Dar al-Islam. I would... I don't know. If he was here, I will, I will sleep with him!" He collapsed onto the carpet, laughing so hard he made no noise. "Sleep," he repeated, slowly. "With."

"Why?"

"Eh?"

"Why do you like him so much?"

"Ah."

"Because of 9/11?"

"No, no, no. There is no proof bin Laden does this thing. Really. It is Jews, not bin Laden."

"Then why is bin Laden such a good man?"

"Bin Laden? Yes, bin Laden! The most strong man. The best Arab." He said the word "Arab" with a flourish, rolling the *r*, and produced another miniature from his pocket. Not long after, two of his friends came to shepherd him home, to his wife.

Al and I were led onto the all-male dance floor. The rhythm was wild and the bodies around us moved in a frenzied, delirious way. Everyone hurled themselves into one another and bounced off again like human dodgems. It was a brawl where no one swung their fists. An elastic mosh pit. The pair of us spun, freeform, into and off every other body there as the singer urged us on, whooping and cheering. The idea was to put your arms round other men and form lines of two or three, like the front row of a rugby scrum, and go marauding through the crowd like that.

Sometimes the twos and threes would join and form a circle and perform a *dubke*, a dance where everyone stamps the floor in unison. It made me think of Kurdish *peshmerghas* dancing in a line. But I made sure not to tell this to anyone there. Apart from Al, but Al didn't really count. Talking to Al was like talking to myself. I did not tell anyone else about how the *dubke* made me think of Kurdish *peshmerghas* because of a conversation earlier that night during which several men had told me they thought Saddam was "very strong man" because he had gassed so many Kurds. This had been hard to take. It was the most severe test of my Richard-and-Judy, emotionally disengaged style of interview. None of the people around us had ever been to Kurdish Iraq. We had been there three months ago, and watching some of the Bdul men scowl as they talked about Kurds made our time in Sulaymaniyah flood back like a homecoming.

The *dubke* never lasted that long anyway, because the ground was strewn with rubble and when you stamped your foot it hurt.

"Why do you speak English always if you are the Austrian?" asked one Bdul man with his arm round me.

"I'm trying to learn it," I said, bouncing away.

"*Sprichst du Deutsch?*" asked another. I pretended not to hear, gave him a hug and leapt off in a different direction.

After an hour Georgie appeared on the male side of the party. There were no other women there and most of Umm Seyhoun's male population descended on her, grinning and respectful like a pack of well-intentioned, tooth-less hounds to a fox. Everyone wanted to dance with Georgie.

Watching from the warmth of the tent were other, often older men who would disappear every half hour to check what was happening six hundred miles away in Iraq. It was the second night of bombing and there were few images to digest. The live feed to the Baghdad skyline was mostly still apart from the ticker tape that ran across the screen, left to right.

On the dance floor you could sense, after so many months of tense build-up, the resolute yet silent desire to forget about the war for this one night.

The dancing continued until just before dawn, the cold-est part of the night, at which point a cloud-like layer of condensed breath began to hover above the dance floor like a halo.

The first full day of the war was over.

$$\mathsf{C}$$

Onions

FOR THE NEXT TWO WEEKS THE INVASION OF IRAQ gathered pace. The three of us followed it from our village high above Petra in newspapers, on television, in conversa-tions and, when we had the chance, on the internet. Although not slow, the coalition advance was not being met by cheering Iraqis offering flowers for the soldiers' guns.

Every day in Umm Seyhoun was defined by the revised number of people killed. It started with seven Iraqis. Then forty-five. Soon it was seventy-seven and I made a picture with seventy-seven Iraqi faces drawn onto that day's

newspaper with crosses put through them. Not long after it was one hundred and forty-two and I made another picture with the requisite number of faces. Although reading the reports affected me in a thinking and rational way, drawing these faces hit me lower down and much harder, in a way that I could not control. Tears would slide very slowly down one or other of my cheeks, tickling them, as I drew the different faces. I would catch the tear with my tongue as it slid past. It was as if I was peeling onions. It wasn't even that satisfying. A muted kind of cry.

When the count got to one hundred and seventy I tried to make another picture, but couldn't find enough different faces to draw from the library of newspapers I had collected – and I didn't want to repeat any of the faces; I could make them up, but never the same face twice because that seemed to dehumanise what I was trying to do – so I stopped, feeling inadequate. Two hundred and seventy-eight. Three hundred and four. Three hundred and thirty-two. Three hundred and thirty-seven. It felt as if it was easing off. Then four hundred and one. Four hundred and twenty-eight. Thirty-two Americans killed. Nine British. Eleven British. Fourteen British. Four hundred and eighty-nine Iraqis. Five hundred and forty-two Iraqis – and it had only just begun.

As the numbers grew we tried to adjust what we felt, but after a while this felt absurd. That this kind of remote and abstract grief should be something precise did not make sense, and yet it was the only way any of us could begin to process what was happening six hundred miles away in Iraq. We had to try to impose order on this chaos. The most complicated part of this remote mourning for people we did not know was exactly what we were supposed to feel when a British soldier died compared to when an Iraqi civilian died, or an Iraqi soldier, or an American soldier, and how that compared to the people around us, who were glad when an invading soldier was killed and sad when an Iraqi died. Which had a certain logic to it.

The building in Umm Seyhoun where we stayed had been built for students from Brown University in America who used to spend their summers digging up Byzantine remains in Petra. Since 9/11 no one from Brown had come to stay. Our host was called Daqlala and his wife had golden skin, as did their two youngest children. Fatimah, who you met earlier in the book quoting from the Qur'an, spoke good English, was top of her class and had eyes that shone whenever she smiled, something she did a lot.

"Only a child could be like that, with everything that is happening," one of her poker-faced brothers told me.

Every morning Fatimah would come and tell us about something that had happened to her the day before, like the exam she got ninety-nine out of a hundred in.

One morning she bounced into the room while Georgie and I were drinking tea. "Guess what!" she said, looking as though she was about to burst.

"What?" asked Georgie, feeding off her energy.

"I have heard this on the television today. A thousand British soldiers have been killed!"

"Great! I mean what?"

"A thousand British killed."

"Wow."

"I know. It is the best news."

"Killed, just like that?"

"Yes! Killed. Maybe captured, I don't remember. The man on television said they had been taken."

"Right."

"Some more tea?" she asked

"I'm OK actually," I said.

"Georgie?"

"No, I'm fine, thank you."

"Al Arabiya have not talked of it yet," Fatimah went on, "only Al Jazeera, but they are always first."

"Right," said Georgie, unaware that eighteen months later she would be working for Al Jazeera.

"Because I have been thinking," Fatimah said, her young complexion deflowered by a frown. "It is good that the British and the Americans know this is not like holiday. I think they are learning!" She smiled some more.

"Like going to school," I said.

"Yes!" she said, thrilled with the comparison. "Exactly like this."

I spent the morning trying to work out exactly what this made me feel, and whether the grief I experienced for these thousand British soldiers was the same I would feel for a thousand Iraqi civilians; if not, why not; or what would I feel if it was a thousand people killed on the other side of the world by a typhoon?

Later the same day I found out that Al Jazeera had reported no more than a rumour; there were no British soldiers captured or killed that day and I had been grieving for a phantom.

☾

Gates of Hell

As the invasion of Iraq gathered pace, more press attention focused on Baghdad. It had become the jewel in the Iraqi crown, Saddam's lair, the symbolic and political heart of Iraq. As journalists all over the world cheerfully pointed out, the last time anyone laid siege to Baghdad was in the thirteenth century when Mongol barbarians fought their way to the gates of the city. This allowed for headlines like "Barbarians at the Gates" and comparisons between Americans and Barbarians.

Arab journalists were certain that the American and British forces would dig their graves in Baghdad. Baghdad was one step too far, they warned. The Americans might be able to win the war in the desert, but conquering the ancient heart of the Arab world was something else. They reminded their readers of the lavish sums Saddam had spent on Baghdad's defences, and how he had a plan up his sleeve. The old fox. Of course he did. He wasn't called Saddam – the fighter – for nothing!

With every passing day, Baghdad's aura of enchanted invincibility grew.

Non-Arab journalists ascribed to this as well. On the day our exhibition in Amman would have opened, the fifth day of the war, Simon Jenkins wrote a piece for *The Times* called "Baghdad Will Be Near Impossible to Conquer". There were chilling references to Napoleon in Moscow, Hitler in Stalingrad, the Israelis in Beirut, the Vietcong in Saigon, building up to the idea that Baghdad was, as he put it, "a city apparently determined on resistance". "Baghdad... has a fierce survival instinct," he wrote. "Hostile cities don't capitulate," and so on.

I could think of no other place I had read about so often but knew so little about. Not in terms of its history, but in terms of what it was right now. What it looked like. What it *felt* like. All I had was my conversation with the Turkish journalist, the *San Francisco Chronicle* article and shards of conversation with Iranians, Omanis and Jordanians. Baghdad had become a chimera. It was a beautiful city, men and women in Umm Seyhoun would tell me, the most beautiful, with the finest art. As one man in Umm Seyhoun had put it, "If you kill Baghdad, you kill the Arab world!" Perhaps he was getting carried away. I didn't mind; it was grist to my mill. We had to get there, I told Al.

☾

Pulpit

ON DAY ELEVEN OF THE WAR I DROPPED IN ON KHALED. His house was on the edge of Umm Seyhoun and had a superb view over Petra. With his back to the view, he watched the latest from Al Jazeera with several friends. I sat down with them.

"Do any of you ever watch Al Arabiya, or Abu Dhabi TV?" I asked after a while.

One man tutted, jerking his head upwards. "*La*. These people do not tell the truth. They are paid for by America."

"It is true," said Khaled's friend. "Al Arabiya today, they say the Americans are one hundred fifty kilometres from Baghdad. But it is not possible they are this close. The Iraqi army cannot disappear."

"Al Jazeera says the Americans are three hundred kilometres away," said Khaled.

"Al Jazeera tells the truth."

"It is like our brother," said Khaled.

We watched in silence as the headlines were read out.

"You know," said Khaled, the discussion's compere, "if tomorrow Al Jazeera says '*jihad*', nothing else, only '*jihad*', I would go to Iraq. Really. All of us, we would go."

"No, no, no," said the man next to him, laughing gently.

"This is true. Believe me. All Muslims would go."

"*La habib*. No my friend."

"Yes! All true Muslims. I would leave my wife, my children."

"You would go to Iraq to be killed by American bullet?" asked one of his friends.

"If Al Jazeera said '*jihad*', I would go. Really. To be with our Iraqi brothers, to support Saddam. Saddam is strong man, the best man now. He will fight back."

The television cast its spell over the room once again and everyone went quiet.

In 1990 the few Jordanians in possession of a satellite dish watched the First Gulf War in English on CNN. In 1996, after the failure of the BBC's putative Arabic satellite station, Al Jazeera was set up, staffed mostly by the remnants of the BBC venture. By 1999 the station was broadcasting twenty-four hours a day, seven days a week, the first Arabic satellite station to do so, and in late

September 2001, only two weeks after 9/11, it pulled off perhaps the greatest journalistic scoop of all time when it aired an interview with the most wanted man in the world, Osama bin Laden, and his deputy, Ayman al-Zawahiri.

It was now late March 2003 and Al Jazeera's audience was believed to be more than forty million. There was no organisation that held greater sway over the hearts and minds of people in the Middle East. Its reportage was incisive and its brand infallible. To an audience starved of journalism that could say whatever it liked about the different censorious dictatorships within the Middle East – laying into your own government in any Middle Eastern state bar Turkey or Israel remained journalistic suicide – Al Jazeera had arrived on the scene like a fridge in the desert.

It was what happened when Al Jazeera was *not* reporting that was so sinister, as I witnessed that day with Khaled.

In between each editorial segment and bank of adverts shown that afternoon came the same carefully crafted Al Jazeera montage: a "bump", in broadcasting speak. It was accompanied by an orchestral score and had little commentary. Too many words might suggest that you, the viewer, were being told what to think; instead, it was for you to join the dots. Clips of bloodied and mutilated Iraqi children segued into images of equally bloodied Palestinian children and injured Afghans. After this came Israeli or American or British troops, rapidly interchanged to appear as one, shown kicking in doors or pushing visibly Arabic-looking men to the ground. Women in headscarves mourned or looked terrified in front of more Western soldiers in desert fatigues, and in slow motion the Palestinian boy Muhammad al-Durra was shot dead in the arms of his father. In between, bombs fell on Baghdad and the camera zoomed in on each explosion so that the flames filled the screen. There were clips of Muslims from all over the Muslim world who might be protesting or going about their daily life; as long as they were wearing some kind of recognisably Muslim outfit, they were in. This built to a crescendo with the iconic – and so slowed down – shot of men praying as one in front of the Dome of the Rock, and after that we were taken back to the latest from Iraq.

It was the most powerful propaganda I had ever seen or felt. The acerbic power of the images and the vibrato of the violins sent shivers thundering down my spine long before I knew where to direct the emotion.

The footage illustrated Al Jazeera's agenda perfectly. As a station, it wanted to portray a culturally united "Islamic world" that was under attack because of its Islamic-ness. By so doing the station hoped to "wake it up", as Al Jazeera's director once said. Its view was that every Muslim should, ideally, feel some of the cumulative grief from conflicts as geographically disparate as Indonesia's remote Molucca Islands, Chechnya, Afghanistan, Iraq, Palestine, Kashmir, Kosovo, or even Sudan.

Similar yet more substantial visual montages could be found all over the Arab world, be they on cheap VCDs or on the internet.

Just over two years later, Hussain Osman, one of the 21/7 would-be London bombers, was quoted in *La Repubblica* as saying that his motivation to carry out his attack came from films he used to watch with his fellow would-be bombers. These films showed, as he put it, "women and children killed and exterminated by the English and American soldiers, or widows, mothers and daughters who were crying". And so, he felt, "it is necessary to give a signal, to do something".

Amear Ali, brother-in-law of the man who ran the Islamic bookstore frequented by at least two of the 7/7 London bombers, described going to this shop and watching identical videos where, as he put it, "film images clicked by in rapid-fire sequence to a soundtrack of pounding drums: dead Iraqi children, Palestinians under siege, Guantanamo prisoners, snippets of President Bush repeating the word 'Crusade'... You could see how it could turn someone to raw hate... It even started working on me. Then I said to myself, 'Get out. This stuff is poison.'"

The Al Jazeera bumps were part of a new phenomenon, one that was inextricably linked to the technological revolution in the Middle East. This had changed forever the speed with which images and image-based ideas could be disseminated within the region, as well as their reach. Fuelled by the drivelling quality of state-run television, there had been an exponential growth in the number of homes with satellite television during the late 1990s and early 2000s, as well as a proliferation of VCD and DVD players and a dramatic rise in the number of people with access to the internet. Accurate and up-to-date figures on internet use are hard to come by, but in the sixteen months between April 2001 and September 2002 the number of internet connections in the Middle East grew by 88 per cent.

That in itself is neither sinister, nor peculiar. However, the speed with which this revolution took place, combined with the dearth of authentic images preceding it and the supremacy of one media brand above all others, meant that any idea or theory propagated by Al Jazeera at that moment in the region's history had a colossal impact disproportionate to its veracity or accountability.

The reductionist hypothesis underpinning both the Al Jazeera propaganda and the videos that Amear Ali or Hussain Osman sat through was the idea that the world was irrevocably divided between "the West" and "the Islamic world", with the latter under attack from the former. A war on Islam. A clash of civilisations. It was an idea that roughly united

President Bush, Osama Bin Laden, Samuel Huntington, Bernard Lewis and the director of Al Jazeera, to name but five.

The most confusing part of this Manichean worldview was the prerequisite that both "the West" and "the Islamic world" were sufficiently homogenised, in a cultural and political sense, to warrant their labels. This was the bit I didn't understand: the idea that the countries Al and I had travelled through since arriving in Turkey were similar enough to be thought of as part of a single unit. Nothing that had happened to us since leaving London seven months earlier suggested the label "Islamic world" had any empirical weight beyond an academic historical discussion or perhaps a religious address. Even then, it was more precise to talk about the *ummah*, the body of believers. What jarred was the way we had felt compelled to adapt to a different and highly individualised set of identities, prejudices and sensibilities every time we had crossed a border within the so-called "Islamic world".

The other problem with this catch-all label was the linguistic insinuation that whatever went on inside the "Islamic world" was "of Islam" and so, like Islam itself, timeless. With that, the inhabitants of the "Islamic world" appear to have timeless characteristics. This idea that the character of a twenty-first-century Muslim can be explained using historical data from, say, the eighth century is at the heart of most Orientalist misconceptions about the region.

Buried in all of this was something that struck at the heart of both how Al and I should be making art and how people in the Middle East were perceived by themselves and by people outside the region. Sitting in front of Al Jazeera that afternoon I understood – in that I witnessed it, tasted it, felt it – the role of an image within the construction and perpetuation of a myth. I could see, right before my eyes, how a series of images was able to transform an otherwise whimsical idea, a pub rant, a notion, into something with life-affecting reality, a policy, an action. The alchemy was stunning.

Something else became obvious, in a way that once I'd realised it I felt stupid for not seeing it sooner, which was that the most powerful artists in the Middle East at that moment – in terms of their ability to affect vast numbers of people with images, emotionally, and to a precise end – were the men and women running Al Jazeera. No one else came close. What was so brilliant about their bumps was their wordlessness, as had been the case for the young Esfahani artists staging their protest. As with most great art, this meant that you, the viewer, felt as though you were reading these images for yourself and coming up with your own interpretation rather than being told what to think, and yet the communication between artist and viewer was impressively precise.

☾

Halas Yani

AFTER MORE THAN TWO WEEKS IN UMM SEYHOUN, WITH THE battle for Baghdad about to begin, we left Jordan and got on a boat to Egypt. Georgie had flown home on day five of the war after her parents had managed to fix her return flight, something she was not happy about at the time.

In Cairo on 9 April 2003 I watched an American flag being draped over Saddam's statue in Firdawsi Square in Baghdad. *Firdaws* means paradise. The statue was then pulled down by an American armoured personnel carrier. I watched the event in the lobby of a high-ceilinged, mostly empty hotel next to an effete receptionist who up until then had been flirting fastidiously with the few guests staying there.

"*Halas yani*," he said, slowly, no longer in the mood. "It is finished."

We continued to watch in silence as the stars and stripes were removed. The reporter relayed a rumour that this flag was the same flag that had flown over the Pentagon on the morning of 11 September 2001. I groaned. It couldn't be true. Surely the American military did not, in their professional opinion, think that Saddam Hussein was behind 9/11? It was like a joke in bad taste. The one about someone's mother that, whichever way you told it, was not funny.

"Is it good that it is finished?" I asked the receptionist.

"I do not know," he said, continuing to stare ahead, his words devoid of any feeling, an armada of buses "not in service". "I am not happy Baghdad falls so fast. I cannot understand this. Al Jazeera told us it would never fall. Al Jazeera told us the people of Baghdad would fight to the death. But... But it is finished. *Halas yani*. They have taken Baghdad. Maybe the Americans can go home now. Maybe they have what they want. I don't know."

He shrugged.

Part Four
Arabian Summer

*From Amman via Damascus and Aleppo to Beirut,
where Yasmine is almost killed*

Corrida

YASMINE STARTED WITH THE THIRD TURN OF THE KEY. FOR the last three weeks she had been parked in Aqaba while Al and I were in Cairo watching the end of the war and getting knowingly lost in that lovely, bustling and peeling metropolis that made me feel both anonymous and at home.

Four hours after leaving Aqaba we were back in Amman. Our show in the Orfali Gallery – the show that would have opened on the fifth day of the invasion of Iraq – had been rescheduled by Rana and would now open in two weeks' time. The Orfali was big and we had a lot of work to make to fill it.

For the two weeks that followed we were put up by Jane Taylor, a legendary English photographer who had lived and worked in Jordan since the early 1980s and had a light and airy house near the centre of Amman that had a balcony with a commanding view over downtown Amman. The balcony was also home to a terracotta army of pots that, with their lived-in patina and European-looking inhabitants, reminded me of home. Getting back to Jane's at any time of day felt luxurious.

Each day we commuted from Jane's to a studio on the opposite side of the valley in the basement of Darat al Funun, an international centre for Arabic arts housed in a stately, tall-windowed building that, like Jane's balcony, overlooked downtown Amman. Its director, Ali Maher, an enormous Circassian with a Father Christmas laugh that made your ribcage shudder once it got going, had agreed to let us work there.

All of which meant we were living out an artist's dream: as well as having a place to stay, a studio to work in and all the materials we could possibly need, we had an enormous space to fill, heads bursting with ideas and, most important of all, we had a deadline. Every artist needs a deadline. Oh, and I almost forgot, the war was over. That changed everything.

Ali told us that T. E. Lawrence wrote some of *The Seven Pillars of Wisdom* in the Darat, even if no one else I spoke to seemed to think he did. At one point in the book Lawrence decided that the Arabs "were limited, narrow-minded people, whose inert intellects lay fallow in incurious resignation. Their imaginations were vivid, but not creative. There was so little Arab art in Asia they could almost be said to have had no art."

So there was something faintly pleasing about the fact that the Darat was now a centre for Arab art. In the basement beneath the spot where Lawrence was rumoured to have begun his tome, we got to work.

Almost everything we made in the Darat dealt with the invasion of Iraq and our experience of watching it. Those two-and-a-half weeks in Umm Seyhoun and Cairo had been extraordinary in the way they brought to the surface so many of the fears and longings of the people around us, like debris from a shipwreck bobbing up unexpectedly; those two weeks also revealed many of our own insecurities and crises of identity, all feelings that might otherwise have remained blanketed beneath the veneer of giving and receiving hospitality.

The piece I spent most time working on had a bull with *banderillas* in his back and blood pouring down his side. I painted him on top of a montage of Jordanian newspapers I had collected during the war.

Setting aside for one moment the well-worn supernova of sexual metaphors read into every charge, pass, shimmy and impotent blunder of a *corrida*, watching the invasion of

Iraq on television had been just like watching a bullfight. As Al Jazeera beamed in the latest from Iraq, the glass of the television screen had become the wooden board running round the ring, the disconnect, and in both the bull-ring and the Jordanian living room I was the spectator, unable to do anything more profound than cheer, boo or cry as scenes of mortal combat unfolded in front of me. In the bullring the crowd wanted each bull to be strong and resilient in his death, yet at the same time they wanted the matador to perform with the grace of a ballerina and the precision of a surgeon. In the same way, the men watching Al Jazeera next to me wanted the Iraqi army to put on a powerful display, to give the Americans a bloody nose, but when it came to defeat they wanted the victor to be both ruthless and elegant. Few believed Saddam's army could destroy the US army, and it was this treacherous sense of cheering on both sides of a one-sided duel that was so sickeningly familiar.

The bulk of Al's contribution to the show was his latest crop of "nature-cultures". This was his most recent concept, following on from his paint-feeling phase, and easily the strongest body of work he had made so far. The idea had come to him in Oman. Each nature-culture was a sculptural installation that involved some sort of juxtaposition between nature and culture; hence the title. The relationship between the two – most of all the point of contact as well as the way you the viewer engaged with an object according to its setting – was the best expression of everything Al was trying to do with his art, as he explained, displaying the same winning conviction with which he had introduced his paint-feelings.

To make these nature-cultures Al would go on long walks with his Omani walking stick and a plastic bag. He would fill the bag with objects he liked the look of – leaves, combs, shoes, phonecards, cigarettes, flowers, fish-heads, playing cards – before positioning them somewhere that would change their meaning – in or on boats, walls, roads, roadsigns, buildings, trees, forts, caves, seedpods, mosques and so on. The peripatetic part was important, because it took him farther away from the remote learning of libraries and the insularity of studios that he disliked so much.

Once he had placed one of his objects in its new setting, he would photograph it and leave it for someone else to find. It was important that he never took one of these sculptures home with him, no matter how much time he had spent manipulating it or securing it to that particular spot. What happened to him while he made these sculptures and the way people reacted was fascinating and worthy of a book in its own right. He stored his growing collection of photographs on his computer, calling it his Pitt Rivers of Rubbish, or his library of ghosts.

A bank of these photographs would fill one of the walls in the Orfali. Other walls were filled with an eight-foot tall homage to Kaveh Golestan, the Iranian filmmaker who had come to our Tehran opening and who at one point was going to make a short piece about us. Less than a month before, he had been killed in Kurdish Iraq working for the BBC. Most of the artists we had got to know in Tehran attended his funeral. There was also a clock that had had its minute hand and hour hand removed and the second hand turned into a cigarette. Everyone smoked more than usual during the war. Then there were tens of paintings of the places we had been before the war, paintings about the different stations of prayer, the ninety-nine names of God, and a piece called *Catharsis*, for which Al painted a canvas red with a blue rectangle in its top left corner before taking it into the street outside the Darat.

Having secured it to a wall he began to hurl Pepsi bottles filled with white paint at it. They exploded only if you threw them really hard, as if pitching a baseball with your left knee up by your armpit, and when they did explode the paint would splatter over the canvas and dribble down in wobbling tendrils. Some of the exploding paint got onto the bonnets of nearby cars. It was my job to dab it off with white spirit.

"It just feels so good, you know, throwing it like that," he said, lining up another bottle. "Proper release, after three weeks of war watching and feeling pissed off, power-less, pretending not to be British, feeling torn in two directions, and..." he hurled another bottle. SMASH. "And wanting everyone to stop telling you to go home and... And just wanting to..." SMASH. "I don't know." He looked over. "I'll shut up. It's better when I paint it." SMASH. Once the paint was dry and the canvas stretched, the piece was turned on its side so that it looked a little like an American flag.

Al also worked detail into several cheap Orientalist-style paintings he had picked up in Cairo, subverting their meaning with tiny F16 fighter jets in the background, or discreet barbed-wire tattoos on the arms of "Oriental" women. When Rana first saw these she didn't get them. She said we should probably leave these pieces out of the show. Then she saw what Al had done. She exploded, "Al, they are brilliant! The best pieces in the show! Bravo! *Alf mabruk*, a thousand congratulations!"

Outside the studio the garden of the Darat sprawled over a steep terraced hillside. The scent of jasmine filled pockets of this succulent, well-watered space, while else-where there was the sound of water being hosed into each flowerbed. Once the bed was saturated, streams of water would trickle over the scorched stone turning it a warm, rotting colour. Eddies of dirt and petals would fuss about in gossiping cabals before carrying on down the slope towards downtown Amman; none of the hoses ever seemed to be turned off.

The garden was lovingly looked after by Rageb, who did his gardening in a smart shirt and trousers with a crease ironed down the front of each leg. Every time I greeted Rageb his smartness made me feel like a paint-smattered urchin. Most men in Amman dressed like him.

Beyond the Darat al Funun, Amman was different to the city we had tasted before and during the war. Georgie and I had stayed with Jane on the night bombs first fell on Baghdad and it was on Rainbow Street outside Jane's house that we had been shouted at. Now every morning leading up to the show Al and I would get into Yasmine, parked in the same spot she had been on the first day of the war, and the students from the café opposite would come over to tell us what a good car Yasmine was, or that I looked like a dervish because of my beard. Some of them asked if they could hide in the back of Yasmine and come to London with us.

No one mentioned the war: it had become taboo.

☾

View

THE PRIVATE VIEW WAS PACKED. THERE HAD BEEN A LOT OF press, mainly because of our nationality, but also because there weren't many other exhibitions going on so soon after the invasion of Iraq.

The British Ambassador opened the show and talked about the importance of this exhibition by British artists after "the recent, very traumatic and heart-rending events".

He did not say the word "war". The room ummed in approval and that night we sold thirty-one pictures.

Walking around the show later, tipsy, with one or two latecomers still working round the room, I felt as though a weight had been lifted. It was as if I had got the war out of my system and now I was desperate to get out of Jordan.

"Well, let's go," said Al. "Let's go tomorrow. We don't have to stay here while the show's up."

"Great. We're going."

"I feel like I've been in Amman too long anyway," said Al, speeding up. "And at the same time I feel like I'm on the verge of something of a... I don't know how to put it, of an understanding. I've got this sense of being just about to see what it is we're actually doing."

"What do you mean?"

"In the way that I think we're about to reach some kind of conclusion. Or resolution."

"Which is why we need to go to Baghdad," I said.

"Will you stop going on about Baghdad? You're obsessed by it. We don't have to go there to resolve what we're doing, and anyway, who says we can right now? It might be too dangerous. What I'm talking about is how much it's changed. Not Baghdad, but what we're doing. The way we set off whatever it was, nine months ago, waving our pamphlets at people, driving a shiny yellow-hooded Yasmine, off to make a new portrait of the heart of the Islamic world, and then look at us now. Ha! We've spent the last three months lying about our nationality, scuffing up Yasmine, wearing disguise, changing the way we work and... And... Realising that we can't make a complete portrait of the post-9/11 Middle East. Ever. Because of who we are. All we can do is record the parts that we attract."

"You think?"

"Yep. Let's go to Syria. To Beirut. You'll see."
With that, he went to find Rana.

☾

Mission Accomplished

LESS THAN TWO WEEKS BEFORE OUR SHOW OPENED,
President George W. Bush landed a jet on board the USS
Abraham Lincoln off the Californian coast. He made what
is known as a tailhook landing, with his plane catching the
last of four steel cables and coming to a standstill 400 feet
later. Just below the cockpit window on the S-3B Viking jet
were the words "George W. Bush Commander-in-Chief".
Hanging from the bridge, in a considerably larger font, was
a banner declaring "MISSION ACCOMPLISHED".

Having got out of the jet, the President greeted various
sailors and pilots, thanking them, slapping some on the
back and shaking hands with others. At one point he held
up his hands to the observation deck where hundreds of
sailors had gathered. They roared their approval, like a
crowd saluting their favourite gladiator. He must have felt
fantastic.

"Great job," he was heard to say again and again. Or,
"'preciate it".

Several hours later, showered and changed, he made a
speech on the flight deck. He confirmed that major combat operations in Iraq had ended. Iraq was now free, he
added.

He did not, however, declare the war in Iraq to be over
and although he did not mention it, the watching world
knew very well that the Iraqi leader Saddam Hussein and
his clique of Ba'athist cronies were still at large. Already
there were reports of an Iraqi resistance. Thousands of

"foreign fighters" were rumoured to have crossed into Iraq: transnational *jihadis* from countries like Saudi Arabia, Egypt, Pakistan and Jordan, all of whom were desperate to oust the occupying coalition or, in the words of 50 Cent, die trying.

☾

Love Thy Neighbour

KINAN WAS A YOUNG CHRISTIAN ARAB GOLDSMITH WHO lived in Damascus, the capital of Syria and only a few hours' drive from Amman. What little hair he had had been shaved off not long ago. His head shone like something semi-precious beneath the workshop lights and around his neck hung an enormous gold cross.

For most of the first hour of our conversation he explained, in detail, how backward the Muslims he shared Damascus with were, before moving on to how crazy it was that "the British" were allowing so many of these Muslims into their country. It was like being at a British National Party rally. What annoyed Kinan most was that as a Christian Arab living in Damascus, he felt under siege. Not from the government – they were Alawite and as an ethnic minority rarely picked on other minority groups in Syria – but from the Muslims he shared the city with.

During the war in Iraq more and more casual exchanges in Damascus's Old City (neatly divided between its Christian and Muslim quarters) would finish with a Muslim saying something chippy to a Christian about the American Bishop Mr Bush, or the Christian Crusade. Graffiti had begun to appear on walls in the Christian quarter quoting Qur'anic *ayah* about what will happen to the non-believers at the Final Judgement, regardless of whether or not they were People of the Book; that is, Christians and Jews as well as Muslims.

Christians and Muslims had lived side by side in Damascus since the seventh century, though rarely had they lived as equals. For most of their coexistence the Christians in Damascus, like most non-Muslims living in a predominantly Muslim city, enjoyed lesser legal status and were obliged to pay *jizya* – a poll tax imposed on non-Muslims in return for not being required to defend the city – rather than *zakat*, a wealth tax that contributed to social welfare. Needless to say, *zakat* was a lot less than *jizya*. This political inferiority eased only when the Islamic Caliphate collapsed in the early twentieth century, but by then Christian numbers were in decline. It had become easier for a Christian Arab than a Muslim Arab to emigrate to Europe, Australia or America. It was also attractive in a way it had not been before. By the last quarter of the twentieth century, "the West" had become an exotic and viable other, a land of wealth and hedonistic indulgence that appeared like a rainbow whenever a storm was brewing in Damascus.

I walked with Kinan through the darkening streets of the Christian quarter, past glass cabinets moulded into the wall with statuettes of Issa lit by yellow bulbs. Kinan would kiss his hand and touch the glass as we walked past. The Christian women we saw looked licentious with their hair out. Kinan told me about the Muslim boys who came to the Christian quarter every Thursday or Friday – the Syrian weekend – to leer at them.

Just before we got to Kinan's car we passed a church. On its black cast-iron door I saw the word "Allah" in Arabic next to a white cross.

"Wow," I said, tutting. "Look at that. That's awful."

"What?" asked Kinan, who had not stopped.

"This, here." He started to walk back. "Someone's gone and put graffiti on the church door."

I looked closer. The "Allah" had not been painted on but was made of iron and had been carefully welded to the door.

"Why do you say that?" asked Kinan.

"This is a church, yes?"

"Yes," said Kinan, looking at me rather than the door. "So the priest had 'God' written on the door. Allah is Arabic for God. We can write God on our churches, no?"

"Sure. But I thought..."

"Henry, we are Arabs, we speak Arabic. Our services are in Arabic. It is normal to write something in Arabic. We worship the same God as the Muslims."

There was nothing remotely tree-hugging or conciliatory about the way he said this.

"You know that, right?"

I did.

We walked on in silence, me sucking in my lips, as I do when I know I've said something stupid.

KINAN'S BEETLE GROANED AND CURSED AS IT RUMBLED through narrow alleyways towards Kinan's friend's house, where he went most nights. In a tall-ceilinged flat on the third floor, six or seven men were sprawled out watching television. Most were unemployed. All were bored. They reminded me exactly of tens of identical young Arab men we had spent time with over the last four months, all part of the same pear-shaped Middle Eastern demographic, all educated, unemployed, wifeless and, understandably, feeling anxious and at times emasculated by all of this.

One of Kinan's friends was on the internet chatting up an American girl, telling her no, he wasn't just after a visa and yes, she was the only one for him; while on the adjoining window he told Karen in Ohio that he was going to love her forever.

On television there was a grainy VCD montage of different belly dancers from Iraq, Syria, Lebanon or Egypt, though most were Egyptian. One had leaden implants and a plastic-surgeried face. None of the men slumped on the sofa thought she was any good. She kept smiling anyway.

One of Kinan's friends showed us a cartoon he had just been sent. Everyone there had already seen it and said things like "That's so true" or "It's already happening, man" as the attachment opened. The first frame showed a fierce-looking sheikh presiding over two pretty and blushing brides who cowered by his feet. Above it was the caption "The Past". "The Present" was a skinny man at a table whose food was being thumped down by a matronly woman. "The Future" had a woman reclining in an armchair being waited on by her husband, who was covered in bandages and had a black eye.

"That's you, Kinan," someone said, grinning and pointing at the husband in "The Future".

Kinan turned to me. "Christian women don't take any shit," he said.

"Um." I lowered my voice. "Why do they say that to you? I thought everyone here was Christian."

"Oh no, I'm the only one," said Kinan, looking away.

"Hang on," I said, "so these guys are all Muslim?"

"Sure."

After the church door incident I thought it best to let this sit before I said anything else.

"But," I said, having gone over it in my head a few times, "what about everything you said before, about the Muslims being backward and stupid and how they shouldn't be allowed into Britain?"

"Oh, I don't know," said Kinan, reclining in his chair. "I don't really think that. I just didn't want you to get the wrong idea. Some foreigners think that because I'm an Arab, well, I must be a Muslim. My best friends are Muslims so..." He trailed off. "I suppose the only Muslims I don't like are the religious ones, you know, because every time you start to tell a story they always go off to pray. It's so antisocial." He looked at me.

I looked back.

"It's a joke, Henry."

"Right. Sorry."

"You know, if you want to laugh."

"Yes. No, sorry, I was..."

☾

She Called It Him

SABA WAS WAITING OUTSIDE THE LE PONT GALLERY. Though they had been done up for the occasion, her eyes looked sad. She wore an ivory-coloured coat and a tight dark-blue headscarf that cut in sharp beneath her jaw. No one I could think of wore it that tight, be it in Tehran or anywhere else; except, perhaps, Princess Susan, who wore it that tight if not tighter. Where Saba's headscarf finished and just before her coat began you could see a triangle of flesh. A silver pendant marked its centre. Saba seemed nervous as we walked to the derelict factory in Aleppo, a city in the north of Syria near the Turkish border.

An open-back truck of workmen drove past and some of them shouted at us.

"What are they saying?" I asked.

She looked tired. "They are say rude things. About you and me. They have bad minds."

"Ah."

"Lazy minds."

"Yes."

We carried on in silence.

The factory had been gutted of its machines and its partitions, making its proportions tall and giving it the feel of a cathedral or a railway station. On the walls were shards of black and white tiles or scraps of agitprop posters with slogans from the 1950s or 1960s of an Arab Nationalist, quasi-socialist bent. Hovering over this at eye level were artworks by twenty-eight female artists from around the world, all contributors to the fifth Women's International Aleppo Art Fair.

We were the only people there. I asked Saba about where she came from and she began to tell her story in a hushed voice, her words echoing around the space as if lost and looking for a place to hide.

Saba was twenty-nine and had finished university five years ago. Originally her family had hoped she would marry one of her cousins, but she didn't like any of them and had dithered; now they were all married. Her family lived in a village to the west of Aleppo and it was because of them that she had to wear her headscarf.

"But your family are not here," I said, cautiously, not wanting to offend her. "They won't know if you stop wearing it."

"Yes, but I live with my brother." She looked away. "I call it him."

I didn't understand.

"Your brother?"

"No."

"Who?"

"Him," she said, tugging at her headscarf. "I call it him. He strangles me." She looked away. "It is also because of my family that I cannot publish my poems. But this is the only thing I want to do. The only thing I *can* do. They say my poems bring shame on family. But there are no bookshops in my village." She looked mutinous. "Nobody there can read anyway." She pulled at her headscarf once more. It was where it came in under her jaw that it seemed to chafe the most.

As Saba went on to explain, a woman's clothes in middle-class or working-class Syrian society, as in Jordanian society or Arabic society – as much as such a thing exists – had a huge bearing on her reputation, as well as her experience of any space outside her home. Her home was her citadel and the moment she left it, whether or not she wore a headscarf was the opening line of her visual statement to an arena in which she was no more than a guest. The male outdoors. Within this first line there were few shades of grey: you either did or did not wear a headscarf. In the un-Armenian parts of Aleppo or less cosmopolitan areas of Amman or Damascus, a woman without a headscarf would have dirty things thought about her or whispered at her by bored shopkeepers. For a lot of men, by not wearing a headscarf the woman had chosen to enter the realm of foreign, non-Muslim, non-Arabic women who ground away on MTV; foreign prostitutes, women from countries where it was unusual rather than usual to be a virgin on your wedding night. Or worse, they reminded them of the women they had seen in foreign porn who went "Oh my God" over and over again.

It was the Madonna/whore dichotomy articulated by uniform. A woman wearing a headscarf – without a foreign man by her side, Saba added, glancing at me – was placing herself within the Madonna canon of good mother and respectable wife.

Within this headscarf-wearing sorority, the second line of the visual statement, there were many shades of grey. Some headscarf-wearing women might dress conservatively, others revealingly, so there was nothing peculiar about a woman choosing to emanate a hint of to-be-looked-at-ness, as Saba did that day, while at the same time maintaining respectability by wearing *hijab*. For a lot of women this was the most powerful way to dress.

Wearing a headscarf was also what the families of most girls would want. Within more traditional or less well-off families, by looking "honourable" the daughter became a better prospect for marriage, which gave her a better chance of marrying above her social or financial rank; whereas a girl who did not wear some kind of headscarf was the exception and the people around her – her extended family, her neighbours – would gossip like fish-wives about why she chose to be the exception. The mere suggestion that the daughter of a family was, well, open to suggestion could damage the name of that family, or its "honour".

Just before leaving Jordan and several weeks before meeting Saba, I had read a report in the *Jordan Times* about a court case in Amman. A twenty-year-old man from Amman had been in Aqaba, on the coast, when he heard that his unmarried sister was pregnant. She had been raped by her neighbour some months before. Her family decided that she should marry her assailant: the idea of a child born out of wedlock or an abortion now that word had got out was far too scandalous. The brother of the girl who had been raped returned to Amman later that day, where he was taunted by other men in the neighbourhood. They called him "the brother of a slut". The next morning he strangled his sister to death with a telephone cord.

This particular case had made the papers because the court could not decide whether or not this man was, legally, in a "fit of rage" half a day and a night after hearing about his sister's unwanted pregnancy. If it was adjudged that he was in a fit of rage, it would be an honour killing. If not, murder.

In the end, the court decided that he was, legally, in a fit of rage and so ruled that "the actions of the victim [his sister] were an unlawful and dangerous act that brought disgrace and shame to her family" and that "he [the brother] could no longer control himself and became very angry".

Several weeks after we left Amman, the man was sentenced to a year in jail. This was later reduced to four months, as it usually is for any man convicted of an "honour crime" in Jordan.

In Aleppo I found the story on the BBC website. Every detail was reported verbatim, as it had appeared in the *Jordan Times*, until the end of the article. After a brief description of honour killing, the piece concluded with a single, free-standing line:

"Most of these killings occur in Muslim countries."

That made me screw up my face when I read it. There is nothing in the Qur'an that mentions, let alone condones, honour killing. It is wholly un-Islamic.

Although there is one Qur'anic *ayah* that says a husband may strike his wife only as a last resort in response to "high-handedness", there is no mention in the Qur'an or the recognised hadiths of maintaining family honour by killing off your close relatives. Jordanian law in effect sanctioned this "honour killing" not because of its religious content, but because it was seen to uphold traditional local moral values – pre-Islamic Arab traditional values – rather than Muslim values, something borne out by the fact that in Indonesia, home to the world's largest Muslim population, honour killing is unheard of. Even Ayatollah Khamenei, the Supreme Leader of Iran, once declared it "un-Islamic".

In a similar sense, the headscarf that Saba called "him" had its roots in a pre-Islamic Arabia. Headscarf wearing is not, by any means, a prominent part of the Qur'an. It is alluded to no more than three times and even then the Qur'an does not explicitly describe a headscarf or veil that must be worn at all times; instead it describes a *hijab*, in the house of the Prophet, which is a screen or curtain that divides the room. In another verse a *jilbab* is mentioned, but it is not clear whether this is the same as the long overgarment worn by some Muslim women today. This should be worn so that the believing women in Yathrib (later Medina) could be "recognised and not insulted".

Saba's headscarf also represented the part of Muslim female identity I felt most affinity for, to some extent because it was something we had seen everywhere we went, in its many different forms and names; also because of its wordlessness. On a more practical level, it was something I was drawn towards because the few women we had got to know were happy to talk about it at length.

What I found so interesting were the different reasons for a woman wearing a headscarf or a veil. Some might wear one to protect their reputation, or their family's reputation; others might wear one to appease a husband; maybe to get a husband; to avoid being leered at; to save money; to look good and follow fashion; to affirm their identity in a foreign setting – to themselves as much as anyone else; to make a political point; because of peer pressure; because their government demanded it; as an adolescent protest against their parents; or they might cover themselves purely out of what they perceived to be religious piety, even if the Qur'an puts far more emphasis on believing in the oneness of God, performing the prayer, charity, respect, honesty and so on than it does on wearing a headscarf.

Saba did not wear her headscarf that day because she felt her religion demanded it. She wore it because of her parents and her brother.

"You know," she said as we were about to leave the factory. "There is a woman I hear about, the most beautiful woman here in Halab, who her husband asks to wear *abaya*, you know, the full black cloak. This *abaya* is no eyes, no hands, nothing. Whoomph." Her hand shot down her front. "And he says he will pay her one million dollars if she does this. One million dollars!" Saba's face worked itself into a precise mixture of disbelief and joy, as only the thought of one million dollars could bring on. "You know I meet this woman some weeks ago?"

"Really?"

"Yes. And I tell her I will pay her one dollar not to go into *abaya*."

"And she took it?"

"Yes. I give her this money. She say now she will not go into *abaya*. Then I say her about him. I say he strangles me. She say if she has a million dollars she will pay it to my family so I can live without him." She sighed and smiled and looked at her watch. Her face became empty.

"I must go. My brother is home soon."

C

Thoroughbred

A BOY WALKS ALONG A STREET LEADING WHAT LOOKS LIKE A thoroughbred horse. A rope is tied crudely around its neck. It is hot and the boy laughs at the camera. His hair is short and ruffled. Behind him, another boy is dragging a fabulous armchair with golden rococo ornamentation and silk upholstery. You can almost hear the legs scraping and skirling on the road. Behind them the sky is an over-exposed blue and some of it is hidden by a plume of black smoke. The caption seems unnecessary: "Young looters leaving one of Saddam's palaces in Baghdad."

In another picture, two men are bent over as they push a cart loaded with several tables and a large cabinet. Their tower of loot looks precarious, but they don't seem to mind. They are grinning like two students who have been caught moving a traffic sign: they don't object to the picture being taken, but would prefer if it wasn't. In the background a building has been bombed. It looks like a wedding cake that has had a watermelon dropped on it.

With the plundering of Saddam's palaces over, looters in Baghdad are concentrating on shops or the homes of the wealthy. Men with guns protect buildings. At night there are pitched gunfights between rival gangs of looters staking out their territory. A lot of these men are criminals released from jail by Saddam in the days before Baghdad was attacked. The city is in a state of lawlessness. The power supply is intermittent. The water is off for most of the day. American soldiers patrol the streets, but are unable to enforce order.

It is April 2003 and suicidal attacks on coalition targets by men driving vehicles loaded with explosives are also becoming more frequent.

And the Baghdadi artists? I don't know. I could find nothing on the internet or in any Syrian newspaper about them. I imagine they are in their studios, taking it all in and wondering when the galleries will open again.

☾

Dancing to Stand Still

WE ARE THE MOST OVER-DRESSED PEOPLE IN THE ROOM. WE didn't mean to be. We tried to dress smart enough to get let in to this Beiruti club and then blend in, but we've gone too far. I am in my border-crossing suit. Underneath is a shirt with marks of paint on it, from when I put a brush in my mouth like a pantomime pirate with a dagger, forget about it, turn my head and get paint on my left shoulder. It happens a lot, but the marks are hidden beneath the jacket so nobody knows. Al is in a suit he had made for him in Aleppo with some of our winnings from Amman. The boys and girls around us wear faded jeans, white shirts and designer scruff.

We are in Beirut, the capital of Lebanon, and yet again we have not quite adjusted to our visual surroundings. Give us a few more days. The venue is BO18, a club situated in a gutted, underground hangar that looks like a Bond bad-guy lair. The roof is open to the sky, as if the laser designed to destroy the moon is about to be wheeled out. Forty-five seconds to go. Forty-four. Forty-three. All around us are beautiful people. Lots and lots of beautiful people dancing on tables. Forty-two. It looks like an over-subscribed casting for a high-end modelling shoot. Some of them have reserved tables, so you can't just go and dance on any table you like the look of. You have to ask first. The chichi watchfulness of it all is mesmerising.

The music is techno-trance but nothing too hard, please. Nobody's here for the music. They're here to dance, something they do with an urgent kind of insouciance; and yes, such a thing is possible. They are doing it now. I can see them. Urgent insouciance everywhere I look. It is as if there's a rule against looking self-conscious, but still everyone manages to people watch while they dance. They are all secretly watching everyone else people watch; all night long they've been people watching and dancing, but nobody is drunk. Not cool to be drunk in Beirut.

Earlier we went to a bar called Red. The owner gave our half-Irish, half-Lebanese host Paddy Cochrane a wink and a hug as he arrived, saying, "You've got a nice table, man. Real nice." I didn't get it. Our table looked ordinary: four legs, not much of a view, seats you sat on.

After half an hour, eleven of the most beautiful women I have ever seen filed past and sat down at the reserved table next to us. They perched – or did they float? – a little forward on their seats, each one a bundle of legs and arms and hair. Like celestial half-beings they seemed to glow. This was Beirut's élite model agency on one of their rare nights out. Sitting on the edge of our group, I was next to one of them. The woman on my right was the model-turned-agency-director who had positioned herself at the one unavoidable point of contact with the outside world so she could watch over her sirens, something she did with the poise of a brooding mother hen. She told me that in Beirut it was a little rude to start talking to someone without being introduced. I said I was sorry. She said it was OK.

Her girls seemed unaware of their beauty, as if they had not looked in the mirror for the last six years and in their minds were still gangly flat-chested twelve year olds. It made them even more attractive. Perhaps they knew this.

Behind them men did double takes, bumped into each other, spilt their drinks or just stood and stared, their faces blank and eyes drooling.

Stroking either her hair or a bizarre furry pendant round her neck that very nearly ruined the magic of the moment, the agency director told me about her modelling days and about the buzz – the *incroyable*, eye-rolling buzz – of walking down a catwalk and feeling all those eyes on you. She missed that. She growled a little as she described it. Thoughts of modelling and being looked at triggered something else and her mood changed as she began to tell me about her recent trip to Iran. It had been her first time there and she had been required to wear *hijab* when outside.

"And I hate this thing. My God. It stopped me from thinking like human being. Hate it. Hate it. And this is why they do it, it is to put down the woman." Her eyebrows went up as far as they would go. "But they cannot! It is in the blood of the woman to be looked at. You cannot change this. They are crazy people in Iran. Ugh. You know to punish the woman in Iran they put the feet in the bucket of these things, the... er, the cockroach?" She was no longer stroking anything. "The Iranians they are, how do you say, they are like people who live in caves. Like animals. Do not go there, OK?"

I didn't know what to say. If I had told her Iran was the most friendly and artistically rich place I had ever visited she would have had me thrown out of the club. That or she would have turned away and I didn't want that, so I said nothing.

Not for the first time, I felt morally glib. Where was my righteousness? My banner-waving spine? Why did I not get on my soapbox and defend Iran, telling her about Moonlight, about Ruya, about Marjan, about the parties? The problem, I realised, as the Beiruti agency director told me where the different girls were from – Russia, Venezuela, Italy, Lithuania and Lebanon, it turned out – was the state of novocained, wide-eyed enquiry that Al and I had slipped into. At times it was like being in a coma. In almost every encounter or conversation during the last ten months both of us would try to reveal as little as possible about ourselves. We would unconsciously paint ourselves out of the exchange and instead mould ourselves around the person we were talking to because that way we seemed to learn more, though I was not sure how much longer I could keep this up. Something was about to give.

The agency director went to join her sirens and they danced around their table, self-consciously, each of them making sure to stay close to the mother ship and not to let any of the boys get too near.

C

Consumption

THE NEXT DAY IN BEIRUT I MET SHAWKI YOUSSEF. HE RAN A fashionable boutique in northern Beirut and used to make art for a living.

"But it is hard to live off your art in Lebanon," he said, sounding blasé about it. He was in his late twenties with a mischievous grin and pale skin that looked more Phoenician than Arabic.

"The way Beiruti high society loves contemporary art, let me tell you, it won't last. For them it is like the latest fashion. It won't last like going out or looking good. Or any other kind of conspicuous consumption. That is the true Lebanon," he said, nodding. "Conspicuous consumption, my man. I read it in a magazine. That and not being sure where we are, as a group, you know. It's an exciting time and a nervous time," Shawki went on. "No one mentions their religion any more. These days in Beirut I can hardly tell if someone is Druze, Maronite, Shia, Sunni, Greek Orthodox, Greek Catholic, Armenian Catholic, Armenian Orthodox, Chaldean, Syrian Orthodox, Syrian Catholic, let me see... Baha'i, Jewish, I don't know. From their name I can tell, but that's different."

"What do you mean about not knowing where you are right now?"

He liked this question and let it sit for a while.

"The best way to think of where we are right now, culturally, emotionally, it's with the dance. All anyone does in Beirut is dance. We're addicted to it. And you know why? Because we want to forget about the past and at the same time we don't want to think about the future. The future scares us, so does the past. We dance to stand still. You can only think of the present when you dance. Unless you're doing it wrong." He grinned.

For several hours we carried on like this, with Shawki telling me about Beirut, Lebanon, the veiled tensions, the tensions of veiling, the relationship with all things Syrian and the faddishness of Beiruti high society. But when I said goodbye and went to find Yasmine parked outside Burger King, what he had said seemed to sit in my head only as a bank of ideas, or just words. There were few images with which to flesh them out.

☾

Latest Craze

WHEN I GOT THERE I FOUND THE STREET OUTSIDE THE Burger King where I had parked Yasmine cordoned off. Beyond the waist-high yellow tape were several police vans and an army truck. I went up to the crowd of soldiers, policemen and Burger King employees and peered through the crowd gathered behind the tape. Beyond them was a car parked by itself, Yasmine. The cars that had been next to her earlier had disappeared.

"What's this? What's going on?" I asked the nearest person, a girl wearing a Burger King cap.

"This pick-up truck, you see with *Mashallah* on its side, it has the bomb inside it."

"What!?"

"Sure, there's a bomb inside."

"What are you talking about? There's no bomb inside it."

She frowned at me.

"In the past hour the police have had seven calls about this car."

"But it's mine! She's my car."

"What?" said an army lieutenant just in front of us, turning round. "Your car? You from where?" He moved towards me. Others stepped away.

"English."

"Show me your passport."

I put my hands in my pockets. Shit.

"Um. I don't actually have it on me. It's in the house I'm staying in, up in the hills."

"What are you doing here?"

I told my story. A crowd gathered. The army lieutenant asked why Yasmine looked the way she did. I tried to explain. He didn't believe me when I said I had driven to Beirut from London via Iran.

"Show me the car," said the senior policeman who had joined the catechism. He began to edge the lieutenant out of the way. I took first the policeman and then the soldiers on a guided tour of Yasmine.

"It is very unusual, this car," the army lieutenant said, half to himself, half to me. "And when the people see *Mashallah* on it, and they see it near Burger King, and they see Syrian flag..." In Damascus Al had stuck a plastic eagle painted in Syria's colours onto Yasmine's dash. "They think this car is from Syrian fanatic. Maybe he wants to bomb Burger King."

Yasmine was searched first by a team of soldiers and then a group of policemen. Both sets of men pulled out anything that caught their eye, such as the skull of a goat Al had picked up in an Omani desert, Happy Meal toys from various McDonald's – possibly incriminating as Burger King's arch-rival – a sticker of Issa, a Qur'anic inscription, an egg that Al had kept from Iran (he wanted to see what it looked like when he opened it up at the end of the journey), fake greenery that we had hung all round the cab giving it the feel of a cheap Thai restaurant, a poster of Shakira, pint glasses, the copy of *The Sun* we had bought the day we left London, a copy of *Orientalism* and an Imam Husayn medallion.

The army lieutenant told me that if I had arrived five minutes later, Yasmine would have been towed away and destroyed. The thought of it made me shudder. Later it made me feel physically sick.

The army lieutenant left, at which point the senior policeman, who was less friendly, said he wanted to arrest me. I told him I didn't want to be arrested. A crowd gathered and we began to argue.

Opposite Burger King was an apartment block that had been painted scallop pink and although there was no sun on them, the metal shutters on the lower floors had been pulled down – to protect the residents against the expected blast from Yasmine. As the argument between me and the policeman grew rowdy, two elderly women staggered onto their balcony and began to yell. At me. In between pleading my case to the policeman, I shouted back at them what I thought were mollifying words, though the eyes of both women had long ago glazed over with an unassailable anger, an anger that I had never felt before. In their tirade I heard the word "Musulman" – Muslim – again and again.

In lieu of my being arrested, the policeman agreed to take me to Shawki's shop because I said Shawki would vouch for my identity. Shawki duly did and the policeman left, his face insentient.

"Well, my man, that's Beirut for you," said Shawki as the door swung slowly shut, as if in a daze. "We're so desperate to be Western we even copy Western paranoia. We're terrified of someone with *Mashallah* on their car. Being scared of Muslims is, I've heard, the latest craze."

I set off to find Al.

On the drive back into the centre of town, I became cross with myself in a sanctimonious, penitent way for not realising the implications of parking Yasmine next to a Burger King in Beirut with Syrian flags on her dash and *Mashallah* on her midriff. It felt obvious now. But, I told myself, there was something useful to come out of this. What had just happened seemed to confirm Al's idea that everywhere we had been over the last nine months, the events or experiences that had affected us the most were always the ones that happened as a result of *us*, be it our appearance or our actions. We had lost any delusions of being able to glide through the region, invisible, stealthy, a fly on every wall, jotting down the reality surrounding us. That was impossible. If anything, we were bulldozing our path through the region and carefully recording the way different people dived out of the way. So to speak.

Understanding that began to change how I thought about our journey, or indeed any journey, in terms of what we could achieve. The artistic end point was much closer now than I'd realised.

☾

Flying from Roof to Roof

"YOU KNOW MY FATHER, HE SMOKES ONE HUNDRED cigarettes every day," Hassan announced, dragging deep on his latest cigarette, clearly proud of this statistic. "One hundred. For Palestinian, if you don't smoke it is like you don't care about what is happening."

We were on the roof of Hassan's house near the centre of a Palestinian refugee camp in south Beirut. It was nighttime and we could hear little or no traffic as there were no cars in the camp, the lanes were too small. Hassan had lived here all his life. He was roughly the same age as us and had neat hair; beneath his eyes bags were beginning to form. His camp was one kilometre square and surrounded by a no-man's land heaped high with rubbish. The men and women inside could not expand sideways, only up. Most of the buildings were now three or four storeys high and on the load-bearing corner of each roof were clusters of rusted steel tendrils awaiting the next floor. They seemed emblematic of a people and a place in limbo. On a roundabout beyond the no-man's land there was a scaled-down cardboard model of the Dome of the Rock; one of its walls had recently fallen down. Next to us on Hassan's roof was a deflated dinghy obscured by the gloom of the night.

"You know about the flying carpet?" he asked. Between us we nodded. "One day I am turning this into the flying boat."

He lit another cigarette.

"So everyone here smokes?" I started.

"Yes."

"Just cigarettes?"

He cocked his head to one side. "Most of my friends smoke other things," he said. "But what else is there for them?" He sounded defensive. "The ones who don't smoke like this, they join Hamas. These are the best people. So pure. So good." He thumped his heart with his right hand.

"So are you going to join them?"

He laughed. "No, no. I am not good enough to be in Hamas. Look at me! I drink, I smoke, no. It is not possible. Maybe one day this will change, but not now. Listen, OK, I have friend who is the artist. Before, he smoke all day. He drink, he never pray, I don't think he is know how to pray, and two years past, at start of *intifada* he turn to Islam. Now he does not smoke, he does not drink, he prays and he has joined Hamas."

"And does he still make his art?"

"No. No, it is in Qur'an you cannot do this."

"Do what?"

"Make the picture."

"Where in the Qur'an?" I asked, sitting up in my chair.

"I don't know. I am not imam. Somewhere in Qur'an."

"It's not, you know."

"It is," said Hassan, sounding unimpressed.

"It really isn't."

Since leaving London I had asked almost every imam or religious student we had met whether or not there was any Islamic injunction against the representation of living creatures. This was something I had been told again and again before setting out. "So you're going to the Middle East to paint? Bit risky isn't it?" people would say. "They cut your hand off if you paint a picture of someone, don't they?"

I knew now that there was nothing in the Qur'an that proscribes the representation of humans or animals. The closest the text gets is in Surah 5, Ayah 90, where *al-ansab* are forbidden. Al-Nasafi's commentary suggests *al-ansab* are inanimate idols – like the pagan stones positioned round the Ka'abah, the central structure within the Great Mosque, in the years before the Prophet took Mecca – rather than images or statues representing human beings. There are a handful of hadiths concerning idols and idol makers, and not surprisingly they stress that *al-musawwiran* – those who make idols designed to be worshipped – will be tormented on the Day of Resurrection; while the most often quoted hadith on this subject is about the angel Jibril, or Gabriel, who refused to enter a house because there was both a dog and an image inside. This was the hadith quoted to me by the only person who asked not to have his portrait painted on religious grounds.

One of the other most relevant hadiths – relevant to any Muslim artist or artist making art about Muslims – is one narrated by al-Bukhari that describes the Prophet asking his wife Aisha to pull aside a curtain that had *suwar* (representations) on it. The Prophet complained that the images were appearing in his mind while he prayed. That seems to sum up the basic premise underlying most if not all Islamic doctrine regarding images and image making: you should never worship a human being, be it directly or indirectly and regardless of his apparent or real link to God.

"But this is not important," Hassan went on. "So many people have turned to Islam now. It is good. Islam is waking up."

"Sure," said Al. "In fact, people have been saying that all over the Arab world."

"Why do you say that?" asked Hassan, bristling once more. "This is not Arab world."

Al looked puzzled. "What is it then?"

"I am not Arab," he said, his eyes narrowing in the gloom. "Arabs are fucks. Don't ever call me Arab. I am Palestinian. I don't care about Saddam giving money to Palestinians. I don't care about Arabs saying they love Palestine. They do not. Arabs do nothing for us. Nothing!" He was now out of his seat. The atmosphere was charged. "Arabs look down on us only. It is the Palestinian who knows true suffering. I am not allowed into my home for fifty-five years." Hassan was twenty-three. "Fifty-five years and no one listens! I have been bombed by Israel, I have been bombed by Lebanon. I have starved. I have eaten meat of donkey, of rat, of goat, of cat, it does not matter. I will eat my own hand to survive. The Arab knows nothing of this." He tutted. "The only Arab I talk to is bin Laden."

He produced a photo from his wallet. "Look. Me wearing *imama* like bin Laden." In the photo he also wore bin Laden's trademark camouflage jacket.

"But why do you like bin Laden so much?" asked Al.

"Because bin Laden, he has made Islam political. Now Muslims read the Qur'an and pray like as protest against America. 9/11 has shown all the world that Islam can fight America! It can destroy it. Lebanon cannot do this. Abu Ammar [Yasser Arafat] cannot do this. Abu Mazen cannot do this. Only Islam can fight back and because of bin Laden we know this, we see this on the television. We see this place, the World Trade, fall to the ground."

"Like a proof?"

"Yes. Exactly. Like the proof."

In silence we looked out over the rooftops of the camp. I thought back to Fatimah in Umm Seyhoun being taught the same thing in school.

"Ah," sighed Hassan, sounding keen to change the subject. "This place is so small. You fart here and everyone knows about it." He chuckled to himself. "I think I know something about, maybe, every roof you see here."

"What about that one?" I asked, pointing at a rooftop fifty yards away.

"Hmm. Perhaps not that one. The one next to it I know. There is a woman there who I sleep with when I am sixteen. I used to climb over these roof to get there." He showed us his route. "And she was married. Can you imagine what this is like for me? The sixteen year old sleeping with a married woman!"

"What if you got caught?"

"The husband, he would kill me. It finish after three months because she is worried her husband would find out, even though he is in Dubai." He shook his head, smiling. "But the girl who take my heart, *yani*, she was different. She was same age as me. I meet her when I am eighteen. That was different. Very different. We used to meet in secret every morning." His face began to melt. "Six-thirty outside the camp." He was whispering now. "We talk just for ten minutes and then go. But for all of the day after, oh my God, I am so happy. And after six months, we kiss for the first time. Ahhh."

It was a soft moan. A vulnerable moan. After all of his chest-thumping Palestinian machismo – the highlight of which was him telling us that Palestinians, as a race, always have more sons than daughters because they are so manly – this was, for a moment, an unmanly moan. He seemed to have transported himself to the very moment when his lips first touched hers. He was floating just at the thought of it.

"Oh my God, I remember that day." His face continued to soften. "My feet did not touch the ground. I was like

Aladdin! I am flying from roof to roof. I could not sleep, no way. This was the best thing I have ever felt. Oh my God. I want to marry her, I want to die for her, believe me. I want to... I don't know, do everything in the world for her. But I do not have the money. I was still young man. So... So when her brothers hear about what is happening, they say if I talk to her again they kill me. Either I marry her or they kill me. So. *Halas yani.*" He clapped his hands together before lighting another cigarette. "She has married other man now." He drew deep on his cigarette and his expression and tone of voice hardened once more.

Back in political mode he told us about Faris Ouda, a Palestinian boy shot dead throwing stones at Israeli tanks, before moving on to Mohammed Al Dura, a Palestinian boy shot dead in his father's arms while a television camera was trained on him. I nodded and listened, but my head was elsewhere. I was still with Hassan as an eighteen year old, in love, flying from roof to roof. That he had found this intensity of feeling amid this uncertainty, this melancholy, this pessimism and this longing to be elsewhere, the more I thought about it, made me want to fly.

A week later we returned to Amman. We had some money to pick up from Rana and a dilemma to resolve.

Part Five
Baghdad and Beyond

From Amman to Baghdad, Jerusalem and home

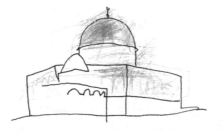

To Go or Not to Go

WHETHER OR NOT WE SHOULD GO TO BAGHDAD WAS THE biggest decision Al or I had ever made. Perhaps this was a sorry reflection on our lives up until then, lives free from any dilemma more demanding than should I or shouldn't I buy that pair of trainers, go to that party, paint the picture this way or that, write that essay now or later; at times it felt as if all we had ever had to do was turn up. In the past ten months the decisions had been harder, certainly, but they had not been impossible. The decision to go to Kurdish Iraq was easy: Sulaymaniyah felt dangerous only when we were there. Choosing to remain in Jordan while the Anglo-American coalition rolled into Iraq was, in reality, depressing rather than life threatening.

To go to Baghdad at that moment was dangerous. We knew that. Foreigners in Baghdad had been killed because of their foreignness. We would be risking our lives by going to Baghdad and, what was more, we did not have to go there. Whichever way up we held our map of the Middle East, Baghdad was not on the way home. We would be going out of our way to put our lives at risk.

"I asked Rana," said Al, gazing out over downtown Amman.

"Asked her what?"

"Whether or not we should go."

Once again we were on Jane's balcony. If there was a balcony anywhere in the world on which momentous decisions should be made, this was it. Something about the size of it, its hushed light and the panoramic sweep over the heart of the Jordanian capital made every conversation there feel epic. Asking someone what time it was on Jane's balcony was profound.

"What did Rana say?"

He laughed. "She just said 'No.'" He shook his head at the thought of it. "She said, 'It is suicide to go now. You are not going. No way. No, no, no.' Then she asked her mother. She also thought it was suicide. Then an Iraqi artist came in who had been there last week. He said it was suicide as well. So yes. They all think it is a bad idea to go to Baghdad right now. They say it is not beautiful now."

"What do you think?"

"I want to go. You know that." He glanced over at me. We did most of our talking side by side, looking at the same thing, so for him to make eye contact gave whatever he was about to say added clout. "I think it's important. And anyway, as I think we both know, if one of us is going to get killed it's clearly going to be me," he said half to himself, looking away again and beginning to smile. "For history to repeat itself."

☾

Lights Out

AFTER SEVEN WEEKS THEIR ROUTINE HAD BECOME EFFICIENT. The man leading the cutting party would take a bearing with his compass – of 110° – and choose a tree or a creeper about a dozen paces ahead of him before hacking through the undergrowth towards it. The two Brazilians behind him would widen the path by removing any stray saplings or other undergrowth he had missed. Once the man leading the party had reached the point he was aiming for, he would take another reading from his compass, 110° as before, and the process would start again. They would carry on like this until an hour before sunset, when they would get to their hammocks and settle down before being benighted.

It was 1961. The Iriri River Expedition, led by a tough young Englishman, Richard Mason, was moving through unexplored Amazon rainforest near the geographic centre of the Amazon basin at the speed of an icebreaker through middle-aged ice. With Mason were my father (John Hemming), Kit Lambert (who later formed and managed The Who) and a team of eight Brazilians including three government surveyors and five hired woodsmen. My father and Richard Mason were both 26. They had been at the same university and had travelled together before – they had even driven through the Middle East on one of their previous trips and gone to Iraq – but they had never both travelled as part of an expedition, and never into a part of the world for which there were no maps.

The aim of the expedition was to locate the headwaters of the Iriri and follow this uncharted river until it joined the Amazon, as every body of water in that part of the world, no matter how small, eventually must. This would flesh out a blank on a map. The Brazilian government had agreed to support them, had provided three experienced surveyors and given the expedition permission to name any geographical features they found. The Brazilian Air Force was providing transport.

Hacking through virgin rainforest was hard, mono-tonous work. It was harder still towards the end of each day, when the temperature beneath the canopy was at its worst. Arms tired. Brows welled with sweat. Creepers that might have dropped to the ground earlier in the day at so much as the sight of a machete now taunted the men who swiped at them, flinching from their touch like a shy date.

Most days the expedition would advance two miles, if that, but for the last eight weeks they had maintained steady progress, driven on both by the novelty of what they were doing and Richard Mason's example and charisma.

After two months the expedition's supplies were running low and the three men agreed that my father should go back to Rio de Janeiro and arrange for new supplies to be parachuted in. He retraced the expedition's trail back to an airstrip at Cachimbo, where they had started, and from there flew back to Rio de Janeiro, where he persuaded an air force colonel to parachute 150 kilos of supplies to a spot near Cachimbo. My father also managed to get the exact time and date of the parachute drop read out on Brazilian national radio, so that the rest of the expedition, tuning in from the middle of the forest, would know when to light smoke beacons in order to guide the pilot to the drop zone hidden beneath the forest canopy.

The plane, fully laden with the expedition's supplies, got halfway to Cachimbo when the President of Brazil unexpectedly resigned. Every Brazilian Air Force plane, including the one carrying my father and the expedition's new supplies, was recalled to base in case of any political unrest that might follow.

Unaware of this, Richard Mason continued to wait at Cachimbo. The drop never came. After staying there for a week he decided to return to the camp, 35 kilometres away along the trail that the expedition had spent the last eight weeks cutting.

The latter part of this trail led through more mature rainforest where the canopy was dense and let little light through to the forest floor far below. At one point, about three kilometres from the camp, the trail cut through a patch of open land, a pocket of savannah no bigger than two football fields side by side. At first you would be blinded by the light. The smell was different too. You could see the sky once again, the sky you had almost forgotten existed, and you could feel the sun on your skin. Then at the other side of the clearing the trail took you back into the subterranean gloom of the undergrowth. It must have felt like someone turning out the lights.

Just before re-entering the forest at the far end of this clearing, on 3 September 1961, Richard Mason was ambushed and killed by a hunting party from an un-contacted tribe of Amerindians called the Panará. The men from this hunting party attacked him with fifteen heavy clubs and some forty seven-foot-long bamboo arrows, which they then laid next to his corpse. His body was found when the Brazilians and Kit Lambert went looking for him.

Having been granted a flying boat from the only section of the air force not to be grounded – the Air–Sea Rescue – to fly both him and his supplies to the drop zone, my father was in the air when the attack happened. The news came through to the pilot of the plane. They were in a storm. With the plane lurching this way and that and the sky flashing white with lightning, as if a team of celestial paparazzi were flying alongside waiting for a reaction, the pilot clambered back into the unlit hold. He told my father things were black. He told him that his friend Richard had been killed by Indians.

Several days later, my father and the others on the expedition carried Richard's embalmed corpse back to Cachimbo and from there it was taken to the British cemetery in Rio.

The Panará tribe was contacted twelve years later, and twenty-five years after this contact my father met with the only surviving member of the hunting party that had killed Richard (I was with him when this conversation took place). It turned out that those in the hunting party had been travelling for several days and were a long way from their usual hunting ground when they came across the trail cut by the expedition. None of them could think who or what would make such a trail. To them it looked like a motorway, even if it was only two feet wide. They found a spot at the far end of the clearing and lay in wait to see who or what would appear: Richard entered the clearing. He was the first white man any of them had seen. He was unlike anything they had ever seen or, within reason, imagined. He was wearing clothes and his jeans made a swish-swish-swish sound that none of the Indians had heard before. As he moved through the clearing, the hilt of the revolver that was tucked into his belt flashed in the sun. The Indians hidden in the forest could not understand either of these things: they had neither clothes nor metal tools.

There was whispered, hurried discussion in the forest about what to do and then a young tribesman fired the first arrow, of his own volition, and the rest of the tribe followed his lead.

I had heard this story plenty of times. Not because my father loved to tell it, but because I would ask for it again and again until I knew it inside out. Al had heard it too.

The two of us had talked about these events intermittently over the last ten months until both Al and I had a strange, semi-superstitious and in many ways macabre sense that history would in some form repeat itself and that one of us would die during our journey; Al would always say it would be him to keep the parallel intact.

This story resonated with a lot of what we were doing. We recognised in ourselves the same impulse to go somewhere foreign to what you know or feel comfortable in and to immerse yourselves in it, and to do this as young men not long out of university; just as we recognised the urge to go on an adventure with your best male friend, both of you brimming with young-man optimism-confidence-chutzpah. Or was it hubris? Being described as explorers was familiar as well. The headline for an article in the *Oman Observer* had dubbed us "21st Century Explorers", though this was little more than a euphemism for us being softer and less macho than the Wilfred Thesigeresque young Englishmen the journalist might have been expecting. More than anything else, Richard Mason's death haunted us because he was killed as a result of what he appeared to represent, not because of something he had done.

The only real difference between what had happened to Richard and what could happen to us if we went to Baghdad was that he and my father had been assured there was little or no danger of them being attacked by uncontacted tribes in that part of the Amazon. There was nothing foolhardy or ill advised about what they had done. The prospect of us going to Baghdad was wholly different.

So why couldn't we just forget about this city, deny it had some fetishistic hold on us and head for home? Over the last ten months we had made an enormous body of work, had accumulated conversations and encounters that had already permanently disfigured our perspective on the world, we had staged three exhibitions and generated a mountain of press; it seemed we had done most of what we had set out to do. So why couldn't we just give in to the prevailing advice and admit that running round the streets of Baghdad making pictures at that moment in the city's rich and chequered history was not a good idea?

☾

Two Become One

"YOU TELL ME, WHY SHOULD WE GO TO BAGHDAD?" I ASKED Al, my words more clipped than I wanted them.

"Was hoping you'd tell me that."

The sun was a little lower now and Jane's balcony that much cooler.

"Well, let's work it out. Come on. Why should we go?" I asked again. "Our lives are going to be in danger if we go, so there has to be some reason beyond 'it sounds exciting'. That's not a reason to risk our lives."

"I never said it was."

"I know you didn't. But still. Why? Why do you want to go to Baghdad?"

"I want to go because... Because we have to go. That's why. Because of what we are. Because of what's changed since we left London."

"What?"

"When we started out, I think we were using our art as a way in, as a passport into our setting. It was in the pamphlet, remember?"

"Sure," I said.

"Well, the last ten months of making art, of having people project artist-ness onto us and of feeling that, as well as all the other artists we've been with, it's changed something in me. It's made me realise, um..." He smiled. "Without sounding like a self-help book, it's made me realise what I am. I'm an artist, in that I make art and try to live off it. I couldn't say that before. So if we come at it from that angle, that we're artists, nothing more, and we just want to keep on making art, then the only logical thing to do is try to make the best art we possibly can. We have to keep on trying to do that. Otherwise we go backwards, right?"

"Right."

"And because our work is about going to a place and expressing what happens to us in that place, then all we have to do is work out the most artistically relevant place we can be right now, at this second in time..."

"I think I can see where you're going with this," I said.

"Yeah, well done. It's Baghdad. The art-making capital of the Arab world. That's the most relevant place we can be making art in right now."

Long pause.

"So let's go." I said. "Let's go now."

"But," said Al, sounding as though he hadn't worked this bit out. "There's one other thing."

"What?"

"We still have to work out whether the art we might make in Baghdad is worth getting killed for. Which is the premise of this. Of this conversation."

"Yup."

"Hmmm."

"That's a biggie."

"And..."

"What?"

He looked pained for a moment. "Well. The only thing holding us back, really, is a fear of death. Isn't it?"

"Yes," I said slowly.

"But why do we not like the idea of dying? I mean, why do we fear it? That's what it boils down to. If you strip away everything else. Or *do* we fear it?"

The next part of this conversation is hard to relate. I wrote it down immediately afterwards in the same way I would record any other conversation and I can remember the feel of it, the taste it left in my mouth, everything I would want to recall about an important conversation; but it doesn't make sense when I set it down in direct speech. It sounds wrong. Cold. At times sick.

The gist of it was that we all die at some point, and as we saw it then, you either die old when happy and fulfilled, or you die young when relatively unfulfilled. If you're going to die young, it would be best to do so when you

have as few people as possible who might be upset by you
no longer being around. We realised that we were both, at
that point, at a pinnacle of unattachedness in our lives.
Between us we had no wives, no children, no galleries
queuing up to sell our work, no publishers desperate for
our story, no army of collectors awaiting our return. We
had very little to lose. Relatively. And for the handful of
people who would notice if we didn't reappear after our
year away, the last ten months had in many ways been a
practice death. We were out of sight and barely in contact.
So, we decided, if we were going to die young, now would
in fact be a perfect time to do it. Also, if we were to die
now we would do so aware of death. By going to Baghdad
we were living life with a heightened awareness of death,
which gave every moment we remained alive an added
intensity; which, in a strange way, was something we were
both getting addicted to.

"The other thing," said Al, "is to think about what anyone we look up to would do if they were in our boots right
now. What would, say, a Basquiat, an Ofili, a Duchamp, a
Kienholz... I don't know, a... a Chatwin do if they were
where we are now?"

"I know exactly what they'd do."

"Right."

"They'd go to Baghdad. All of them, I reckon. They'd
go find the artistic renaissance there. In fact, they'd have
been there weeks ago."

"So we're going."

"Yup. We're going."

"To Baghdad."

"Done."

It was a weird conversation. I had to leave the balcony
to take it in properly. It was also the defining moment of
our journey: going to Baghdad was, as I realised then, the

embodiment of both everything we wanted to be and everything we wanted to do with our lives.

Next we had to decide how to get there. Taking Yasmine was not an option. Too many people we had spoken to thought she would get stolen in Baghdad. Most of these people thought we too would get stolen. Or just shot.

We decided to take the bus.

The following day I went to the British Council to get a letter explaining we were artists in case we ran into any trouble that a letter could get us out of. Tim Gore, the director, was reluctant. "These two artists are..." he dictated to his secretary. "What are you? Idiots. Shall I put that in?" His face was knotted into an uneasy half-joking, half-angry conundrum. Perhaps more angry than joking. Tim didn't think we should go to Baghdad.

He rang a friend at the British Embassy in Amman. He handed me the phone once he had got through.

"So you're going to Baghdad?" asked a serious-sounding voice on the other end.

"Yes, we're going to go make art there. We're artists."

I said the last bit with a new-found conviction.

"Right. Well, my first piece of advice is don't go."

"OK."

"But if you do decide to go, all I can say is make sure you cross the border at dawn, and when you're in Baghdad watch out for the eleven o'clock curfew. Other than that, there's a party at the British Club here tonight. Twenty-five dinars, all you can eat and drink. Theme's Hawaiian. Should be a lot of fun. Be great if you could make it. Or are you leaving for Baghdad tonight?"

"We are, actually."

"Oh well."

The thought of barbecue and beer with balding, middle-aged British expats was enticing in a way I had never thought possible. Tim's secretary gave us copies of the letter he had dictated in Arabic and English and the aroma of barbecue in my mind began to fade. We went back to Jane's to get ready.

C

Die Another Day

THE ROAD FROM AMMAN TO BAGHDAD ROSE AND FELL IN A smooth, rocking motion as the last flickers of settlement were extinguished. With my face right to the glass of the window and my hands cupped to my temples, all I could see was a blank broadside of desert. On a screen at the front of the bus the latest Bond film, *Die Another Day*, skipped intermittently as the bus continued east.

Sitting next to us on the night bus to Baghdad were Iraqis who had watched the war from Amman and were now going home. All of them were pleased about this. One Iraqi told me he would rather be killed in Baghdad by an American than spend another day in Amman with the Jordanians. Everyone who heard this laughed, heartily, like Turkish army officers talking about Turkish villagers.

Not long after the bus had rocked me to sleep, we arrived at the Iraqi border. It was three in the morning and the crossing was busy. Half asleep, we shuffled past kebab shops and piles of cardboard boxes and suitcases stacked between buses and lorries and taxis, all of them pointing east, into the immigration hall, where we handed our pass-ports to the officials before waiting alongside several hun-dred men and women either hunched forward or leaning right back in their plastic seats. Names were read out over a loudspeaker. Cigarette butts and pistachio shells fell to the floor like fat from a spit roast. One by one, everyone went to collect their passports.

Since leaving Amman a few hours ago, both Al and I had told everyone on the bus we were French. This Frenchness came to an abrupt and unexpected end after a break in the flow of Iraqi and Jordanian names being read out, a whispered consultation behind the microphone and a resigned "*Britanni. Wayn Britanni?* British. *Itnin Britanni.*" British. Where are the British? Two British people. The hall exploded into a drumming, murmuring sound and everyone woke up. I looked at Al. He grimaced. We got up to walk the length of the hall and collected our passports. On the way back to where we were sitting, if looks could have killed we would have been shot to pieces.

Back on the bus, no one seemed to mind our schizophrenic sense of nationality. The family opposite said we were their guests and offered us yet more cartons of fruit juice and sweets as the vehicle chicaned through the remainder of the border crossing and out onto an empty motorway. With a triumphant roar, the driver ground through the gears and we accelerated towards Baghdad.

I slept through the sunrise and woke a hundred kilometres outside the capital. Out of the window were signs to Ramadi and Falluja. This was the most dangerous leg of the journey, the part where most of the carjackings or kidnappings occurred, and for the next hour everyone was glued to their window.

The bus arrived at the Baghdad central bus terminal and we stepped out of its whimpering cool into the furnace of Baghdad at midday in the summer. The heat was fantastic. It enveloped you, swirling round you and smothering you like two king-size double duvets. We got into a taxi and asked for the Al Rasheed Hotel. Nick, who we had met in Amman and who was now working for the Coalition

Provisional Authority, was staying there and had said he might be able to get us a floor to sleep on.

The streets around the bus station were gridlocked. Occasionally you saw a policeman in a crisp airtec shirt waving gloved and ineffectual hands at the traffic jam like someone practising tai chi; otherwise men would jump out of their cars and direct the traffic themselves. Having got it moving they would hop back into their vehicle, race forward twenty yards, hop out and start again. Boys walked past pushing wheelbarrows with pillars of ice balanced on top. My mouth watered. The power went off in the middle of the day in post-Saddam Baghdad, I remembered being told, but only now did I or could I understand what that meant.

By the side of the road people queued and paid to splash cold water on their faces. Elsewhere I saw torched cars abandoned outside buildings to keep out looters. Shops had been bricked up. Cars drove on the pavement. In the distance were the gargantuan pillars of a mosque Saddam had begun to build that in its infancy looked like a ruin. Only a megalomaniac could build on that scale – "Look on my works, ye Mighty, and despair!" – something we felt socially conditioned to tut at. A thousand years hence, had he finished it, we would have cooed. Around us cars honked at each other or broke down in the heat. With Baghdad still recovering from the anarchy that had followed the fall of the city nine weeks earlier, the streets were full of spluttering wrecks that might not have been allowed out in the days of Saddam.

After half an hour we saw our first GIs. We both leapt over to one side of the car. These were the lions of the safari. Al took some pictures. I got out my sketchbook. They looked much bulkier than they did on television, with their layers of padding, body armour, helmets and heavy boots. It made their form strangely unhuman and instead android, or *Star Wars* stormtrooperesque. Their guns moved slowly over the traffic like the beam of a lighthouse scanning every face and car, including ours, once per rotation. You couldn't see their eyes behind the mirrored sunglasses. Baghdadi urban myth had it that these glasses allowed the soldiers to see through women's clothes.

At first Baghdad looked like Damascus or parts of Cairo in its concrete, its pocket teahouses, its broken pavement, its bustle and the tart intensity of its light; but when you looked harder you could see the effects of both a decade of sanctions and the recent invasion.

Though there were fewer bombed-out buildings than I had expected, the buildings that had been hit had been obliterated. Often the buildings on either side would have had no more than their windows blown out. The problem was which buildings had been selected for annihilation. Nobody knew why the supermarket near the National Theatre had been neatly flattened, nor did a man I spoke to understand why the house seven down from his had been destroyed by a bunker-busting bomb that killed everyone inside. Without raising his voice or sounding pissed off, he said simply that he did not understand.

Men in Umm Seyhoun, in Jordan, where we watched the war on Al Jazeera and Al Arabiya, had gone red in the face and trembled with rage as they described the bombing of Baghdad, a city none of them had ever visited.

Although the streets were busy, a lot of the shops were shut. Those that were open sold a more ascetic selection of wares than their equivalent in a neighbouring Arab capital. A chicken *shawerma* in Damascus would be carved out of a glistening pillar of prime breast from tens of different chickens. In Baghdad three chickens would be skewered, bones and all, and propped up as a bulimic pillar.

This would change – not while we were there, and perhaps not for several years – but the country's borders had opened and slowly Baghdad was being swamped by a free-for-all of cheap, imitation brands and men on the make. They sold mostly televisions and satellite dishes. Thuraya satellite phones were also popular.

At the Al Rasheed Hotel a crowd had gathered at the first of many checkpoints.

"OK, people, OK, stand back!" an American soldier shouted at the crowd of Iraqi men and women, most of whom were trying to get work as interpreters.

"Hi," I said, from near the front of the crowd. "We're here to see Nick..."

"Sure, sure, I'm gonna need to see some ID," the sergeant barked back, glancing at me and doing a double take. "Say." He looked harder. "Tell me. You some kind of radical?"

"What?"

"Radical?"

"Er. No."

"Certain?"

"Artist."

"Artist, eh?" he said, smiling and flicking through my passport. "Well, I see that beard and I'm thinking... OK soldier," he gestured to the boy next to him, "search their bags." As directed, the soldier hunched over our bags and began to pick gingerly through their contents. "C'mon now, Private," said the sergeant, with the measured delivery of a stand-up comedian. "We're looking for CX4 explosives here, not a bobby pin."

"Sir," the soldier squeaked back at him.

At the next checkpoint I took a photo of a GI who grinned a lot and had gold-plated front teeth.

"Man, you gonna put me on the cover of *Time* or something? Huh?" he asked as I snapped away. "Yeah. I'd like that, make me famous, do that. And make sure my teeth look good. I want a nice shine on them. Anyway, what the hell you boys doing here? You don't look like no two soldiers."

I told him.

"Artists! You know this is a war zone?" he asked. "Where you from?"

"London."

"London, England?"

"Yeah."

"Course you are. They'd be British, wouldn't they?" the gold-toothed GI said to the soldier next to him who had more spartan dentures. "Making goddam artist paintings in a war zone. Ha!"

Several checkpoints later, having steered through a maze of barbed wire and concrete barriers, we arrived in the lobby of the Al Rasheed Hotel. American soldiers of every rank and colour and gender walked back and forth in floppy hats, their weapons hanging from their shoulders. In one corner was Uday's, the nightclub where the nastiest of Saddam's sons used to let himself go.

Nick was out, so I spoke to Karen who was in charge of hotel logistics. There was nowhere for us to stay. She had a rash on her neck and trembled a little as she told me to be very careful in Baghdad.

"Don't trust any of the civilians, y'hear? Just yesterday two of our men were in a crowd of children. Everyone laughing, you know, and two guys came up to them from behind, popped up their helmets and shot them in the back of the head. Just like that." Her eyes were red. She had either been crying that morning or was suffering from an allergy. She wished us luck and we walked back through the concrete blocks and razor wire to the crowd of interpreters outside the hotel. Someone suggested a cheap hotel on the other side of the river, so we took a car there. Although there were official taxis in Baghdad, with so many people out of work almost any small car that drove past would take you in return for a few purple notes with Saddam's face on. During our time in Baghdad we would hail anything that moved. Apart from a Humvee. Or a tank.

The Majalis Baghdad was a long way east down Saadun Street, past the Palestine and Sheraton hotels where most journalists stayed, past the money changers and past the Ali Baba roundabout. The hotel was run by three Kurds who had put up posters of Sulaymaniyah where two months ago there had been portraits of Saddam. On television was Hero Talabani's KurdSat. The man at reception beamed when I said we had met Mrs Talabani and been put up by her in Sulaymaniyah. I told him the Majalis Baghdad was as beautiful as the Sulaymaniyah Palace Hotel. It wasn't. He purred. Most of the hotel guests were men down from Kurdish Iraq who were visiting Baghdad for the first time since the early 1990s, which gave the place a subdued holiday atmosphere.

Our room looked out over an expanse of golden-retriever-yellow Baghdad roofscape dotted with the green of date palms, the emblem of Iraq, as every artist we met in Baghdad would tell us with a hint of grandeur. Opposite our room was the curving spire of a church. Every morning priests in cassocks with cream-coloured ropes hanging from their haunches would distribute food to a queue of local residents. On the horizon was a plume of burning oil and on either side of it several tall chimneys, each one crowned by a ball of burning gas.

For the first time in Baghdad we could breathe. We had made a base. In the Majalis we felt hidden, most of all because we were away from the journalists and the other foreigners in the city, apart from two freelance journalists who were also staying at the Majalis, one French, one British. They both warned us about the curfew. As the man in Amman had suggested, it started at eleven.

Sure enough, by ten past eleven that night we heard distant bursts of gunfire. By eleven-thirty it had got going on Karada Street, less than a hundred yards away. This was the street I had read about in the *San Francisco Chronicle*, the epicentre of the so-called Montmartre I had been told about all those months ago in Istanbul. Without realising it, we had checked ourselves into a hotel within shouting distance of the place I wanted to find most of all.

The gunfire was much louder than it ever is on television or in the cinema. Much sharper too. Each shot was a proper crack, like a steel girder being snapped in two. I sat listening to it all on the balcony of our room with the curtains drawn behind me, mouth open, every part of me agog. I had never before heard sustained, live gunfire like this. Men firing guns in order to kill one another. I was inhaling the same air as them, listening to it all. It was extraordinary, both thrilling and terrifying, although after half an hour I was less scared by the gunfire than I was by the part of me that was enjoying it so much.

On the other side of the street a man came to the door of a brothel and pulled the grille shut for the night. Soon after, I went back into our room.

☪

Esam

ON OUR SECOND EVENING IN BAGHDAD, THE FRENCH freelance journalist staying at the Majalis introduced me to an artist called Esam, who came round most evenings to teach him Arabic.

Esam Pasha al-Azzawy looked like a king. He was tall and broad with long hair, a beard and dark, bewitching eyes that made him stand out on a Baghdadi street like an elephant in an aviary. All his life he had been mistaken for an Afghan, or a Turk or an Iranian. The one time we ate with him, the man serving us thought he was an Israeli. When I first met him he swore I was French.

Esam suggested Al and I should come to his studio, on the other side of town, so the following morning we took a taxi there.

The studio was small and cluttered. Esam had spent the war there by himself, sketching, drinking tea, smoking Miami cigarettes, praying and listening to classical music or Enya. All of his neighbours had gone to stay with relatives outside Baghdad, but Esam had felt it was important to witness this invasion.

"And now I do not spend enough time painting. It is sad, you know. I am too busy, much too busy."

"Why, what are you doing?" asked Al.

"All day I am translating for the Americans. I should be making art. Making art and making love. That's what I should be doing," he said in a matter-of-fact way. "But instead I am... What am I? I am the go-between for people who don't understand each other."

"Soldiers or contractors?"

"Oh, soldiers. I'm with a National Guard unit from Florida. The money is good, and they are not bad people. Only I don't know how long I'm prepared to risk my life for them," he said, his English immaculate and at times poetic in its delivery. "These days I hear about translators who are killed for working with the Americans."

"Even in Baghdad? I didn't think that happened so much here."

"It happens here as well. Believe me."

Al continued to sift through Esam's pictures.

"Tell me," Esam started, fixing us both with those eyes. "Have either of you seen the film *Elizabeth* with Cate Blanchett?"

We hadn't.

"Ah, this is one of my favourites. It is very strong. And there is a scene in it that I cannot stop thinking about now. It is in my dreams every night," he said, sounding anxious. "It haunts me."

"Which scene?"

"The one where the Pope has sent an assassin to kill Elizabeth. You see the assassin, and you know he is trying to kill her. Then you see Elizabeth, but she does not know and... It is so strong." He shook his head. "There is this silent energy. It expresses how I feel now. I cannot take this feeling out of my head, the feeling of someone trying to kill you, plotting, but you don't know about it and you can't see them. It is hidden."

"Have you seen *La Haine?*" I asked.

"No, tell me about that."

"There's a scene in it that I can't get out of my head. The one where two guys are falling off a building, and midway through one guy says to the other, 'So, how's it going?' And the other guy looks back and says, 'So far so good... So far so good.'"

"Mmm," said Esam, his eyes lighting up.

Al picked up a painting that showed a man with a sword. "What's this one about?"

"Ah," said Esam, straightening. "That is... Yes. That is *Brutus*. It is about my ex-best friend. In January of last year he stole my girlfriend." He sat down. "Yes. Think of it. My ex-best friend with my ex-girlfriend. To lose her was OK but to lose him was very sad. I think for any man to lose his best male friend is very sad." He looked at Al. "And you know, last month I find out my ex-best friend used to be spy for Saddam. Can you believe this? He was writing reports about me all this time."

"Where is he now?"

"Oh, no one knows. He disappeared when the Americans arrived. Maybe he has moved to a different country. I think this is best for him."

Al and I continued to pick through Esam's studio, past a distinguished-looking humidor that was a stand-in for a fridge in a city with little or no power, empty packets of Pringles that held paintbrushes and a dog-eared copy of *Sophie's World*. Esam didn't like how little Eastern philosophy there was in it. On top of a Baghdad Monopoly board, with the Al Rasheed Hotel where Marylebone Station might otherwise be, there was a judo trophy. Esam used to compete at national level, though he made sure never to do too well. Everyone knew what happened to members of Iraqi international sporting teams when they lost in the days of Saddam and his sadistic sons.

Hidden beneath a chair was Esam's most precious possession: a box of forty *Hello!* magazines that a Romanian collector of his work had provided.

"You know *Hello!?*" We knew all about *Hello!* "Ah, this is the best magazine," Esam said, his regal composure slipping away. "Really, I love reading about these people. It is my favourite thing." His face melted. "To see what they are doing, to see who is most beautiful, who is marrying who, to see the princesses, the princes, the actors as well, although many of these actors I don't recognise."

Al and I flicked through different issues. "And she. She is the best," he went on. "My favourite. Please meet Gabriella." We crowded round. "Lady Gabriella Windsor." He shook his head. "She is the most beautiful of all the princesses in the world. The most elegant. The most...

Hmm. If she married me she would lose her title and become a countess, but maybe she would not mind. Please. Look at her."

The three of us gazed in silence. "You see, I come from an important Iraqi family," Esam went on. "My grandfather on my mother's side was Nouri al-Said Pasha, the Prime Minister of Iraq for many years. He was very close to the British. Our family is Ottoman, that is why my name is Pasha. So maybe one day I will meet her. Who can tell?"

We stayed in Esam's studio for most of the day and by the time we left, our heads brimming with stories, ideas and of course images, both Al and I felt something familiar. Again, it was as if we had known this man for months, not hours, as it had been with almost every young artist we had met during the journey.

For me, Al and Esam, the experience of thinking of ourselves as artists had, among other things, conditioned us with a sense of artist-ness that owed a lot to the universal caricature of the artist as the expressive, liberal, belligerent, sex-crazed and emotionally tortured loner who smokes a lot and whose head if you opened it up would be a crazy, flighty, Joycian stream of consciousness. "Oh, you're an artist. Right. Well, that explains the beard." Or, "You're not that weird for an artist."

Like a Palestinian being told over and over that the only language he or she, as a Palestinian, fully understood was that of violence, or a Muslim being told that the "Islamic world" was under attack because of its Islamic-ness, it is hard not to believe in a myth if it is projected onto you consistently from a position of authority. Even more so when there are images that appear to confirm the myth. Once enough people believe in the myth it becomes self-perpetuating and before long, as somebody who makes art for a living you feel compelled to act a bit tortured or have moments of weirdness so that you feel, in a passive and societal sense, more like an artist. Ditto as a Palestinian.

Over the last ten months our most charged and intimate encounters had involved other artists. Always, it was a sense of shared history and kinship that had allowed us into the lives and heads of these people. It made them feel as if they were talking to an old friend, and vice versa, which flew in the face of how Al and I had been conditioned to group ourselves. At any moment we might belong to thousands of different groups, be they real, imagined, abstract or fleeting, but it seemed as though throughout our lives up until then we had been pushed towards placing gender, nationality and religion above any other grouping. Age might be the fourth. When we were around artists in the Middle East these groupings fell into abeyance and were made to feel irrelevant. In Esam's studio, as before, all had been superseded by our shared artist-ness.

There was nothing mawkish about this. No one had been passing the peace pipe, and there were some things about Esam that we did not feel close to; but his artist-ness, there was no denying it, made him feel like a long lost friend and there was something extraordinary about this.

It also made me want to get to Karada Street even more.

☾

Ja'afar

ONCE SHE REALISED WE REALLY WERE GOING TO BAGHDAD, suicidal as our decision may have sounded, Rana put us in touch with Zainab. Zainab ran a gallery on the banks of the Tigris. Al and I went to meet her in the apartment she had rented in Amman while the invasion of Iraq ground through its motions. She would stay there until it was safe for her and her daughters to return to Baghdad. She told us to go and visit her gallery, which was opposite a statue of Scheherazade, the heroine of *The Book of One Thousand and One Nights* (sometimes called the *Arabian Nights*), who had told stories with cliff-hangers so tantalising that she managed to defer her own execution for the eponymous 1,001 nights, before being exonerated.

On a sheet of lined A4 paper Zainab had drawn for us a map of Baghdad, marking her gallery and the studios of her gallery's artists with a series of overgrown crosses.

"And this street, Karada," she had said, pushing the biro hard into the paper, making sure whoever else used the pad would also be able to find their way round Baghdad. "It is like the Montmartre, you know, the Montmartre in Paris. Most of the artists on this street, they are bad artists. They don't paint well. Realist stuff with these awful colours." She had rolled her eyes. "But on this paper I have marked the ateliers of the, er, how do you say, the good artists."

Two weeks later Al and I stepped onto Karada Street in our Baghdadi outfits. For me, Diadonas tracksuit bottoms with "diadonas" written in an Adidas font and four stripes running down each leg (rather than the Adidas three), into which I tucked a collared T-shirt. For Al, fake Nike tracksuit bottoms and a shirt with an oversized collar and tacky patterning that looked as though it would come off in the wash. If he ever washed it. Which was unlikely, because with clothes this cheap Al preferred to buy new ones than wash old ones. All clothes models' own, bought at second-hand stalls in downtown Amman or Damascus.

Instead of a backpack I carried a black plastic bag. When I was by myself and dressed like this, people in Baghdad would ask me for directions. It happened twice and both times it felt unreal. For a few seconds I had assimilated. Fully. Finally. When I was with Al, neither of us would be asked for directions because the colour of Al's hair and the piercing blue of his eyes made it hard for him to pass for a local.

We found the building that seemed to match one of the crosses on Zainab's treasure map, the largest cross, the one she had gone over several times as if beneath it was the greatest prize of all. Around its hem were several shops. We asked around for the artist's studio and the man from the fruit-juice shop took us to a stairwell and pointed up it. The steps were bare and swept and the sound of our footsteps echoed clumsily ahead as if we were cats with bells round our necks. Next to the cross Zainab had written the words Ja'afar Muhammad. Al practised saying the name, whispering it to himself as if it was a mantra until we arrived at a door that was a little ajar. Inside were voices.

I knocked on the door hard enough to push it open: a sneaky knock-push that was more of a push than a knock. A man in his thirties with a stubbly oblong head came to the door. He wore a white singlet and round his neck was a towel that had once been bright and white but now looked like sandpaper.

"*Salaam Aleikom, tekhi Inglizi?*" said Al in his best pidgin Arabic.

"Yes, yes, we speak some English," the man said, harvesting the latest crop of sweat from his head. "Who are you?"

"We've been given your address by Zainab, Zainab from Gallery Dijla."

"Ah!" his face lit up.

"She said we should come and visit you," I said, nodding and waving her map as if it was a contract. "But you have no telephone. I could not call."

"No, no telephone here."

"And no power."

"No power."

"Right. And Zainab says hello."

"Good," he said. "But what are you? You are soldiers?"

"What? No, no we're not."

"Tourist?"

"Sort of, um... *Ana resam*. Artist."

He let out a sigh, held out both arms and gave first Al then me a sweaty hug.

"That is good. I am Ja'afar."

"That's what Zainab said. Ja'afar Muhammad."

I still wanted to show him the map. As if it was proof.

"But why you here? Why here in Baghdad?" he asked, ushering us in.

As Ja'afar led us upstairs we told him our story, both of us taking it in turns to narrate different parts, with the words tumbling out like lines from a poem that we had both learnt by heart long ago but were no longer moved by; the lines were now hardwired into our collective unconscious and had since lost their barb.

Ja'afar's studio was on the top floor. Before taking in the room, all I could think about was the heat. The power in Ja'afar's studio had gone off earlier that morning, as it had done most mornings since the city fell to the soldiers with mirror sunglasses and body armour rumoured to have in-built air-conditioning, and the heat was thick. A concrete ceiling was all that hid us from the midsummer Baghdadi sun, and instead of protecting us from it the roof seemed to magnify its glare. The ceiling was charred and black, adding to the sense of having just walked into an enormous oven, and the room smelt of turpentine, oil paint and cigarette smoke.

The space was wide and there were canvases stacked up against the walls. Fragments shored against his ruin.

Wherever you looked you could see the familiar paraphernalia of an artist's studio: half-broken chairs, stools, paints, mediums, palettes, masking tape on the walls, rags, marks of paint on most walls or clothes, and bins full of cigarette packets and ash. Ja'afar had smoked a lot during the war. He smoked Sumer cigarettes that came in Safavid-blue boxes.

On one easel was a canvas divided into a series of small squares, half of which had been painted; the others awaited Ja'afar's brush.

"But I do not like these pictures," he said, dismissing them with a shrug. "*Yani*, people buy them. I make them."

Elsewhere there were portraits, sketches, abstract expressionist work and mercifully little of the crossword-clue artistic symbolism we had seen so much of in Amman, where a pigeon represented peace, scales were for justice, a kite was Palestinian freedom and so on.

"But I cannot make the painting with the oil paint now. Not since the fighting."

"Why not?"

"Because of the oil. Before, in the first attack by the Americans in 1991 there is, *yani*, big black smoke that fills the streets here in Baghdad." His arms flailed above him. "And when my paint is drying, it becomes black as well."

Unprompted, Ja'afar began to describe the artistic revival that had accelerated since the first Anglo-American invasion of Iraq in 1991. Although this was the moment I had been trying to imagine for so long, hearing the Baghdadi artistic renaissance described to me by one of its artists, in Baghdad, there was something missing. It wasn't the satisfying full stop I had thought it might be. I had not yet thrown the ring into the fire.

Ja'afar told us there had been only one commercial gallery in Baghdad in 1991. Now there were fifteen. Even if the sanctions imposed on Iraq meant they had to use poor-quality Chinese paint that was said to crack after thirty years, Ja'afar and Ahmed's artistic careers had blossomed since the mid-1990s.

"It's amazing," said Al. "But I still don't understand why this artistic revival started. With the sanctions and so on."

"Well," said Ja'afar, speaking with a sententious slowness perfectly in keeping with the sapping heat of the studio, "with the sanctions, for the rich people in Baghdad it is not good to spend the money on the car or the swimming pool, or the things like this. It is better to spend the money on the art. It is luxury but it is, *yani*, it is more pure. More of Iraq. The Iraqis are artists. For them to make art is like to breathe. With the sanctions, everyone is hurt. It is like when it rains all the people get wet. The rich people and the poor people. But," he went on, remembering, "after the sanctions there is more prayer also, more imams. Maybe from 1993 or 1995, I think. But it is the same thing, when Iraqi people are at their most pure. When it rains on all the people some make the art, some make the prayer." We nodded. "I make the art!"

With that he lit another cigarette. He offered me one. I declined. Ja'afar tutted and told me I was an artist so of course I should smoke. I took one.

Like almost every Baghdadi we spoke to, Ja'afar was happy Saddam was gone, but at the same time he did not like the American soldiers. He said they were trigger happy and was cross that they had not fixed the power. Throughout our time in Baghdad the sight of an American soldier made every man we were ever with tut, instinctively, as did the experience of having to pull over to the side of the road as a convoy of Humvees roared past like a herd of runaway rhinos. Different Baghdadis told us how they would love to kill an American soldier, although they talked about it in a rhetorical way, just as someone who threatens to commit suicide rarely does.

"Also," Ja'afar began, "the Americans, they have not given everyone the mobile phone."

This was one of the many pre-invasion rumours that had been put about.

"Where did you hear that? On Al Jazeera?"

"No, no," he smiled. "We don't have Al Jazeera. No satellite with Saddam. But for the first time, this week, I see this Al Jazeera." Again he tutted, lifted his head and closed his eyes, all in one movement. "They have the, er, the man in Iraq. On TV. And it is like I am watch another country! I do not see Iraq." He was animated now. "Al Jazeera says like we are religious people, like Saudi, like Iran. Crazy people who read Qur'an all day."

He tutted again. "Al Jazeera, I think they are like *jihadis*. They come from Saudi, al-Maghreb, al-Jazeer, these places, you know? They have their own idea about Iraq and that is it. *Halas*. They do not talk to the Iraqi man unless he is saying 'Allahu Akbar! Allahu Akbar!' And they are cross we don't fight against America. Why? Why don't Al Jazeera fight America? I will give them the guns! Really! I will say, 'Here are your guns. Now go fight with these people.' I will not die for Saddam. No. It is like the pictures I see of the man in Jordan. Argh." His face was red. "He is saying, 'Saddam! Saddam! Saddam!' How can he say this?" Ja'afar was angry now. "They are stupid people, the people in Jordan. Saddam kills his own people! How can they love this man?"

I thought back to Umm Seyhoun and the Jordanian who had told me the Iraqis were like his brothers, and how Saddam was the most strong man.

With the prominent vein on Ja'afar's forehead beginning to pump blood to his brain that bit faster, Al got out a pad and started to draw our host.

"I am going to make painting of you also," said Ja'afar, inspired, pointing at me and putting on his glasses.

"Fine. I'll make a picture of you too," I said.

Ja'afar's friend Ahmed shuffled into the studio. He wore boxer shorts and a stained singlet and looked as though he had just woken up. He greeted Ja'afar and waved at me and Al. Seeing the portrait triangle that had just begun, he announced that he was going to make a portrait of Al. He hunted around for some paper. Al decided to draw Ahmed. Soon all four of us were either drawing or painting each other. Four mirrors set up in opposition.

The conversation fell away. The room became silent. We were like four children who had just been given new toys; we were consumed, jaws hanging loose in concentration. All you could hear was the scratch of pencil on paper, the swish-swish-stab of brush on canvas, or the scratch of a match being lit followed by the sound of a cigarette being sucked to death.

Although I did not realise it then – and I wish I had – *this* was the moment I had been dreaming of since December of the year before. Now the ring was in the fire. This was the microcosm of everything that had happened to me and Al since leaving London ten months earlier. It felt like every one of the paintings, drawings, photographs, stories, installations or amateur videos we had made since then could be forgotten as long as this one moment remained. We were in Baghdad, the place that we originally thought we would never get to, with two artists whose careers had blossomed during an artistic revival that very few people outside Iraq knew anything about – a hidden part of the Middle East, something you wouldn't get on the international nightly news – and we were making portraits of those artists while they made portraits of us. In trying to make a portrait of the post-9/11 Middle East, we had ended

up sitting for our own portrait; we could never make the exhaustive or dispassionate account of the region we had once dreamt of. And we were making pictures of artists, of all people, because it was in them that we saw ourselves. Everywhere we went in the Middle East we had been drawn to places and people in whom we saw ourselves.

With midday drawing close the temperature got worse. Beads of sweat on my forehead and the sea of them on the small of my back began to prickle. I wiped a trail of sweat from my brow. Ja'afar tutted and told me not to. He had just got to my eyes.

Outside a distant, nasal drone that had been there for a while detached itself from the hubbub of the street. It grew until it drowned out everything else, at which point an American Black Hawk helicopter flew past the window. With a yelp Ja'afar ran to the window, where he began to fire an imaginary machine gun at it. He stood with his legs propped wide and let loose what would have been enough ammunition to shred the thing. His body shook as the invisible weapon hammered into his shoulder. His face spluttered with the sound effects. I was about to jump up and help feed a steady flow of bullets – to make sure the gun didn't jam – when the throbbing hum of the helicopter died and the machine flew out of sight. Ja'afar's arms fell limp to his side.

"Next time," he said quietly, half smiling, half grinning, the lines around his mouth becoming pronounced as he glanced at each of us.

Henman Out of Wimbledon

AL GOT UP EARLY ON 4 JULY 2003 AND HAD LEFT THE HOTEL before I woke up. It felt like the harbinger of something. I got a car to Esam's studio and together we went to the British Embassy where I was hoping to get written permission to make art in one of the ex-presidential palaces. Esam wanted a British visa.

It took a while to get there, because the street leading to the embassy had been cordoned off after a bomb had exploded there earlier that morning. Two GIs had been killed. Perhaps the significance of that day, Independence Day, had not been lost on the Americans' reclusive and increasingly suicidal enemy.

The British Embassy compound was bordered by tall walls and beyond the grille of its main gate were five or six troops, some of only a handful of British troops in Baghdad. They sat behind sandbags and monitored the crowd before them, most of whom were there just to stare at the soldiers and their guns and their enormous arms.

"What's that, mate?" said a trooper in a thick Geordie accent to one of the children on the other side of the gate. "No focking way," he said, laughing. "You can't have my gun. And no, I won't give you no money neither." He gave him a square of chocolate instead. The sergeant next to him bantered in pidgin Arabic with the other children, telling them not to become Ali Babas: thieves, looters. "Ali Babas *la quais*, they're bad, mate."

It was different to being around American soldiers. The British troops had none of the swagger of the GIs, who would cheerfully tell us about the other day when they were "bustin' some skulls" in such and such a street, or pose for photos smoking cigarettes back to front. The GIs we met spoke endlessly about how much they wanted to go home. The British troops were more tight-lipped. One GI told Al he was also disappointed by the girth of the Iraqis he had seen. Before the invasion he and his buddies had been told that Saddam was starving his people. "But man, 'tween you and me, I've seen some of these 'raqis and, well, let's just say there ain't no hu-man-i-tar-ian crisis goin' on." His pitch went right up. "I mean, some of these guys, they got them their big bellies on them, bigger than guys I know back home! They ain't starving. Man, they need to go on a diet, that's what."

I asked one of the British troops if I could speak to the ambassador. With his gun trained on my chest, he told me to wait. Ten Humvees pulled up at the house opposite the gates to the embassy. The crowd scattered. The soldiers behind the gate took up defensive positions. The most dangerous place to be in Baghdad was near an American soldier. I squatted down where I was while I heard the squaddie nearest to me mutter to himself "Not gonna get focking killed for no focking Americun cunt", as he rearranged his sandbags and shot anxious looks at the American soldiers who were clambering out of their Humvees and beginning to wander around. They looked a little lost as they stretched and took in their new setting, like a group of tourists piling out of a coach.

The gates opened and the British commanding officer strode towards the American colonel. In desert fatigues and a soft, peaked hat the British officer looked naked next to his opposite number in helmet, mirror sunglasses and full body armour.

"Um," the commander started in a declamatory, public-school voice. "I need to know what you are doing here. We haven't been told anything about this."

The man smiled at his British counterpart. "Don't worry about it. Won't be here long. Some meeting about sewage. We got civil contractors in."

"Right. Well..."

The British officer marched back and the gates shut behind him. I stayed where I was.

Once the American convoy had departed, the gates opened and Dave from the embassy staff, who wore shorts that day, fielded questions. Most of the men wanted work. One explained, his language stripped of cant, "I fish man. No money now. No fish in Baghdad. No business. Business here?" It summed up the feelings of most men there. One man had brought his baby daughter. He cradled her in his arms. She smiled at something she had seen on the ground while her father asked if there was any gardening he could do in the embassy grounds. Another wanted compensation for the damage done to his house by some American soldiers.

Esam asked about a visa, dropping the name of his grandfather, Nouri al-Said. Dave had not heard of him. He told Esam they would not be functioning as a consular embassy until an Iraqi government was established. I showed Dave my British Council letter and was ushered into the walled compound after arranging to meet Esam in an hour.

Dave led me towards several portacabins opposite the long and low Ottoman building on the banks of the Tigris that had been the embassy building. It looked like a dilapidated Palladian farmhouse in the Veneto and had lain derelict since 1991; it was now being refurbished. Nearby, beneath the piercing sun, four soldiers with skin coloured postbox red plodded round a tennis court in shorts and heavy boots swatting tennis balls at each other. It was midday.

"Mad dogs and..." said Dave under his breath, following my gaze. "Oh, and you know Tim Henman got knocked out of Wimbledon yesterday?"

We got to the portacabin, where Dave handed me a copy of the *Daily Mail* before going to put the kettle on.

"Milk and sugar?"

"Milk, one sugar. Thanks."

It all felt very homely.

Chris Segar, the stand-in ambassador, said he could not write a letter giving me permission to make art in any of the former presidential palaces because they constituted an American military zone and the American military was, at that moment, on high alert. Instead, he told me about several other interesting places I could go and draw, including al-Faris al-Arabi Square. There was a decapitated statue of Saddam there. It would make a great picture, he thought.

He also told me about the British paratroopers who had taken the embassy compound in April just as the looting began. During the two weeks they were there they had visited every house within two hundred metres of the compound walls. They had worn berets rather than helmets and had taken tea with each family.

That evening in Saddam's Republican Palace, having got in without any embassy-sponsored letter of permission, I told this to an American soldier, who did not believe me. "No soldier would ever do that," he laughed, "Gullible artist" appearing in a thought bubble above him. But he liked the idea of British soldiers going on a marathon tea-drinking binge. "Goddam yellow-toothed Brits," he said.

I smiled, trying to keep my teeth to myself.

From the embassy compound I crossed the Tigris and found the Shahbandar Coffee House where Esam was

waiting. Around him were men engaged in lofty conversations, smoking *nargileh* and drinking coffee. There was no
television and on the walls were paintings of Baghdad, *surah*
from the Qur'an and pictures of former Iraqi monarchs and
presidents. But no Saddam. There were also tens of people
reading newspapers and one reading a book. It was a
remarkable sight. I had not yet been in a café anywhere in
the Middle East with more than two or three people reading
a newspaper, and could not think of the last time I had seen
anyone reading a book. But this was Baghdad. As the saying
goes: Cairo writes, Beirut publishes and Baghdad reads.

Esam told me about a Miró painting that had been
looted from the Saddam Art Centre in the days after the
city fell. He knew it was still in Baghdad – part hunch, part
shred of evidence – and was determined to get it back for
Iraq. The way he said this was a monument to one of the
few positive things that might have emerged from the last
months. In their shared experience, in some ways like the
people of Lebanon, the ethnically disparate Iraqis we had
met now felt a little more Iraqi than they had before. The
idea of Iraq splintering into three ethnically homogenous
segments – Kurdish, Sunni and Shia – seemed remote
when Esam talked about buying back a Miró for Iraq, or
about friends of his who were doing the same.

The following day I met the director of the Hewar
Gallery, who had recently sold his car to buy back as many

of these looted paintings as possible. But perhaps this was just a Baghdad thing. "These Mirós are our heritage," both men told me.

Outside in the bustling book market there were coffee-table books on Picasso, Cézanne and Impressionism, *The Marsh Arabs* by Wilfred Thesiger, cheap English novels, copies of the Qur'an, Shia commentaries, magazines with luscious, pouting women on the cover, and the latest issue of an array of newspapers that had started up since Baghdad fell. There were also stalls selling Chinese oil paint, reminding me that I had made it to the art-making capital of the Arab world.

☾

Get Him

I GOT BACK TO THE MAJALIS AND WENT UPSTAIRS TO OUR room, where I found Al grinning nervously and pacing up and down.

"I'm leaving," he said as I walked in.

"What?"

"Getting out of here. Baghdad. I'm going tomorrow."

"Why, what's happened?"

"It's..." He sighed. "It's been a bad day. I almost got killed. Twice. Anyway, I've made all the art I want to, I've got to get out." He sighed once more, his breath shaky. "It's like that slogan under the old Saddam statue."

"I don't know it."

"No, you do, the one in big letters, 'All donne, go home.'"

"OK, I do. But what happened?"

"All done. Go home," he said again, dazed. "Um. Where do I start? I got up early." He slowed himself. "I got up early because the light's better and because it's not as hot. And I went down Abu Nuwas and found this bombed-out building near the Tigris. So I was making some nature-cultures in there, and there were all these amazing things to sculpt with, gorgeous bits of rubbish, chequebooks, pictures of Saddam and so on, when I saw these three enormous, unexploded bombs. Huge things. They were just sitting there in the rubble. Right in front of me. It was the weirdest thing. I almost stepped on one. At first I thought 'Get out', but I was just drawn to them. I can't explain it. I really couldn't tear myself away. I tried to leave a few times but they kept pulling me back, like they were magnetic. There was something about them, these huge objects of just, just destruction. They were so clean and smooth and... I don't know. Anyway. Eventually I left. So I was quite weirded out by the whole thing, when on the way back I passed that American base on Abu Nuwas, you know the one?" I nodded. "And as I walked by, I saw these three hookers chatting up some GIs."

"Really?"

"Yeah. So I snuck in behind this tank and started taking pictures of them."

"How far away were they?"

"About fifty yards. I got some great shots when the commander starts yelling, 'That guy there! That guy! Get him! GET HIM! GET HIM!' and the two soldiers start waving their guns in my direction."

He did an impersonation, eyeballs like marbles. "At first I thought there must be someone behind me. So I spin round. But there was no one there. Then I realise they're talking about me. He was shouting at them to shoot me. I couldn't work out what to do. My brain froze. It's, God, it's one of those impossible things, like, I don't know, like hanging onto a hot-air balloon as it floats away.

You know that every second you hang on it's getting worse. So I just, man, after about ten seconds I put my hands up and stepped out from behind the tank, going 'DON'T SHOOT! Don't shoot!' And I'm just waiting for that impact. I've got my eyes closed. Waiting. And that feeling. Jesus, that feeling. Of waiting for the BOOM of a bullet tearing into you."

He thumped his breast with his palm. It made a hollow sound like a muffled bass drum. "And being totally defenceless. Totally and utterly defenceless."

He was breathing deeply now, forcing each breath out like it needed a push.

"What did the soldiers do?" I asked.

"They started shouting like crazy, told me to drop my bag, told me to put my hands right up and walk as slowly as possible to the checkpoint. Then they erased the pictures I'd taken, the ones of them with the hookers. That was the most annoying bit. Really pisses me off, actually. They also told me I was a 'stupid fucking asshole', and that they would have shot me if they'd seen me sooner. Apparently they've got orders to shoot on sight anyone they don't like the look of."

"Christ."

"Yup. The last few weeks insurgents have been taking reconnaissance photos of checkpoints before planting bombs there. They're all on edge and, well, to be fair to them, they do keep getting blown up. And then the hookers. Oh my God. It got even weirder. They were still there while this was all going on. And this one girl was desperate to get one of the GIs. You'd think she'd be worried or something."

"What did the GIs do?"

"Not much. They weren't having any of it. Or they sort of weren't. Not with their commanding officer there.

Apparently in the US army only marines get to go with hookers. So the GIs start telling me to have a go. And one of the girls starts coming up to me, telling me to come back to her place round the corner, taking my hand, and the GIs were egging me on and everything, saying 'Go for it, go for it', but no way! Can you imagine? Then on the way back these five kids see me and start shouting '*Americi! Americi!*' Argh. Just after almost being shot by the fuckers. And I'm like 'No, no, no way, *ana la Americi. Nemsa. Nemsa.*' But they just got louder. Then their friends turn up and there's this crowd of people following me chanting '*Americi! Americi!*' I'm shitting myself now. So I just sprint back to the hotel. And here I am. Don't really want to go outside now."

"Wow."

"So I'm going back to Amman. Tomorrow."

"I'm staying."

"Your funeral."

"Don't say that."

"Sorry."

"At least come along to the party tonight."

"Sure. I wouldn't want to miss that. Maybe I'll bump into the guys who were going to shoot me. That'd be nice."

☾

The Fourth of July

THAT EVENING WE MET UP WITH NICK, WHO HAD PROMISED to get us into the Fourth of July party in Saddam's Republican Palace. Four bored GIs manned the entrance to the Green Zone.

"I'm gonna need to see some ID for these two," said the well-built sergeant as Nick explained his credentials. A few

minutes later he had talked us into what was formerly
Saddam's palace complex, out of which the Coalition
Provisional Authority now operated. We were driven down
a wide and leafy avenue that was smoother and cleaner
than any other road in Baghdad. On either side of us was
a series of enormous palaces and ministries, each one a
crude triumph of testosterone.

The Republican Palace was more feminine in that it
curved gently, in some ways welcoming you. Running
along its parapet were four busts of Saddam wearing a
spiked Sumerian helmet, as if doing a shoddy impersonation of Kaiser Wilhelm II. The gaze of each overgrown
head was trained on the entrance to the palace and all four
seemed to frown at us as we walked through Saddam's former front door.

Nick led us down extravagant passageways decked out
in fake marble, gold and yellow light, and everywhere we
looked there were echoing tall ceilings, chandeliers, mirrors, pillars and plush, red armchairs with rococo flour-
ishes on each foot. The whole building was a shrine to
porn-magnate neo-classicism. On the wall in among this
faux grandeur were more recent mosaics of CPA notices
about meetings and sewage and administration.

In the former ballroom stood a lone ping-pong table
and beyond it a darkened dormitory where GIs slept and
others played computer games in a fug of foot and sweat.
In the games they played the idea was to kill as many people as possible. We walked through the dormitory and past
a room decorated with pictures of Saddam's biggest and
baddest missiles, which had been turned into a chapel.

Al and I were in heaven, an art-making heaven.
Everything around us was the most delicious treat and
Nick was having trouble keeping the three of us together.
There were far too many things to look at. For me and Al

this was Willy Wonka's Chocolate Factory, the deluxe version. We were all gasps and sighs as each new room or corridor presented itself and before long Al disappeared. He had run off to explore a passageway he liked the look of. Nick went to find him and told me to wait near some of the magnificent red armchairs. I asked a passing soldier to pose in one. I was sprawled on the floor trying to get a better angle, when an American colonel came over to ask what my credentials were.

"Um. I don't have any. I'm with my friend Nick, he's just…"

"No. I said who do you work for?"

"I don't work for anyone. Really. I wish I did."

"Well, who the hell are you here with?" His eyes narrowed.

At this point Nick reappeared with Al and apologised to the colonel. He told Nick not to let either of us out of his sight. Chastised, we moved on to the pool area where the party was.

Standing and sitting all over Saddam's soft and spongy lawn were several hundred soldiers, contractors and administrators. Most of the soldiers had rifles slung over their right shoulder and a beer or burger in either hand. On every available wall were American flags and A4 notices reminding the partygoers to clear their weapons. As we walked onto the lawn we were each given miniature American flags that came with a message from the Ladies Auxiliary District 5, Colorado: "A flag for your pocket, so you will have a piece of home to carry with you. We are praying for you and are so proud of you for all that you are doing to protect Our Freedoms. GODS speed for your safe return."

Our Freedoms. It made you wince. Not in a predictable anti-American way, not at all. This was something else.

Before us was a representative fraction of an army a long way from home drowning in a semantic soup of peace-keeping, liberating, War-on-Terror-fighting, Weapons-of-Mass-Destruction-finding, self-defending and democratising. Although I had not thought it possible beforehand, it was hard – at that moment, in that place, with the message from the Ladies Auxiliary District 5, Colorado in my hand – not to feel extremely sorry for some of the GIs getting drunk and jumping into Saddam's pool. The less calculating ones at least. Some of them genuinely did not understand why so many Iraqis wanted to kill them. Surely they were the good guys? Hadn't they just got rid of the bad guy?

The music came out of an iBook and was rock, light to heavy. There was also a band with a trombone and a banjo that went round the party giving the evening a canapé-sized taste of the Deep South and making some of the soldiers homesick. Elsewhere there were crates of food and beer and a whole table of sauces for the burgers and hot dogs. In the middle of the pool was a fountain that men threw themselves at. Others backflipped or bombed from the diving board.

"Just can't stop bombing Baghdad, can we?" said Henry, a contractor from Alabama, chuckling to himself. He told us to come and stay if we were ever in Alabama. He cooked a mean burger, he said. Made it himself. Secret recipe. Best burger in Alabama. Made you fart all night though.

Lewis Paul Bremer III, the administrator of Iraq, strolled through the party wearing a neat blue shirt tucked into khaki trousers. He looked like a middle-aged model from a mail-order catalogue. We had been promised Arnold Schwarzenegger, but Arnie only made it to Baghdad airport. Bremer was good enough. At one point he was within two yards of us, which was our dose of celebrity for the night.

We chatted to marines with elaborate, Maori-looking tattoos on their biceps, administrators getting paid triple wages for being so far away from home, a British SAS soldier, more marines, a South African running Baghdad Zoo and three American soldiers originally from Mozambique, who were standing next to Saddam's pool in their swimming trunks arguing in Portuguese about a girl back in Maputo. They had just found out that all three of them had been with her. At different times. Or had there been an overlap? At one point it looked as if the argument might get out of hand.

When we left the Republican Palace it was past ten o'clock and by the time we were out of the Green Zone it was ten thirty-five. Already the roads were deserted. Curfew started at eleven. Either we could walk back to our hotel or we could sleep in the Green Zone. We decided to walk back to the hotel. We both had several Budweisers inside us and Al was certain we could get back in time if we hurried.

We set off at a brisk march. By the time we had crossed the Tigris we realised we were not going to get to the hotel before eleven. We had screwed up. We thought we had gone too far to turn back (looking at a map later we were in fact only a third of the way there), so we carried on down Saadun Street, quietly and fast. Ahead of us, on a parallel street, we heard gunfire.

"Shit," I hissed at Al.

It was about two hundred yards away and it was loud. We kept on walking. The only vehicles driving past were Humvees, but they would not stop. For a moment it was excruciating to think we had been drinking and chatting with their colleagues less than an hour ago, that they were our new best friends and we theirs, yet now all we could do was register in their night-vision cross-hairs as "civilians". If only we could tell them. But we couldn't. That was the whole point. We were again in a place where the only language that mattered was that of silent semiotics. We knew that now. The last ten months had been a masterclass in it.

Ahead of us was more gunfire, only this time there were different-sounding guns that responded to each other in short bursts. A little like the song on one of the tapes in Yasmine with its call and response, I told myself, the imagery doing nothing to calm me. We were the only people on the street and we were scared. What should have been trouser-wetting fear turned into adrenaline. Lots and lots of adrenaline. We knew that the only thing we could do was continue to walk, quietly and fast, keeping close to the buildings and scanning the street ahead of us for movement. We could not turn back. Not now. So we carried on. Quietly and fast. Quietly and fast. The rest was out of our hands.

For ten minutes we continued like this, neither of us saying a word. The street around us was warm and silent except for bursts of gunfire that kept getting louder. The warmth was off-putting. It made me think of holidays. Of a summery night in Italy. Another burst of gunfire would shatter the thought. Our ears were now hypersensitive and any noise louder than a footstep made us jump. Sometimes we would hear the mumble of a television from a house as we hurried past and it made me think of people snug behind concrete walls; thick, friendly concrete walls that would keep out bullets. All we had were our clothes. They would protect us like a cardboard fence against a tsunami. I began to long for Yasmine: she would get us home, she'd keep the bullets out alright.

In the distance I saw a vehicle with one of its headlights broken. The broken headlight meant it was unlikely to be a coalition-issue GMC Suburban or a Humvee. Like two trainee matadors who had skipped the first lesson, the one where they go through the basics, we ran out into the road and lined ourselves up to be gored, both of us spreading our arms to widen the target. Another burst of gunfire.

The car stopped. We told the man where we wanted to go and he asked for what seemed like a lot of money. I argued. Al swore at me. I stopped arguing. We got into the car and ten minutes later we were back at the hotel, out of breath and high on adrenaline and Budweiser.

The men at the hotel unlocked the door and told us we should not be out so late in future. It was very dangerous. By midnight the gunfire was on Karada Street again; it felt louder than any other night, and again I sat on my balcony with the curtains drawn behind me.

☾

Iconoclasm

AS PLANNED, AL LEFT EARLY THE NEXT MORNING AND GOT on a bus to Amman. Now I was alone in Baghdad. One of the hotel owners told me that three people were killed on Karada Street last night, but they were Ali Babas, looters, he said with a shrug, so it did not matter.

I took a car to the decapitated Saddam statue in al-Faris al-Arabi Square that the stand-in British ambassador had told me about. In the centre of a concrete field stood the mangled colossus he had described. The mustachioed former president had been sculpted wearing army slacks that flared a little over his boots. Round his waist was an over-sized revolver. Both of his arms had been hacked away, leaving skeletal steel rods that made him look like a head-less scarecrow.

The iconoclasm that had gone on throughout Baghdad over the previous two months was phenomenal. Every statue or painting or mosaic of the former president had been either torn apart, painted over or smashed, and there were a lot to get rid of. One of the only faces I ever saw on the side of a building in Baghdad was David Beckham's. He had been painted into a sky of fluffy clouds above an image of the Dome of the Rock.

Soon after I sat down to draw, a crowd of thirty to forty men gathered behind me. I don't know where they came from. They were loud, laughing and play-fighting, and I laughed along with them. The man who had helped remove the head from the statue struck poses in front of it, pushing out his chest as far as it would go while I drew him and took photographs. He looked like a Page 3 model with his chest out like that. Everyone roared with laughter. Not because he looked like a Page 3 model, that made *me* laugh, but because he was a funny guy and any impersonation of the man in the statue was funny because it was so risqué.

One of the men there spoke good English and told me he had a brain tumour. He would soon lose his sight. His face was gnarled. He was confused by my clothes.

"Why do you leave them dirty like this?"

"They're not too dirty, are they?"

"Yes, but this paint."

"I don't mind the paint."

"Ah," he said. "I understand. You are like the *bohème*."

At one point the crowd inadvertently closed so I could no longer see the statue. The man with the brain tumour cleared an opening. He also tried to shoo away some of the more rowdy spectators as he was worried they were putting me off. They wouldn't go. After remonstrating with them for a few minutes, his tone changed. He turned back to me.

"Mister. This is bad place for you. You go now. These people bad people. They are poor people. Go now."

The play-fighting carried on and as before it felt innocent. I was happy where I was. The man repeated his warning, but this time there was something in the way he said it that stung. I felt a need to get out. I packed up my things, bowed to my audience, thanked the man with the brain tumour and went to flag a car.

I had no idea what was happening a few kilometres away at that exact moment.

In a white Beetle with a hole by my feet through which you could watch the road rush past, I was driven to Firdawsi Square, where the statue of Saddam was famously pulled down by an American APC and a crowd of Iraqis apparently trucked in for the occasion. There was one more thing I needed in Baghdad.

I asked one of the money changers in the square about getting hold of a large painting of Saddam. He said he knew a man who could get me one, a nice big painting. He called over a boy from a neighbouring stall, to whom he gave instructions.

"OK *habib*," he said, looking at me, frowning, and buttoning up my shirt one button. "That is better." He moved back, satisfied. "Go with this boy, Ahjam. He will take you to the man who can give you painting."

Ahjam was about ten and set about his task calmly. We got on a bus that went down Saadun Street before turning into streets I did not know. After twenty minutes, with both of us watching the road carefully – me to remember the way, Ahjam for the stop – we got off.

The man I wanted to see was not in, so the pair of us waited in the street outside his shop and threw stones at a distant bit of paper to pass the time. When the man I wanted turned up, he said he did not have any paintings. Oh. I asked again, but no, he had nothing. Oh again.

A man opposite invited me into his shop and gave me a cup of Pepsi, before sitting me down in front of a VCD of Kadem Alsaher, an Iraqi singer – "So good, so beautiful, and he sings in London, in US, everywhere!" – before making enquiries on my behalf.

A little later he came back to say the man opposite did have a painting of Saddam, a nice one in fact. The latch on the door clicked shut and one of his friends pulled out a folded canvas from a black bin liner. He opened it out. It was a gorgeous, eight-foot tall painting of Saddam in his famous 1920s Chicago gangster get-up firing a shotgun, with the Dome of the Rock in the background. There was a puff of grey smoke at the end of the gun to show it was actually being fired.

As they so often did, Saddam's eyes had the grandfatherly warmth and good-looking loveability of a US senator.

Whatever his defects, Saddam's understanding of portraiture, uniform and appearance was inimitable. Over the past few days I had seen hidden-away pictures of Saddam in everyday clothes, Saddam as an affably full-cheeked kebab seller with a goofy grin, while at other times his face and expression were lean as he did his army general pose. He could do white-robed sheikh, gangster, devout Muslim on *hajj*, lounge lizard, Sumerian king, but his favourite was plain old late-twentieth-century paranoid dictator.

The painting was exactly what I wanted. The price started at $200 and finished at $50. With the sale done, the shopkeeper reached into his desk and pulled out a sub-machine gun. My heart stopped. He pointed it at the painting of Saddam and pretended to fire. Everyone laughed and slapped him on the back. I slapped him on the back too, before pulling out my camera. The man leapt back as if I had aimed a revolver at his head.

"No!" he said. "I will be killed. No, no, you cannot take picture of me like this. Maybe Saddam come back. You must not tell anyone I do like this, OK?"

I left, feeling I had committed an awful gaffe. On my way back to the hotel, clutching my portrait of Saddam, I stopped at the Sheraton to check my emails.

One of my messages was from Nick. At first he thought it might have been me because of the description – young, British, male, 24, freelance – and had panicked and tried to find out which hotel I was in to come and see if it was me. He had since found out it was not.

Earlier that day a British freelance filmmaker, Richard Wild, had attended a meeting in the Iraqi National Museum, less than two miles from al-Faris al-Arabi Square. At more or less the exact moment that the man with the brain tumour had suggested I leave al-Faris al-Arabi Square, Richard Wild had walked out of the National Museum and crossed the road to a traffic island, where he had tried to hail a taxi. Behind him was a crowd of students.

As he tried and failed to find a taxi or passing car to take him, a man walked up to him, put a gun to his head and shot him in the base of the skull. Several hours later the news of his death appeared on the BBC website.

The news of Richard Wild's murder hit me hard, not like a sudden or sharp blow but as something that builds inside you, accelerating and taking several minutes to reach terminal velocity, at which point it knocks you sideways with the force of an electric shock. The longer I sat in front of the computer in the converted conference hall in the Sheraton with the portrait of Saddam Hussein by my feet, the harder it shook me, the memory of being in al-Faris al-Arabi Square warping in my mind and becoming something sickening and awful in every way. It was like Oedipus thinking back to his night of passion, in that there was no reversing what had happened, and this memory that had once been so playful and light was now hideous. The face of the man with the tumour made me sense panic, disaster, imminent death. I felt naïve and reckless.

I thought of the man in *La Haine*. "So far so good... So far so good." It was as if he had just looked down and seen the ground racing up at him. So far so not so good. I could taste it, I was there, plummeting, with my stomach somewhere far, far above me I was falling so fast. But it was a trick of the eye. An illusion. I had to keep on telling myself that. There was a little farther left to fall.

Richard Wild had committed no crime, yet in the way he dressed and the way he had his hair he had become a symbol. An icon. For his murderer to walk up to him and shoot him in the back of the head was akin to tearing the head off a Saddam statue. It made me think of Richard Mason in the Amazon, of my father, of Al. In spending so long in al-Faris al-Arabi Square I too had become a statue, an icon, an emblem of the unknown. I had allowed that group of men to stand behind me long enough for them to see me as a symbol of Britain, of foreignness and of invasion.

Another email was from a friend in London who had also heard the news. He had passed my address on to Richard Wild only two days previously and Richard Wild had written back saying he would get in touch either tomorrow or the next day.

Feeling shaken and empty, I walked the mile or so back to the hotel where I took a seat on the steps outside with a glass of tea by my side. It was bitter and reminded me of both Sulaymaniyah and Rana back in Amman. Her mother was Iraqi and the tea in the gallery was made to her taste.

I decided to leave the next day. I had to leave the next day. My confidence had been shot to pieces and I felt very alone in Baghdad. The thought of Al relaxing in Amman made me wince with envy.

Although the sun was low and the shadows long, the street continued to give off most of the immense heat it had soaked up during the day. Outside the brothel opposite, an argument became noisy. A beautiful girl was screaming at a man wearing a wifebeater. I had seen her the day before on Karada Street and had walked behind her, feeling invisible because everybody's eyes were on her; it had been the best disguise yet. She had worn clogs.

Now she threw herself at the man in the wifebeater. He remained unmoved with his arms folded as she sobbed and screamed at him. His shoulders were large yet flabby and the skin covering his upper arms was hairy. Several men who were watching joined in the shouting, only I couldn't tell whose side they were on. None of the men watching behind me knew what was happening. Some began to hypothesise in Kurdish, pointing at the different players in the drama unfolding before us.

As the theories grew more elaborate, a man stepped out of a taxi parked nearby. He looked very similar to the man in the wifebeater, same features, same gait. A brother, perhaps. He took a revolver from his belt and fired it into the afternoon sky. As if starting a steeplechase. Nobody moved, except for the girl who fell to her knees as though she had been scythed down. The revolver went back into the belt of the man who had fired it and I thought of Richard Wild again. I thought of Richard Mason with the revolver in his belt. The man in the wifebeater strode past the girl who had once worn cork shoes into the brothel. She stayed where she was, broken, her body crumpled and her face buried in the black of her cloak. After a few minutes, she got to her feet and staggered inside.

All was still.

With a thud and a whirr, the electricity in the hotel behind me came on. The men sitting next to me went inside to watch television, as the evening news on Mrs Talabani's KurdSat was about to start. I stayed outside.

Ten minutes later, the man in the wifebeater walked out of the brothel, slowly, with his arms crossed as if he was cold. His shoulders were a little hunched. He and I were the only people on the street and he glanced in my direction, before turning away from the lowering sun and moving down the road. His frame moved gingerly; it was as if he was measuring his pace. Then I saw what was in his arms: a baby. It had no more than a few strands of hair on its head. For a moment it looked as though the hairs were still wet, that it had just left a womb somewhere inside – but no, I looked harder and saw that it was several weeks old.

The girl came to the door of the brothel. Her eyes, dark as before, were now teary and around them her make-up had run. She moved a few steps after the man in the vest and her baby, before falling again to her knees, her face creased as if in labour. She buried her face in her *hijab*.

There was something familiar in her expression and her pain, something I had seen throughout the eight days we had been in Baghdad. For most Iraqis when Baghdad fell it was as if a new country had been born. It had since been taken away.

I left at dawn the next morning.

☾

Misadventure

AFTER BAGHDAD, JANE'S BALCONY IN AMMAN WAS A bastion of calm and cool. Beyond the wisteria-entwined balustrade and pots of hibiscus that had just flowered, cars honked in an orderly fashion, the driving was neat and there were fewer people out on the street. Birds sang from the ash trees and fir trees beneath the balcony, while above the horizon opposite I could make out two, three, no five, finally eight kites winding back and forth in the mid-afternoon sky like birds of prey pondering their next meal. They were being flown from one of the Palestinian refugee camps.

Al and I were exhausted, physically and artistically, and in different ways shaken by our time in Baghdad. But there was still one more thing we had to do before we could go home. Watching Al Jazeera in our hotel in Baghdad we had seen montages of Hasidic Jews in black hats, dread-locks and glasses backed by sinister music in a minor key, which had reminded us of the new "them" that had formed in our minds, against our wishes, over the last ten months. To burst this bubble we had to go to Israel. It seemed to be the final piece in our art-making jigsaw.

After one night at Jane's, we got a taxi to the Israeli bor-der and took with us enough clothes, paper and film for a few days' work. We arrived at the busiest crossing between Jordan and Israel, the King Hussein Bridge, just after it closed for the day. An extravagantly fat taxi driver told us that if we hurried we could get to the Sheikh Hussein crossing before it closed. We got into his taxi and half an hour later we were there.

The Jordanian side of the crossing was quick and we were soon on a bus that ferried us across the River Jordan to the Israeli side of the border. As the bus slowed to a halt, two officials in shorts with machine guns over their shoulders began to point at us and talk into their walkie-talkies. We had not yet stepped off the bus. They had not seen our passports. They knew nothing about us beyond what we looked like, but that was enough. Of course it was. I knew that by now.

"Yes, sir. You, you two. Come this way," said one as we got off the bus. We were led to a special area. Memories of the Slovak border flooded back, one by one, like an embarrassing drunken night you are trying to piece together the morning after. Not now, I thought. Not again. Not after everything that had happened since then.

The questions came fast. "Why are you travelling so late? Why do you have so few bags? Who do you know in Jerusalem? Why do you not stay in a hotel when you are in Amman? So you have Arab friends? Why do you go to Baghdad? Iran? Saudi?"

We were not being let in. There were full, groping body searches aimed mostly at areas where it would have been biologically impossible to hide a gun or a bomb, our shoes were X-rayed, my phone was taken away and every name and saved text message was inspected. Separately we were asked how long we had known each other. I said ten years, Al said nine. This was levelled at us as a discrepancy in our "story". Everything in our bags was examined, unearthing several things we had both forgotten were there, including a pocket Qur'an at the bottom of my rucksack. There was a lot of muttering and words in earpieces while teams of tanned, pumped-up men continued to stare at us, as if our faces might suddenly reveal something. The border crossing closed and before long its entire staff stood before us, sizing up the odd couple in front of them. The Qur'an-carrying odd couple.

Al's bag of objects he wanted to use in sculptures in Jerusalem aroused almost as much suspicion as my translation of the Qur'an. In his bag were two Iraqi plugs, a rusty coil, an empty can of Titanic vodka he had found in Iran, a poster of the Dome of the Rock, playing cards, matches, a picture of J-Lo, toy soldiers, an Iraqi chequebook, several knives and a tube of superglue. In fact several tubes of superglue.

Looking back at it, of course this looked unusual and suspicious, but at the time we thought that leaving Yasmine in Amman was the disguise masterstroke that would get us into Israel. Anything more seemed like overkill. We were also dazed after our spell in Baghdad, so our disguise-making heads were not properly screwed on.

After inspecting Al's materials, the border guards moved on to my sketchbook. On one of the pages someone in Damascus had drawn a map showing us the way to the nearest petrol pump. He had written the street names in Arabic. None of the guards read Arabic and so, perhaps understandably, they imagined this was a map showing us where to go in Jerusalem in order to blow ourselves up or to meet someone who could show us how.

We waited for half an hour while an Arabic translator was driven in from a nearby town.

"And you are British," said a humourless Russian girl with freckled, alabaster skin and red hair.

"I'm sorry about that," I said. "I can't help it. But, um, what does being British have to do with getting into Israel?"

"Because of the history between our country and yours!"

I paused. "I don't understand. With the greatest respect, I always thought our country had a good history with yours. I mean, I thought it had helped in the creation of your country, no?"

"No!" she howled. "The present history. Not the ancient history! Two months ago your country sent two suicide bombers into Israel. That is the real history."

She was talking about Asif Mohammed Hanif and Omar Khan Sharif, the Britons from West London and Derby who had studied in Damascus before one of them blew himself up in Israel. The other was found dead on an Israeli beach several days later. Like us, they had crossed at the Sheikh Hussein Bridge late at night. They had told the border guards they were part of an international peace mission. We were trying to convince them we were artists.

Just two weeks after these two British suicide bombers hit the headlines, we had spent time with the British Muslims they had studied with in Damascus. They were a small group and most were wary of us. The previous week, Damien McElroy from the *Daily Telegraph* had flown out to Damascus to befriend several members of their group, before filing what one of them referred to as "a proper hatchet job" that suggested they should all be charged under the Terrorism Act 2000 for appearing to condone – in conversation – what their fellow students had done and so not be allowed back into Britain. When we spoke to these men they were adamant that what Hanif and Sharif had done was "not of the right path".

That our Britishness made us potential terrorist suspects was interesting. It was in many ways a shrewd portent of the London terrorist attacks in 2005, where in the space of two summer weeks the idea that the Middle East was the world's sole provider of suicidal religious militants who claimed the Qur'an as their inspiration was shattered. At least it should have been. It was for me. The threat might come from elsewhere, from within, from Britain and from London, as much as it might come from the Middle East. The Israeli border guards knew this in 2003; it was we who had not yet adjusted.

The Arabic translator sat down between me and Al and began a routine where he would start by chatting in English, friendly, your pal in all of this; and then mid-sentence switch to Arabic, *tekhi Arabi?* or *qayf hallaq?* – "do you speak Arabic?" or "how are things?" – the idea being we would respond in fluent Arabic, thus giving away our true Arabness. This went on for about twenty minutes, each cycle lasting three or four minutes, and by the end of it I could feel myself drifting away from the scene. It felt surreal. And laughably slow. The way this man was trying to trick the pair of us into speaking Arabic was like being pickpocketed in slow motion, with the pickpocket giving you a running commentary on what he is trying to do as he does it.

Yet again, we had become an icon of suspicion because of what we appeared to represent. Only two days ago we had been in Baghdad, desperate not to look like two non-Muslim Westerners; now, at the Israeli border, this was the only thing we wanted to be taken for.

"So," the Russian girl started, once Al and I had been separated. "Are you a Muslim?"

"Nope."

"And do you think you might become a Muslim in the future?"

"What?"

"Do you think you might become a Muslim one day?"

"Um. I have no idea. Probably not."

"But you cannot rule it out?"

"No," I sighed. "Just as I can't rule out becoming Jewish. How about Buddhist, can I become a Buddhist? Baha'i?"

"So at some point in your life you might become a Muslim?"

"I don't understand. Are you joking?"

"No!" she barked. "You think Israel is funny?"

"No. I don't think Israel is funny."

"This is not funny."

"Israel is not funny."

"This is Israel. Everything is different in Israel."

She had said this a few times, as had several other guards.

Just after midnight we were driven in separate police trucks to the local police station. It was clean and warm and smelt like a hospital. On the wall was a large poster commemorating the attack on the World Trade Center, while next to it was a picture of the Western Wall with the slogan "Have Faith in Israel". Al and I were again shown into separate rooms.

Mine was a small room, more or less bisected by a rectangular table. An Israeli detective sat on one side, I on the other. He was in his late forties and had a warm face with lines around his eyes that suggested he liked to smile, though he did not smile just then.

"So you have been on a journey, with a car that you no longer have with you?" he began.

"Yup, she's called Yasmine. She's parked in Amman."

"With who?"

"With Jane."

"Jane who?"

"Jane Taylor." He wrote it down.

"OK. I need to know all the other people you have stayed with on this journey, their names, who they are, what they are."

"All of them?"

"Yes."

"You mean from the whole journey?"

"Yes, tell me about the whole journey. Every person you have been with."

"But that'll take forever."

"We have all night," he said, the one phrase I did not want to hear. I straightened my back and began to talk.

For the next forty minutes I continued to talk until I had given him a complete account of the places we had been to, the people we had seen, where we had stayed and where we had exhibited, the names and places and dates all returning like a piece of music I knew how to play long ago. The longer I went on, the more emotion I began to insert. I told him about what I felt when weighing up whether or not to go to Baghdad, I told him about my dad, I told him about Al nearly being killed, about the Fourth of July, the web of events and emotions and near misses blending into one accelerating narrative until I got to the part where we arrived at the Israeli border – and I stopped. Exhausted. And vulnerable. I felt as though I had told him everything, more than I had told my diary.

Again I thought back to Slovakia. It seemed like a long time ago, and I hardly recognised the person who had stormed after the border guards waving a pamphlet while telling them about our dynamic cross-cultural artistic expedition into the "Islamic world".

"This is a long adventure, I think," said the detective after a while.

I looked around at the pared-down décor of the police cell.

"Um. Misadventure, don't you think?"

He smiled reluctantly.

"Yes. Misadventure."

It was now one thirty-five in the morning and both of us were tired.

"Who is this prince you say?" he studied his notes. "Prince Talal? Prince Hassan of Talal?"

"Prince Hassan bin Talal of Jordan."

"Yes, who is he? He is Saudi prince? Wahhabi prince?"

Just as I was about to answer, I noticed a poster on the wall behind him.

"Turn around," I said.

"Why?"

"Please. You'll see."

"Tell me why."

"Please." I pointed at the wall behind him.

He turned his body slowly, keeping his eyes on me before swivelling reluctantly to face the wall. It was empty but for a poster with an Israeli flag fluttering artfully beneath an image of six men standing on a lawn. In the middle was Bill Clinton and on either side of him were Yasser Arafat, Yitzhak Rabin, King Hussein of Jordan, President Mubarak of Egypt, and on the right, Prince Hassan bin Talal of Jordan. The poster had been issued to commemorate a historic peace agreement between Israel and its Arab neighbours.

"He's the one on the right," I said.

The man nodded, yawned, pulled out his chair with a scrape and left the room.

Ten minutes later he returned, saying we had permission to enter Israel. Al emerged from the room where he had been questioned.

"They letting us in?"

"Yep."

He closed his eyes and nodded.

Two policemen drove us into Bet She'an, where they dropped us at the town's only hostel. The streets were empty but for a pack of well-groomed dogs who patrolled this well-lit suburbia, its gardens carpeted with succulent and spongy grass that reminded me of the lawn in Saddam's Republican Palace. The policemen wished us well and drove back to the police station.

The hostel was expensive, prohibitively so, and just as we were working out which bit of grass to sleep on instead, I heard a bassline in the distance. It came from a building that looked like a bar that was about a mile away. Without a word, we both began to walk towards it. Sleep could wait, the morning and everything it might bring could wait, because the only thing that mattered at that moment was the fact that we had made it into Israel. There was no farther we could go on our journey through the Middle East, and so our journey had reached its conclusion.

From Israel we would fall into a slow and dreamlike drive back to London through Europe in high summer, a continent in repose populated by a people performing their seasonal migration to anywhere-but-here. That was ahead of us. For now we were in Bet She'an, the lawns surrounding us reminded me of Saddam's Republican Palace, and our footsteps were slow.

I FELT WE HAD SOMETHING TO CELEBRATE; PERHAPS celebrate is too strong a word, we had something to feel good about. We had crossed the last border on our journey, and for the first time I allowed myself to enjoy the fact that we had picked up the gauntlet thrown down at the Slovak border, in that we had managed to slip through, over or across all of the borders and divisions that had articulated the different chapters of our misadventure; not just the political borders, but the ethnic borders as well, the cultural divisions, the separations of language, gender, race, religion and social standing that had formed an intricate and at times invisible web linking the different people we had met. Everywhere we had gone we had encountered unexpected divisions, usually in the form of a new "them" that existed over "there", and the more "thems" we had heard about and subsequently met, the more we had become hooked on crossing these divides, until this was something that drove us on. We actively sought out borders in order to cross them. They represented the thrill of the unknown, the thrill of moving on. Each border was a shrine to restlessness. Every time we felt a scab was beginning to form in our way of seeing or thinking, we would try to tear off the scab and go and find a new "them".

Whether we were toing and froing between Turkish villagers and Turkish soldiers, sliding from the polished chic of a Tehrani art gallery opening to the ennui of a dervish hideaway, drinking and smoking on an Iranian ski slope before pleading our way into Kurdish Iraq, being *shalwar kamise*-wearing Austrians sleeping rough in the Saudi desert one moment, polite Englishmen dining in a royal palace the next, or whether we could sit just as comfortably with a woman calling her strangulating headscarf "him" as we would with a Palestinian man telling us that a woman without a headscarf was a slut – every time we had crossed one of these divides a new part of our surroundings had been revealed, as had a new part of "us".

This last bit was important. To different people we had at different times represented terrorists, tramps, artists or spies; we had been ambassadors of paradise and avatars of ignorance, potential punters or possible providers, suitors, scapegoats, jokers, janitors – in the words of Ali Reza, "different things to different people" – all of which hammered home both the possibilities of what we were doing as well as its inherent limitations. Our journey was as much a portrait of our different forms as it was an account of the places we had passed through.

The music coming out of the building that looked like a bar was louder now, a bass-heavy Euro-trance that I hadn't heard for some time. Every fifteen metres the streetlights above doused our bodies in a jaundiced light as we continued towards it. The night air was warm, like someone breathing on the back of your neck, and as we got closer to the bar I could make out figures on the veranda. It looked like they were dancing, their bodies silhouetted by the light coming from within, although it was hard to tell from where we were. We would have to get closer. I began to wonder what they'd make of us.

"O MANKIND! WE HAVE CREATED YOU FROM A MALE AND A FEMALE, AND MADE YOU INTO NATIONS AND TRIBES, THAT YOU MAY KNOW ONE ANOTHER..."

THE QUR'AN, 49:13

Acknowledgements

DURING THE JOURNEY A LOT OF PEOPLE LOOKED AFTER US – certainly we spent more nights in homes than hotels – although most of our hosts and hostesses either don't appear in the text or their names have been changed. So to everyone who put us up, put up with us, fed us or just showed us the way, thank you. Special thanks to: the artists in the Nifl Artists' Colony; James & Onke Wilde; November Paynter; Grace Spooner; Cem & Anne Kozlu; The Reverend Ian Sherwood; Nazim in Yeniyol; Yalda; Nader & Marjan; Amir Ali; Memat & Guiti; Media; Moonlight; Arush; Arezoo; Peter Morgan; Michael Sargent; Nazgol Reypour; Farhad Hakimzadeh; Andrew Greenstock; Hero Talabani; Ala Talabani; Alison Collins; Lorraine Roberts; Hassan Meer; HRH Princess Susan al-Said; Patricia Millns; Robin & Caroline Searby; Stuart & Sibella Laing; Patricia Groves; Larry Wright; Faisal Bajaber; Mohammed Zoheb; TRH Prince & Princess Hassan bin Talal; His Grace The Duke of Muthayba; The Pasha of Amman (Ali Maher); Patrick Forbes; Mizyed Ateigi; Daqlala; Haroun Dhakillalah; Jane Taylor; Rana & Sawsan Snober; (communist) Abdul in Damascus; Issa Touma; Michael Bleby; Muhammad Ishtiaq; George Asseily; Kai Stabell; Paddy Cochrane; Shawki Youssef; Tim Gore; Zainab Mehdi; Esam Pasha; Ja'afar Muhammad; Nick Horne; Arik Kilmeni; Randa al-Khalidi; Hugh & Millie Swire; and Simon & Gayle Jenkins.

Back in London, translating the journey into a publishable manuscript took a lot longer than I thought. Partly because at the time I was putting together a visual account of the journey (*Off Screen*, Booth-Clibborn Editions, 2004), but also because my first three or four attempts at this were not very good. To the people who were kind enough to read through these early efforts I am indebted, and apologetic. Most of all to Bea, my sister, who was – and is – a shrewd and patient editor, to Al for being a blast of fresh air, always, to Mum and Dad for their encouragement, to Tom Fenwick for being a constant inspiration, to Heather and James for being such assiduous agents, to Nick Brealey for being both imaginative and provocative, to Sally Lansdell for bringing in much needed order, and semi-colons; and to Helly, for the way she sees things and the happiness she has brought me, both of which have changed the shape of this book immeasurably.

Without all of these people this book and the journey it describes would not have been possible.

H.H.
January 2007

To see a selection of photos and artworks from the journey, go to www.HenryHemming.com